STUDY GUIDE

Susan Burns
Grant MacEwan College

PSYCHOLOGY
Third Canadian Edition

Carole Wade
Dominican University of California

Carol Tavris

Deborah Saucier
University of Lethbridge

Lorin Elias
University of Saskatchewan

Pearson Canada
Toronto

ISBN-13: 978-0-13-507921-8
ISBN-10: 0-13-507921-7

Editor-in-Chief: Ky Pruesse
Senior Developmental Editor: Madhu Ranadive
Managing Editor: Söğüt Y. Güleç
Production Coordinator: Avinash Chandra

    4 5   13 12 11

Printed and bound in Canada.

I would like to thank Tina E. Stern, Jeffrey D. Green, Jody L. Davis, and Angelina S. MacKewn, who wrote the previous version of this Study Guide. *I have revised and updated it for use with the second Canadian edition of* Psychology, *by Wade, Tavris, Saucier, and Elias. The format of this Study Guide is user friendly, challenging, and practical. It presents students with a variety of assessment techniques and takes advantage of what psychologists know about learning and memory. I hope that you find it to be a useful resource in your studies.*

Susan Burns

iv

CONTENTS

THE BEST WAY TO USE THIS STUDY GUIDE

This Study Guide has been developed utilizing psychological research findings in the areas of learning and memory. The structure of the Study Guide is designed so that students can be actively involved in learning.

LEARNING OBJECTIVES   Learning Objectives begin each chapter. Students should read the Learning Objectives **BEFORE** they begin reading the chapter. Students can also formulate additional questions on a separate sheet of paper by using headings, key terms, and concepts. Students should examine all these questions before reading the text and answer them while reading that particular section of text.

CHAPTER SUMMARIES   Following the Learning Objectives, each chapter has a chapter summary. It provides a general overview of the chapter.

PREVIEW OUTLINES   Each section of the chapter is presented in a general outline format, which students are intended to examine **BEFORE** they read the chapter. Students should preview or survey a section of text before they read it.

CONCEPT MAPS   Each major section of the chapter is briefly organized into concept maps, which helps students to understand the key concepts without a great deal of confusion. These should be used as visual guides.

TABLES   Many chapters have tables that help students organize, categorize, and form associations to the information. The completed table will be a great study aid, but the act of completing the table is just as important; it is another way to make the information meaningful.

IDIOMS AND SLANGS   Each chapter has a summary of difficult-to-understand words and phrases to help students gain a better understanding of the material provided.

THREE PRACTICE TESTS   Each chapter has three practice tests that represent different testing methods. Practice Test 1 is a multiple-choice test. Practice Test 2 is a short-answer test and requires students to recall (rather than just recognize) information. Practice Test 3 requires students to apply, analyze, and synthesize information in essay or short-answer responses.

ANSWER KEYS   Answer Keys for all practice tests are presented at the end of the Study Guide. They were separated from the chapters to encourage students to try to answer the questions before looking at the key.

HOW TO STUDY

TIRED??

* of reading a chapter and not remembering any of the contents five minutes later?

* of fighting against drooping eyelids and losing?

* of thinking you've studied enough only to find that you can't remember anything that's on the test?

* of studying definitions and terms only to find that the test questions don't ask for definitions and terms; instead, they ask for examples that you never saw in the text?

* of test scores that don't reflect what you know?

It would be nice to be able to say, "Guaranteed, 100%!!! Follow these simple guidelines and you, too, can get an A! Simple! Easy! Money-back guarantee! Teachers and parents will love you, and it will change your life!!" Of course, we cannot make those claims, but we can say the following: "YOU CAN change the above behaviours IF you read AND attempt to use the techniques that are described in this section of the Study Guide." Changing your study habits is like going on a diet. First, you must know the details of the diet: How does it propose to help you eat healthier? However, knowing how the diet works and what you are supposed to eat will NOT cause you to develop healthier eating habits. You must implement the diet. In other words, to receive the benefits, you must DO IT! It is not enough to know what you are supposed to do...you must actually do it! It is the same thing with changing your study habits. It is not enough to know the changes you need to make...you must MAKE THE CHANGES!

STEP 1: DIAGNOSING THE PROBLEM

Some students have developed study skills that work well for them, and they do not wish to change their habits. Some students have many study skills with which they are generally satisfied, but they have one or two areas that need improvement. Other students have difficulty with a number of their study skills. Below is a list of some study skills. Review this list and try to identify whether you are satisfied or dissatisfied with each of these abilities. The preface to this Study Guide focuses on study skills and how to use this manual. As you read the preface, focus on the areas in which you need improvement. If this chapter does not cover that particular area, identify and USE the resources that are available on your campus to get assistance. DON'T ignore study problems. It is unlikely that they will just disappear on their own or that they will improve simply by your trying to do more of what you are already doing!

Check all of the following areas that are problems for you:

Reading the text _____

    Comprehending the material _____

    Concentrating while reading _____

    Identifying what is important _____

    Recalling what you have read _____

    Being distracted easily _____

Time Management

    Not planning your time _____

    Not having enough time to study _____

    Not using the time you have allotted to study _____

    Under-estimating the time you need to study _____

    Difficulty saying no to other plans _____

    Not sticking to your study schedule _____

Getting the Most out of Class _____

    Trouble paying attention in class _____

    Not going to classes _____

    Not understanding what is important _____

Taking Notes

    Your notes aren't helpful _____

    Your notes are disorganized _____

Taking Tests

    Trouble recalling information _____

    Test anxiety _____

    Trouble on multiple-choice questions _____

    Trouble on fill-in-the-blank questions _____

    Trouble on essay questions _____

    Trouble predicting what will be on the test _____

    Trouble going from definitions to examples _____

Identifying your problem areas should help you to focus on the skills that you most need in order to improve. Think about your problem areas as you read the preface and apply the information to your particular situation.

ON BEING A LEARNER or DON'T STOP BEFORE YOU BEGIN!

What was the last new skill you tried to learn? Were you learning to play basketball, softball, tennis, or the guitar? Or were you learning a new language? Whatever you were learning to do, it is very likely that you were not very good at it at first. In fact, you were probably **BAD** at it! <u>That is how it is supposed to be!</u> Your ability to do something well depends on gaining experience with that activity; the more you do it, the better you become at the task. This means that it is necessary to go beyond the beginning period of learning when the new skill is difficult and awkward, and you are not very good at it. This can be frustrating for students who often think they already should know how to study, and if they have to learn new study skills, they should be learned quickly and easily. During the early stages of learning a new skill, a person may be tempted to say, "This isn't working," or "This will never work," or "These techniques feel so artificial." **RESIST** those thoughts. Learning these skills may be difficult at first, but no more difficult than continuing to use skills that you already know **DO NOT WORK!!** If you want to change any long-standing behaviour, you will have to tolerate the early phases of learning when the new behaviours won't yet feel like "your own." In university, graduate school, and employment, you will find that persistence pays. So, **RESIST** returning to your old habits and **PERSIST** with learning the new habits. Don't stop before you begin...give it some time.

MASTERING YOUR MEMORY (OR AT LEAST GETTING THE UPPER HAND!)

A great deal of the information contained in most study skills manuals and courses are based on what is known about how human memory works. Experimental psychologists study memory and how it works; therefore, it is appropriate in this course for you to understand the findings of scientific research on memory and how they apply to **YOU**. Ignore these findings at your peril! This section will present a few general findings about memory that are particularly relevant to your studying. This information comes directly from Chapter 10, which will discuss memory in more detail. Information about memory has applicability not only to your psychology class, but to all of your classes.

KEEPING INFORMATION IN SHORT-TERM MEMORY The three-box model of memory suggests there are three types of memory: sensory memory, short-term memory (STM), and long-term memory (LTM). Sensory memory is a very brief type of memory that lasts less than a second. Sensory memory is important because if information does not get noticed in sensory memory, it cannot be transferred into either short-term or long-term memory. The limits of short-term memory are known. Short-term memory can hold seven (plus or minus two) pieces of information for about 30 seconds or less. A person can extend the amount of time information held in STM by repeating it over and over (this is called maintenance rehearsal); however, once you stop repeating the information, it is quickly lost. Think of times that you have called directory assistance to get the number of the nearest pizza place. You repeat the number over and over and hope your roommate does not come along and ask to borrow your comb, because if your repetition is interrupted, you will forget the number. Many professors believe that most students study in ways that get information into short-term memory, but not in ways that get it into long-term memory.

GETTING INFORMATION INTO LONG-TERM MEMORY Long-term memory can hold an infinite amount of information for an unlimited amount of time. **THAT'S** where you want to store all the information you are studying!! The important question is how to transfer information from short-term memory into long-term memory. The transfer of memory from STM into LTM relies upon the use of elaborative rehearsal. Elaborative rehearsal involves more than the simple repetition of information required by short-term memory; it requires that you make the information meaningful. Making information meaningful requires more than saying "This has deep meaning to me." Meaningfulness can be accomplished by interacting with the material in any **ACTIVE** way. Some examples of ways to make information meaningful include putting it into a story, putting it into a rhyme (i.e., "30 days has September"), forming visual images of the information, forming associations with people or things already familiar to you or associating information to other pieces of information, organizing it into categories, putting it into your own words, explaining it to someone else--almost anything that you do with the information that is **ACTIVE**. Being **ACTIVE** with the information and aiming for **UNDERSTANDING** and not simple repetition of the material are the keys. Almost anything you do with the material that is active will help move it into long-term memory. Passively reading the material will not help the information transfer into long-term memory, but that is the technique most students use.

CRITICAL THINKING AND LONG-TERM MEMORY Critical thinking is emphasized throughout this textbook. Every chapter includes information on how to approach topics critically. Critical thinking requires organizing, analyzing, and evaluating information. This may sound suspiciously like elaborative rehearsal. Critical thinking is important for many reasons. In the context of study skills, critical thinking is important because it involves the same processes that promote the transfer of information into long-term memory.

GETTING MORE INFORMATION INTO SHORT-TERM AND LONG-TERM MEMORY One last piece of information about memory has to do with expanding the amount of information contained in short-term memory. To get information into LTM, it must pass through STM, and we know that STM holds only about seven (plus or minus two) units of information. That does not seem like a practical system, since most textbook chapters seem to contain hundreds of pieces of new information in each chapter! Short-term memory holds **units** or chunks of information, and a strategy to increase the amount of information being held in STM is to include more information in each chunk. For example, you can change 26 separate pieces of information (which far exceeds the capacity of STM) into one piece of information (well within the capacity of STM) by chunking! Whenever you use the word "alphabet" to refer to 26 separate letters, you are chunking. If you organize the information you are studying into categories, or chunks, you will improve your chances of getting more information into LTM in two ways: 1) you will increase the information contained in the units getting into STM, and 2) you will be making the information meaningful by the act of organizing it into the chunks! You can't lose! Making outlines is a good way to chunk information. Outlines naturally organize information into categories (chunks) and subcategories. This study guide presents the information in ways that help you to organize information into chunks, which also helps make the information meaningful.

STUDYING WITH THE SQ3R OR STAYING AWAKE, STAYING ACTIVE, AND OPENING THE DOOR TO LONG-TERM MEMORY

The SQ3R method was developed by Francis Robinson, a psychology professor at Ohio State University. It is a method of reading assignments that implements many techniques that promote the transfer of information into long-term memory. The letters "SQ3R" stand for <u>survey, question, read, receive, review</u>.

SURVEY Before you read a chapter or reading assignment, it is important to survey what is in the chapter and how the information is organized. You can do this by simply looking over the headings or the chapter outlines at the beginning of each chapter. This Study Guide also provides more detailed preview outlines for this purpose. It is important that you survey the information before you read, because surveying turns what otherwise would seem like hundreds of independent facts (which far exceeds the capacity of STM) into a much smaller number (probably five to nine--textbook authors know how memory works) of main topics identified in separate headings. Once you have seen the main headings, you have an organizational structure to begin your reading. This helps you organize the information when you begin reading (remember that organizing is one way to make information meaningful, which transfers it into LTM). Surveying a chapter in the text is like going on a trip. Before you arrive at a city you do not know, it is very helpful to look at a map. You quickly can see the location of the airport, your hotel, downtown, the river, and the three important sites you want to see. This orients you to your journey. If you do not look at a map before your arrival, you are wandering around without knowing where you are going. You do not want to wander around a 40-page chapter that contains a great deal of information without knowing where you are going.

QUESTION Assume you are taking an exam that contains a comprehension section. There are several paragraphs for you to read, and then you are to answer five questions about the reading. Would you read the questions before you read the paragraphs, or would you read the paragraphs and then begin to try to answer the questions? Most of you would read the questions first, so that as you read the paragraphs, you could keep the questions in mind and look for the answers while you read. The reasons for formulating questions before you read your text are: 1) to help you read with a purpose, and 2) to help you be more active while you read.

After you have surveyed the chapter, formulate questions by converting the headings, key terms, and definitions into questions. For example, "The Major Psychological Perspectives" is a subheading in Chapter 1. "What are the names and key concepts of the major psychological perspectives?" is one example of changing that subheading into a question. This Study Guide has listed the relevant learning objectives for each. In addition, you should try to formulate additional questions and write them on a separate piece of paper. The intention is that you will write the answers to all these questions while you read the chapter. This helps you read with a purpose: your purpose is to answer the questions. This also helps you to be active while you read. You are being active by looking for the answers to the questions **AND** by writing down the answers as you find them. You will also have answers to all the learning objectives in writing when you go to study for quizzes and exams.

READ You are now ready to read. You have surveyed the chapter in order to know where you are going and how the chapter is organized. You have formulated your questions in order to know what you are looking for as you read. While reading, you will be organizing the information and answering the questions. These are both ways to increase the transfer of information into long-term memory. As you begin your reading, look at your first question. Open your textbook to the part of the chapter that applies to the question and read in order to answer that question.

RECITE After you have surveyed the reading assignment to get the general idea of its content, have turned the first heading into a question, and have read that section to answer the question, you are now ready to recite. Reciting helps make information meaningful (did you ever notice that when you speak in class, you tend to remember the information you spoke or asked about?). Also, it is another way that you can be active (which also makes the information meaningful). Reciting requires that you put the information into your own words, and it is an excellent way to identify what you don't yet understand. There are a number of ways to recite.

Using the learning objectives and the questions that you have formulated, recite aloud the answers to the questions (without looking at the answers). You can say definitions or examples of key terms, terms that are listed in bold, or terms that are underlined as a vehicle for reciting information. You can recite responses to learning objectives. Explaining information to other people, either classmates or patient friends who are willing to help, is also a good way to recite the information. Explaining the information to others also allows you to identify areas that you do not understand well. Remember, your recitation of information should be in your own words and should attempt to give examples of the concepts you are describing. If you simply try to memorize definitions given in the text and recite these definitions, you are simply camouflaging maintenance rehearsal. Remember, getting information into long-term memory involves meaning--so make sure you understand the material and can make it "your own" to get it into long-term memory.

REVIEW The final step in the SQ3R approach is to review the material again. Frequent reviews, even brief reviews, are among the important keys to learning. After at least one hour, review the material once more. This can be done by going over the main points of the chapter (with your book closed), going over the answers to the questions you have written (without looking at them), and reviewing key terms and concepts. Limit your reviews to about five minutes. Reviews can be used in other ways too. Begin each study session with a five-minute review. Before each class, review notes from the previous class for five minutes. At the end of every class, review your notes for five minutes.

SUMMARY The SQ3R method incorporates the information that psychologists know about how people learn and remember. The key points to remember include: **BE ACTIVE, MAKE INFORMATION MEANINGFUL, INTERACT WITH THE INFORMATION, AIM FOR UNDERSTANDING NOT JUST REPETITION, THINK CRITICALLY.** All this can be achieved by writing, talking, thinking, making outlines, forming associations, developing questions and examples and putting definitions in your own words. The SQ3R method suggests that these goals can be achieved if you:

1. Survey the information: Use headings and chapter summaries to orient yourself to the information you plan to read. Give the information an organizational structure.
2. Question: Turn the headings, terms, and concepts into questions.
3. Read: Read each section to answer the specific questions that you asked. Write your answers on a separate sheet of paper.
4. Recite: Close your book and rehearse the information contained in the section by answering the relevant questions or giving examples of key terms or concepts.
5. Review: After at least an hour-long break, close your book, turn over your notes, and list the main points of the chapter and the answers to your questions.

REMEMBER, this may feel awkward or hard to do at first, BUT the more you use this method, the easier it will become.

WHEN AND WHERE TO STUDY

In many courses, several weeks can pass between tests. You might wonder whether it is better to study intensely the night before the test or to spread out your studying time. Memory research clearly suggests that "cramming" just doesn't work. You may know this from personal experience. Rather than studying for hours and hours just before the test, it is much more effective to study as you go along in the course.

In terms of when to study, the best time to study is immediately after class. BEFORE going to class, you should preview the material to be covered, form general questions, and read the text. Study the subject that was covered as soon after the lecture as possible. You will find it easier to master the material and will have an opportunity to test your understanding of the lecture if you study right away. The procedure of continuously studying fairly small chunks will also help you to avoid the nightmare of the infrequent studier--the sudden realization that you don't understand any of what you have been covering for the last few weeks. If you study for a short period after each lecture, you will not have to worry about this. You will also find that tomorrow's lecture will be easier to understand if you study today's material and master the essential points covered by your teacher. Most professors structure lectures so that each one builds on earlier lectures and readings. Studying as you go along will guarantee that you are well prepared to get the most out of each new lecture. It is also a good idea to set a specific time to study. Even if it is for a short time, you should study at a regular time every day.

In terms of where to study, many students indicate that they have difficulty concentrating. Upon further examination, it seems that many students study with their TV or MP3 player on at the same time and place their roommates are having a snack or are on the phone. Some general guidelines about where to study include:
1. Limit the places that you study to one or two special locations. These could be the library, a desk, or a designated study area. They are special in the sense that they should be places where the only thing you do there is study. That means you should not study in places where you regularly do something else (such as the dining room table or bed).
2. Make these places free from distractions, Distractions like the telephone, and other electronic devices or friends can cause studying to be abandoned.

3.   Set a specific time to begin studying and then study in the same place every day. In that way, that place will become a cue to study.

OTHER SKILLS THAT INFLUENCE STUDYING

Many skills influence study habits. The diagnostic checklist at the beginning of this section identifies some of the skills that students must possess to study effectively. Skills that affect studying include the following: time management, note taking, test preparation, test taking, stress management, using the library, dealing with professors, and classroom participation. All of these abilities are important. In fact, they are so important that entire books have been devoted to helping students develop these skills. Many colleges and universities offer various types of academic assistance, from courses on study skills to individual counselling on study skills. One of the survival skills necessary for post-secondary students is to be aware of the services offered by your institution and to make use of them as needed. If you have identified problem areas that influence your performance, you have several choices: find a book on study skills in your library, look for courses at your school that deal with study skills, or identify other campus resources that are available to assist you in developing these abilities.

CHAPTER ONE

What Is Psychology?

LEARNING OBJECTIVES

After studying this chapter, you should be able to do the following:

1. Define psychology.
2. Distinguish psychology from nonscientific and pseudoscientific approaches.
3. Define critical thinking.
4. Explain the eight guidelines for critical thinking.
5. Summarize the early history and development of psychology, using the example of phrenology to illustrate the hazards of not using empirical methods.
6. Discuss the role of empirical evidence in the birth of modern psychology.
7. Describe the goals and methods of structuralism.
8. Describe the goals and methods of functionalism.
9. Describe the basic ideas of psychoanalysis.
10. Describe the major principles of the biological, learning, cognitive, sociocultural, and psychodynamic perspectives in psychology.
11. Discuss the influences of the humanistic movement on psychology.
12. Discuss the influences of the feminist movement on psychology.
13. Describe the three general professional categories that psychologists generally fall into. Give examples.
14. Distinguish between applied and basic psychology.
15. Describe and give examples of the major nonclinical specialties in psychology.
16. Describe the history and the mandate of the Canadian Psychological Association.
17. Describe the training requirements for becoming a psychologist in Canada.
18. Distinguish between a psychotherapist, a psychoanalyst, a psychiatrist, a clinical psychologist, and other practising mental health professionals.
19. Identify the basic areas of agreement among psychologists.
20. Outline five ways psychology can contribute to your life.

BRIEF CHAPTER SUMMARY

Chapter 1 defines psychology and traces the historical and disciplinary roots of the field to its current perspectives, specialty areas, and activities. Critical-thinking guidelines are described, and students are encouraged to understand and apply these concepts as they read the text. The complexity of human behaviour requires that students resist simplistic thinking and the search for simple answers. Five current perspectives and two important movements are identified. The current perspectives include the biological perspective, learning perspective, cognitive perspective, psychodynamic perspective, and sociocultural perspective. The two important movements are the feminist and humanistic movements. Each of these approaches reflects a different emphasis and approach to understanding human behaviour. Students are encouraged to think about human behaviour from each different perspective and use their critical-thinking skills to compare and contrast these approaches. A review of the specialty areas within the field helps students appreciate that psychology includes vastly diverse topics and that psychologists are engaged in a wide variety of occupations. Examples of specialty areas include educational psychologists, developmental psychologists, and psychometric psychologists. The practice of psychology, which helps people with mental health problems, is discussed along with a description of types of practitioners within the field of psychology (e.g., counselling psychologists, school psychologists) and those outside of it. Although psychologists have different orientations and different occupational activities, almost all of them share a fascination with the human mind and behaviour and stress the importance of empirical evidence critical to making psychology a science.

PREVIEW OUTLINE

Before you read the chapter, review the preview outline for each section of the text. After you have read the chapter, close this book and try to <u>re-create</u> the outlines on a blank piece of paper.

I. **PSYCHOLOGY, PSEUDOSCIENCE, AND POPULAR OPINION**
    A. **Psychology** - scientific study of behaviour and mental processes, and how they are affected by an organism's physical state, mental state, and the external environment
    B. **Psychobabble** - pseudoscience covered by veneer of psychological language
        1. Psychology is based on research evidence, whereas popular opinion is not.
        2. Psychobabble confirms existing beliefs; psychology challenges them and deepens our understanding of accepted facts.

II. **THINKING CRITICALLY AND CREATIVELY ABOUT PSYCHOLOGY**
    A. **Critical thinking** - ability and willingness to assess claims and make objective judgments on the basis of well-supported reasons and evidence rather than emotion and anecdote; the basis of all science

B. **Eight critical-thinking guidelines**
1.   Ask questions; be willing to wonder
2.   Define your terms
3.   Examine the evidence
4.   Analyze assumptions and biases
5.   Avoid emotional reasoning
6.   Don't oversimplify
7.   Consider other interpretations
8.   Tolerate uncertainty

What is Psychology?

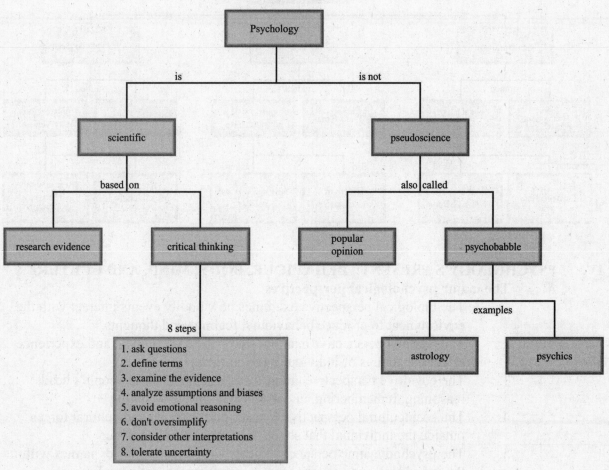

III. PSYCHOLOGY'S PAST: FROM THE ARMCHAIR TO THE LABORATORY

A.   **Early history and phrenology - Hippocrates, the Stoics, Locke**

B.   **The birth of modern psychology and Wilhelm Wundt**

C.   **Three early approaches to psychology**

      1.   Structuralism and E. B. Titchener

      2.   Functionalism, William James, and Charles Darwin

      3.   Psychoanalysis and Sigmund Freud

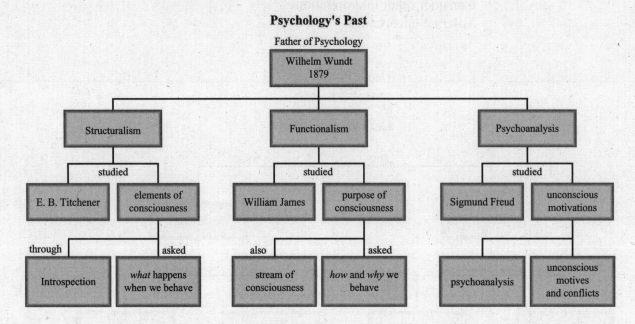

IV. PSYCHOLOGY'S PRESENT: BEHAVIOUR, BODY, MIND, AND CULTURE

A.   **The major psychological perspectives**

      1.   The biological perspective examines how bodily events interact with the environment to produce behaviours, feelings and thoughts.

      2.   The learning perspective examines how the environment and experience affect the actions of individuals (or animals)

      3.   The cognitive perspective emphasizes what goes on in people's heads: reasoning, remembering, understanding, problem solving

      4.   The sociocultural perspective focuses on the social and cultural forces outside the individual that shape every aspect of behaviour

      5.   The psychodynamic perspective deals with unconscious dynamics within the individual, such as inner forces, conflicts, or instinctual energy

B.   **Two influential movements in psychology**

      1.   Humanistic psychology rejects the psychoanalytic perspective as too pessimistic and behaviourism as too mechanistic.It emphasizes free will, personal growth, resilience and the achievement of human potential.

      2.   Feminist psychology analyzes the influence of social inequities on gender relations and identifies biases in research and psychotherapy

Psychology's Present: Behaviour, Body, Mind, and Culture

V. WHAT PSYCHOLOGISTS DO

A. Overview of professional activities
1. Teach and conduct research in colleges and universities
2. Provide health or mental health services (psychological practice)
3. Conduct research or apply findings in nonacademic settings

B. Psychological research
1. Basic psychology - research that seeks knowledge for its own sake
2. Applied psychology - research concerned with the practical uses of knowledge
3. Some major nonclinical specialties in psychology: experimental psychologists, psychometric psychologists, developmental psychologists, industrial/organizational psychologists, and educational psychologists

C. Psychological practice
1. Those who try to understand and improve physical and mental health
2. Practitioners of psychology work in mental or general hospitals, clinics, schools, counselling centres, and private practice
3. Types of practitioners: counselling psychologists, school psychologists, clinical psychologists; Degrees for practice: Ph.D., Ed.D., Psy.D.
4. Types of nonclinical psychologist practitioners: psychotherapist, psychoanalyst, psychiatrist, social worker, marriage and family counsellors

D.   Psychology in the community

What Psychologists Do

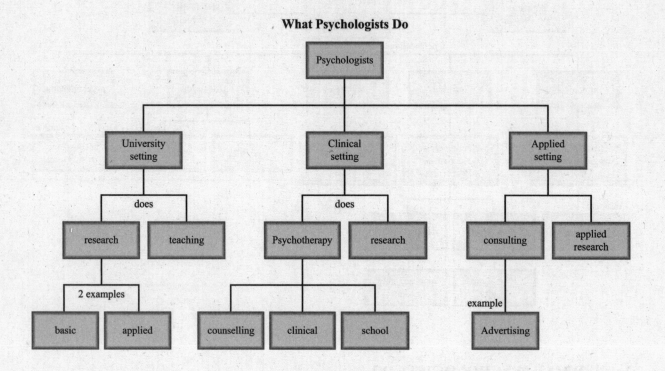

VI.   BIOLOGY AND PSYCHOLOGY: BEYOND THE BORDERS
   A.   **Variety in psychologists' activities, goals, and perspectives creates a mosaic**
   B.   **Though there is disagreement about emphasis, psychological scientists and scientist-clinicians agree on basic guidelines**
      1.   Most believe in the importance of empirical evidence
      2.   Most avoid one-note explanations of behaviour and either-or thinking
      3.   Most share a fascination of human behaviour and mind

PERSPECTIVES TABLE

Complete this table, and then identify similarities and differences among perspectives and movements.

PERSPECTIVE OR MOVEMENT	KEY FIGURES	KEY CONCEPTS AND TERMS	MAJOR INFLUENCES ON BEHAVIOUR
BIOLOGICAL PERSPECTIVE			
LEARNING PERSPECTIVE			
COGNITIVE PERSPECTIVE			
PSYCHODYNAMIC PERSPECTIVE			
SOCIOCULTURAL PERSPECTIVE			
HUMANISTIC MOVEMENT			
FEMINIST MOVEMENT			

IDIOMS AND SLANGS

Psychobabble – Pseudoscience and quackery covered by a veneer of psychological language (page 4) – The textbook refers to psychobabble as a false science that is hidden behind psychological words and language. Quackery refers to the activities or behaviours of an unknowledgeable individual who claims to have knowledge.

Electrical gizmos (page 4) – People are very interested in technological inventions and machines. These gizmos or toys may be a sign of psychobabble.

Examples of flabby thinking (page 7) – The textbook is implying that some people do not practise how to think so they get lazy in their mental skills.

From the armchair to the laboratory (page 17) – This phrase refers to how psychology went from something people talked about to something we scientifically tested.

Blunders (page 17) – While trying to measure behaviour, psychologists made a number foolish or stupid mistakes. One example was phrenology.

Gamut of topics (page 18) – Wundt's researchers could not possibly test the entire range or scale of behaviours, so they had to focus their studies.

Structuralism soon went the way of the dinosaur (page 19) – The textbook is referring to the disappearance of the early approach of studying psychology called structuralism. Like the dinosaur, it became extinct.

The five lenses that predominate in psychology today (page 21) – Referring to the five areas of psychology listed in the textbook, which are biological, learning, cognitive, sociocultural, and psychodynamic.

The social and cultural environment that people swim in everyday (page 22) – Refers to the social setting and cultural influences that sociocultural psychologists study.

The word *psychologist* conjures up an image (page 25) – Typically, a psychologist is thought of as a therapist who helps people with their problems.

Makes people tick (page 32) – Means why people behave or think the way they do.

PRACTICE TEST 1 - Multiple Choice

1. Psychology is defined as
   A. the scientific study of behaviour and how it is affected by an organism's physical state, mental state, and the external environment.
   B. the scientific study of behaviour and mental processes and how they are affected by an organism's physical state, mental state, and the external environment.
   C. the scientific study of mental processes and how they are affected by an organism's physical state, mental state, and the external environment.
   D. the scientific study of groups and institutions in society.

2. The main difference between psychological knowledge and popular opinion is that
   A. psychological knowledge is contained in textbooks, but popular opinion is not.
   B. psychological knowledge is based on research evidence, but popular opinion is not.
   C. findings based on psychological knowledge are often the opposite of popular opinion.
   D. popular opinion is usually very obvious and psychological knowledge is rarely the expected result.

3. "Unhappy memories that are often repressed and then later recalled accurately," "abused children inevitably become abusive parents," and "abstinence from alcohol reduces rates of alcoholism" are all examples of
   A. popular opinions that have been supported by research evidence.
   B. common beliefs that have been contradicted by the evidence.
   C. scientific research findings.
   D. ideas that have been rejected by popular opinion.

4. The ability and willingness to assess claims and make objective judgments on the basis of well-supported reasons and evidence rather than emotion and anecdote defines
   A. critical thinking.   B. psychobabble.
   C. common sense.   D. psychology.

5. All of the following are essential elements of critical thinking, EXCEPT:
   A. Ask questions; be willing to wonder.
   B. Examine the evidence.
   C. Avoid emotional reasoning: "If I feel this way, it must be true."
   D. Reduce an issue to a simple concept.

6. _____ established the first psychology lab in 1879 and is considered the "father of psychology."
   A. E. B. Titchener   B. William James
   C. B. F. Skinner   D. Wilhelm Wundt

7. An early school of psychology, popularized by E. B. Titchener, attempted to analyze sensations, images, and feelings into their most basic elements. This school was called
   A. structuralism.   B. introspection.
   C. functionalism.   D. behaviourism.

8. A second early school of psychology asked how and why an organism's behaviour helps it to adapt to its environment. It was called
   A. structuralism.   B. introspection.
   C. functionalism.   D. behaviourism.

9. Titchener is to James as
   A. trained introspection is to Wundt.
   B. functionalism is to structuralism.
   C. trained introspection is to functionalism.
   D. structuralism is to functionalism.

10. Proponents of the _____ perspective believe that to understand the mind, one must study the nervous system, because all actions, feelings, and thoughts are associated with bodily events.
   A. behavioural   B. psychodynamic
   C. cognitive   D. biological

11. You have recently started psychotherapy with a psychologist who believes in the learning perspective. Which of the following statements would she make?
   A. "To best address your problem, we must identify the behaviours that are causing problems and the environmental conditions including the rewards and punishments that maintain the behaviours, and then we must modify those behaviours."
   B. "To help you we must identify your unconscious inner conflicts, memories, and emotional traumas from your early childhood."
   C. "Your problem has to do with how you are thinking about this situation. You must examine your expectations and try to understand this differently."
   D. "We must examine your problem in the context of the broader culture and how cultural expectations and beliefs are affecting your behaviour."

12. "To understand a person's actions, we must concentrate on the environmental conditions--the rewards and punishments--that maintain or discourage specific behaviours, rather than studying the mind or mental states." This reflects the position of the _____ perspective.
   A. learning   B. psychodynamic
   C. cognitive   D. biological

13. Which perspective or movement has helped people eliminate unwanted habits?
   A. humanism   B. biological
   C. learning   D. psychodynamic

14. _____ theorists combine elements of behaviourism with research on thoughts, values, expectations, and intentions.
  A. Social-cognitive learning
  B. Psychodynamic
  C. Humanist biological
  D. Biological

15. What goes on in people's heads, including how people reason, remember, understand language, and solve problems, are some of the topics emphasized by the
  A. the sociocultural perspective.
  B. humanists.
  C. social-cognitive theory.
  D. cognitive perspective.

16. "To understand the causes of the high rates of anorexia nervosa among older adolescent women, we must consider the influence of society's norms for female beauty and thinness." This statement reflects which of the following perspectives?
  A. sociocultural
  B. humanistic
  C. psychoanalytic
  D. cognitive

17. "The answer to violence and cruelty doesn't reside in instincts, brain circuits, or personal dispositions, but in situational, economic, and cultural factors." This statement is consistent with the thinking of _____ psychologists.
  A. cognitive
  B. humanistic
  C. sociocultural
  D. psychodynamic

18. "Psychological distress is a result of inner forces, specifically unresolved unconscious conflicts from early childhood." This statement reflects the position of the _____ perspective.
  A. behavioural
  B. psychodynamic
  C. cognitive
  D. biological

19. Developed in reaction to Freudian pessimism and behaviouristic "mindlessness," _____ was based on the notion that human beings had free will.
  A. feminist psychology
  B. social learning theory
  C. sociocultural psychology
  D. humanistic psychology

20. Which of the following might be one of the goals of feminist psychology?
  A. Encourage research on menstruation and motherhood.
  B. Identify biases in psychological research and psychotherapy.
  C. Make sure that both male and female subjects are used in research design.
  D. All of the above.

21. Which of the following best describes the difference between applied and basic research?
    A. Basic research examines the basic elements of sensations, images, and feelings, whereas applied research studies how these processes help a person adapt to the environment.
    B. Basic psychological research seeks knowledge for its own sake, whereas applied psychological research is concerned with the practical uses of knowledge.
    C. Applied research seeks knowledge for its own sake, whereas basic research is concerned with the practical uses of knowledge.
    D. Basic research is based on the psychoanalytic perspective, whereas applied research is based on the humanistic approach.

22. Psychologists who conduct laboratory studies of learning, motivation, emotion, sensation and perception, physiology, and cognition are called _____ psychologists.
    A. experimental   B. educational
    C. developmental   D. social

23. A developmental psychologist would
    A. conduct a study on infant attachment behaviour.
    B. conduct research on the role of arousal in the experience of emotions.
    C. develop a new test to measure personality.
    D. design and evaluate tests of mental abilities, aptitudes, interests, and personality.

24. A psychometric psychologist
    A. studies how groups, institutions, and the social context influence individuals.
    B. studies how people change and grow over time physically, mentally, and socially.
    C. designs and evaluates tests of mental abilities, aptitudes, interests, and personality.
    D. studies behaviour in the workplace.

25. Psychologists who help people deal with problems of everyday life, such as test anxiety, family or marital problems, or low job motivation, are called _____ psychologists.
    A. psychometric   B. clinical
    C. counselling   D. school

26. Which of the following is a research area in psychology rather than a practice specialty?
    A. counselling psychology
    B. school psychology
    C. clinical psychology
    D. educational psychology

27. Which type of psychologist would be most likely to work with highly disturbed people?
    A. clinical   B. experimental
    C. counselling   D. school

12

28. A psychotherapist
   A. has specialized training at a psychoanalytic institute.
   B. is not required to have any training at all in most states.
   C. has a medical degree.
   D. is a psychologist.

29. Dr. Iriko believes that Jon's depression is biochemical and writes him a prescription for antidepressant drugs. She is most likely a
   A. counselling psychologist.   B. psychotherapist.
   C. psychiatrist.   D. social worker.

30. Though there are many areas of disagreement among psychologists, which of the following describes one of the guidelines on which psychological scientists and scientist-clinicians agree? Most
   A. agree that psychiatrists are better able to help people than psychologists.
   B. agree that the behavioural perspective is superior to all other perspectives.
   C. believe that applied psychology is more important that basic psychology.
   D. believe in the importance of empirical evidence.

31. The principle of Occam's razor states that
   A. the explanation that makes the fewest unverified assumptions is the best one.
   B. emotional reasoning should be avoided at all costs.
   C. knowledge is useless if it cannot be applied.
   D. simple explanations are usually not the correct ones.

32.
Licensed clinical social workers and marriage, family, and child counsellors ordinarily treat
   A. general problems in adjustment and family conflicts
   B. severe mental disturbances
   C. mental disorders with medication
   D. only patients who participate in research studies

PRACTICE TEST 2 - Short Answer

1. Psychology is defined as the scientific study of _behaviour_ and _mental process_, and how they are affected by an organism's physical state, mental state, and the external environment.

2. Scientific psychology differs from popular psychology in that it is based on _empirical_ evidence.

3. _critical thinking_ is the ability and willingness to assess claims and make objective judgments on the basis of well-supported reasons and evidence rather than emotion and anecdote.

4. Two of the eight guidelines for critical thinking are:
    ask ?'s
    define term, examine evidence, analyze assumpt.

5. Early psychologists, like today's psychologists, wanted to describe, _predict_, understand, and _modify_ behaviour in order to add to human knowledge and increase human happiness.

6. William Wundt's favourite research method was _trained intro spectrum_.

7. Titchener named his early approach _structuralism_.

8. According to psychoanalysis, distressful symptoms are due to _conflict/trauma early childhood_.

9. The _psychodynamic_ perspective is related to Freud's theory of psychoanalysis.

10. The five major current psychological perspectives are:
    biological, learning, cognitive, sociocultural & psycho dynamic

11. The _learning_ perspective is concerned with how the environment and experience affect a person's actions.

12. Unlike behaviourists and psychoanalysts, humanists believe that human beings have _free will_.

13. The _cognitive_ is one of the strongest forces in psychology today, and it has inspired an explosion of research on the workings of the mind.

14. The sociocultural perspective focuses on _social / cutural forces_

15. Within the sociocultural perspective, social psychologists focus on _social rules, roles, groups & authority_, while _cultural_ psychologists emphasize how cultural rules and values affect people's development, behaviour, and feelings.

16. Psychologists from the _feminist_ movement have noted that many studies used only men as subjects.

17. _basic_ psychology is the generation of knowledge for its own sake, whereas _applied_ psychology is concerned with the practical uses of such knowledge.

18. _Industrial / occupational_ psychologists study behaviour in the workplace, whereas _educational_ psychologists study principles that explain learning and look for ways to improve educational systems.

19. Both of the psychological specialties described in question 18 are considered _non-clinical_ specialties.

20. Three examples of practice specialties in psychology are _clinical_, _counselling_, and _school_.

21. In the past, the focus of _developmental_ psychologists was mainly on childhood, but many now study adolescence, young and middle adulthood, or old age.

22. In Canada, the regulation of psychological practice is the responsibility of the _province_. In most cases, psychologists possess a _doctorate_ degree whereas psychological associates possess a _masters_ degree.

23. People often confuse clinical psychologists with _psychotherapist_, _psychoanalyst_, or _psychiatrist_.

24. _psychiatrist_ have a medical degree and may prescribe medication, whereas _psychotherapist_ are not required to have any degree at all since the term is not legally regulated.

25. Other types of professionals who engage in mental-health fields include _social workers_, _school counsellors_, and _family/child counsellors_

26. _evolutionary_ psychology focuses on how genetically influenced behaviour that was adaptive during our ancestral past may be reflected in our present behaviours.

27. The contemporary research area of positive psychology flows from the _humanist_ tradition.

PRACTICE TEST 3 - Essay

1.   Several activities are described below. For each activity, indicate (a) whether it is an example of applied or basic psychology, (b) the area of specialization most likely to be involved, and (c) whether that area of specialization is a clinical or nonclinical area. Explain the reasons for your answers.

   A.   Psychologist David Wechsler designed an intelligence test expressly for use with adults.

   B.   Researchers Hubel and Wiesel (1962, 1968) received a Nobel Prize for their work in the area of vision. They found that special cells in the brain are designed to visually code complex features of an object. Their research involved recording impulses from individual cells in the brains of cats and monkeys.

   C.   Swiss biologist Jean Piaget observed that children of different ages understand concepts and reason differently. Based on his observations, he developed a theory of cognitive development.

   D.   Several researchers have studied work motivation. They have been interested in the conditions that influence productivity and satisfaction in organizations.

   E.   In 1963, Stanley Milgram conducted a classic study on obedience to authority. In subsequent variations of the original study, Milgram and his colleagues investigated the conditions under which people might disobey.

   F.   Strupp conducted research in 1982 to examine the characteristics of effective psychotherapy. He found that the relationship between the therapist and client greatly affects the success of the therapy.

   G.   A national study of 3,000 children in fourth through tenth grades found that over this period of time girls' self-esteem plummeted (American Association of University Women, 1991). As a result of recommendations based on the findings of this and other research, changes in school systems have been suggested.

   H.   Several psychologists have studied the process of career development and use these theories to assist college and university students in selecting their careers.

2. Harold is 17 years old and has been abusing alcohol and marijuana for the past year. He has been missing school and his academic performance is declining. Harold was formerly a "B" student and was involved in sports. He is now getting Ds and Fs and has dropped out of most extracurricular activities. Answer the following question: What influences would each of the five perspectives (learning, psychodynamic, biological, cognitive and sociocultural) and two movements in psychology (humanist and feminist) identify as central to the development of Harold's drug problem?

3. Juanita is suffering from depression and she is interested in seeking professional help for her problem. Briefly describe the general types of treatment that would most likely be utilized by a psychologist, a psychiatrist, a psychoanalyst, and a psychotherapist. Indicate the types of training they are likely to have had.

4. Suppose that your friend Zainab dreamed that she would meet a hero of hers and have a personal discussion with him. A few days later, it actually happens! Zainab is convinced that she is psychic—she has special, paranormal powers. Using the critical thinking concepts, could you explain this event differently than Zainab? Would you give her any advice to help her think critically about this event?

CHAPTER TWO

How Psychologists Do Research

LEARNING OBJECTIVES

After studying this chapter, you should be able to do the following:

1. List the reasons research methods are important to psychologists.

2. List and discuss the five characteristics of scientific psychological research.

3. Distinguish between a theory and a hypothesis.

4. Define the principle of falsifiability and describe its relationship to the confirmation bias.

5. List and discuss the characteristics of descriptive research methods.

6. Describe and give examples of case studies, naturalistic observations, and laboratory observations. Discuss the advantages and disadvantages of each descriptive research method.

7. Distinguish between objective and projective tests. Define standardization and norms.

8. Distinguish between test reliability and validity. Describe two types of reliability and twoz types of validity. Give examples of each.

9. Describe the advantages and disadvantages of surveys.

10. Describe the benefits and drawbacks of using technology in survey research.

11. Define the word correlation. Give examples of positive and negative correlations. List and discuss the characteristics and limitations of correlational studies, specifically noting why correlation does not necessarily mean causation.

12. Distinguish between experimental and descriptive research studies.

13. Distinguish between independent and dependent variables and identify examples of each.

14. Distinguish between experimental and control groups.

15. Describe what is meant by random assignment and discuss the use of placebos.

16. Describe single- and double-blind studies and explain how they improve experiments.

17. Discuss the advantages and limitations of experimental research.

18. List and describe the types of descriptive statistics.

19. Describe how inferential statistics are used and explain statistical significance.

20. Compare and contrast cross-sectional and longitudinal studies.

21. Describe the technique of meta-analysis.

22. Define informed consent. Describe the procedures that experimenters must follow when deception occurs in research.

23. Outline the eight principles researchers must follow with human subjects.

24. Describe some of the reasons for using animals in research.

25. Describe five strategies that one should use when being presented with statistics, to avoid misinterpretation.

BRIEF CHAPTER SUMMARY

Chapter 2 discusses the importance of understanding scientific methodology in the psychological context. The text describes the characteristics of scientific research that should be used to evaluate research findings in psychology and in other fields. Three major types of research studies are described: descriptive studies, correlational studies, and experimental studies. Descriptive studies include case studies, observational studies, studies based on psychological tests, and studies based on surveys. Correlational studies are a special category of descriptive studies that describe relationships between two variables. Correlational research is very useful in making predictions from one variable to another. Experimental research is the best type to determine cause-and-effect relationships because it is conducted in a highly controlled fashion. The components of experimental research include independent and dependent variables, random assignment to conditions, and experimental and control conditions. Potential biases in conducting research are discussed, as well as methods to reduce such biases (e.g., single-blind and double-blind studies). The text explains descriptive and inferential statistics and demonstrates how they help to make research findings meaningful. Finally, the ethical concerns revolving around studying human beings and animals are discussed.

PREVIEW OUTLINE

Before you read the chapter, review the preview outline for each section of the text. After you have read the chapter, close this book and try to <u>re-create</u> the outlines on a blank piece of paper.

I. **WHAT MAKES PSYCHOLOGICAL RESEARCH SCIENTIFIC?**
    A.   **Why are research methods so important to psychologists?**
        1.   Helps separate truth from unfounded belief
        2.   Helps sort out conflicting views
        3.   Helps correct false ideas that may cause people harm
    B.   **What makes research scientific?**
        1.   Precision
            a.   Start with a theory: organized system of assumptions and principles that claims to explain certain phenomena
            b.   From a hunch or theory, derive a specific hypothesis
            c.   Operational definitions: terms must be defined in ways that can be observed and measured
        2.   Skepticism: accept conclusions with caution but be open to new ideas
        3.   Reliance on empirical evidence rather than on personal accounts

4.   Willingness to make "risky predictions" and the principle of falsifiability
5.   Openness in the scientific community so that findings can be replicated

What Makes Psychological Research Scientific?

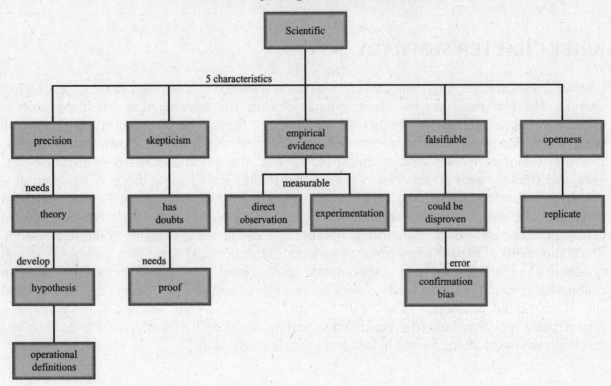

II. DESCRIPTIVE STUDIES: ESTABLISHING THE FACTS
-allow researchers to describe and predict behaviour but do not choose one explanation over another
-include a variety of research methodologies, all requiring selection of representative sample of subjects

    A.   Case Studies - detailed descriptions of particular individuals
        1.   Advantages include producing detailed picture of one individual
        2.   Disadvantages: rely on possibly inaccurate memories, cannot generalize to all human behaviour, do not test hypotheses

    B.   Observational Studies – observing, recording behaviour without interfering
        1.   Naturalistic observation: used to find out how people or animals act in their normal environment
        2.   Laboratory observation: scientist has greater control, but participant might alter his or her behaviour

C. **Tests (assessment instruments) - procedures to measure personality traits, emotional states, aptitudes, interests, abilities, and values**
    1.   Types of tests
        a.   Objective tests (inventories) - measure beliefs, feelings or behaviours of which an individual is aware
        b.   Projective tests - designed to study the unconscious
    2.   Characteristics of a good test
        a.   Standardization - uniform procedures for giving and scoring the test
        b.   Norms - established standards of performance
        c.   Reliability - getting the same results from one time to another
            (1)   Test–retest - giving the same test twice
            (2)   Alternate-forms - giving different versions of the same test
        d.   Validity - a test measures what it set out to measure
            (1)   Content validity - test questions ask about a broad array of beliefs and behaviours relevant to what is being measured
            (2)   Criterion validity - predicts other measures of the trait

D. **Surveys**
    1.   Gather information by asking people directly
    2.   Potential problems with surveys (e.g., bias in question wording, representativeness of sample, volunteer bias, participants lie or forget)
3.   Benefits and risks of using technology in survey research.

Descriptive Studies: Establishing the Facts

III.CORRELATIONAL STUDIES: LOOKING FOR RELATIONSHIPS

A. **Purpose** – to determine whether two variables are related, and if so, how strongly

B. **Characteristics of correlations**
   1. Direction of a relationship between variables
      a. Positive correlation - high values of one variable are associated with high values of the other; low values of one variable are associated with low values of the other
      b. Negative correlation - high values of one variable are associated with low values of the other
   2. Correlation coefficient indicates the strength of relationship between the two variables; ranges from -1 (strong negative) to $+1$ (strong positive)

C. **Benefits and limitations of correlations**
   1. Benefit - allows someone to predict from one variable to another
   2. Limitation - cannot show causation

Correlational Studies: Looking for Relationships

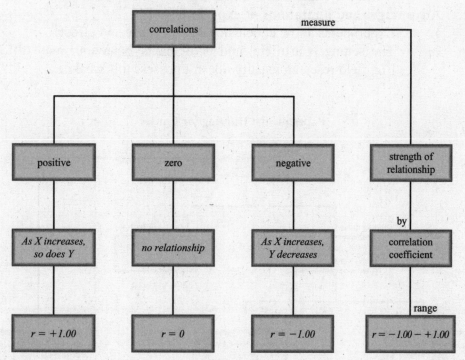

23

IV. EXPERIMENTS: HUNTING FOR CAUSES

A. **Purpose of experimentation** - to look for causes of behaviour because the experiment allows the researcher to control the situation being studied

B. **Experimental variables** - the characteristics the researcher is studying
1. Independent variable - the characteristic manipulated by the experimenter
2. Dependent variable - the behaviour the researcher tries to predict

C. **Experimental and control conditions**
1. Experimental condition - the condition or group in which participants receive some amount of the independent variable
2. Control condition - the condition or group in which participants do not receive any amount of the independent variable
3. Random assignment balances individual differences among participants between the two groups

D. **Experimenter effects**
1. Single-blind studies - participants don't know whether they are in the experimental or control group
2. Double-blind studies - neither the experimenter nor the participants know which participants are in which group

E. **Advantages and limitations of experiments**
1. Experiments allow conclusions about cause and effect
2. The setting is artificial and participants' behaviour may differ from real life; field research usually doesn't possess this weakness

Experiments: Hunting for Causes

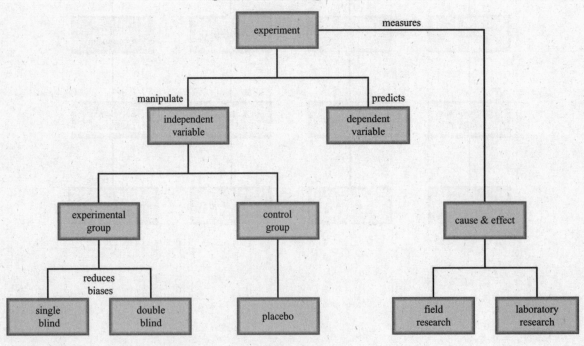

V. EVALUATING THE FINDINGS

A.   **Descriptive statistics: Finding out "What's so?"**

       1.   Arithmetic mean compares group scores between two or more groups

       2.   Standard deviation shows how clustered or spread out individual scores are around the mean

B.   **Inferential statistics: Asking "So what?"**

       1.   Determines the likelihood that the result of the study occurred by chance

       2.   Statistical significance - the result is expected to occur by chance fewer than 5 times in 100; it does not necessarily indicate real-world importance

       3.   Statistically significant results allow general predictions to be made about human behaviour, though not about any particular individual

C.   **Interpreting the findings: What is the best explanation for the findings?**

       1.   Researchers must test a hypothesis in different ways several times

           a.   Cross-sectional studies - compare groups at one time

           b.   Longitudinal studies - study participants across the lifespan

       2.   Researchers must judge the result's importance with procedures like meta-analysis that combine and analyze data from many studies

Evaluating the Findings

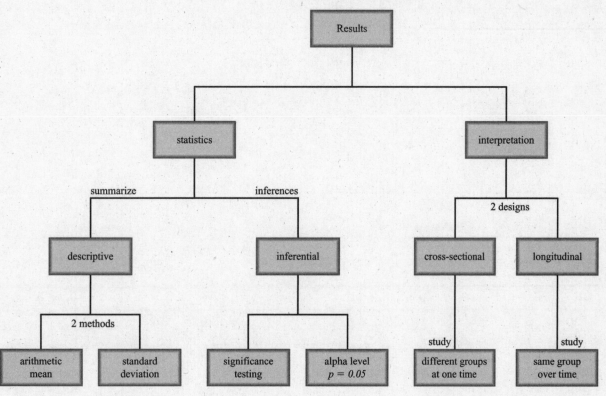

VI. KEEPING THE ENTERPRISE ETHICAL
A.   **The ethics of studying human beings**
1.   The Tri-Council and Canadian Psychological Association
a.   Dignity and welfare of participants must be respected
b.   People must participate voluntarily and give informed consent
c.   Participants must be free to withdraw from a study at any time
2.   Use of deception: Researchers are required to consider alternatives to deception, show that a study's potential value justifies the use of deception, and debrief participants about the study's true purpose afterward

B.   **The ethics of studying animals**
1.   Many purposes exist for conducting research using animals (e.g., basic research on a particular species, improve human welfare)
2.   Canadian Council on Animal Care (CCAC)
a.   Treatment and regulations have improved due to debates over the issues

RESEARCH METHODS TABLE

Complete this table and compare the differences among the research methods.

RESEARCH METHOD	DEFINITION AND DESCRIPTION	EXAMPLE
CASE HISTORY		
NATURALISTIC OBSERVATION		
LABORATORY OBSERVATION		
TESTS		
SURVEY		
CORRELATIONAL STUDY		
EXPERIMENT		

IDIOMS AND SLANGS

Misery loves company (page 39, 40) – This phrase means that people who are sad like to have other people around them who are also sad.

Secrecy is a big "no-no" in science (page 40) – An important characteristic of science is to tell other scientists about your results. This can be done through replication of a study or publishing your results in a journal.

May come smack up against a company's desire (page 41) – The textbook is talking about the conflict between scientists for a drug company releasing all of the results of their studies and keeping them quiet so other drug companies can't steal their results.

Passion is the fuel of progress (page 41) – People who believe strongly in something will work harder to study it and understand it.

Approving some viewpoints and relegating others to the scientific scrap heap (page 41) – Some ideas are accepted, while scientists do not accept others.

Abstract generalizations and cold statistics (page 44) – The textbook is saying that studying individual people may give us more information about human behaviour than numbers and statistics.

Refrigerator mothers (page 44) – These are mothers who do not care about their children. This was once thought to explain psychological problems in some children.

Arguing by anecdote (page 45) – Personal stories are used to argue against scientific results, which is incorrect.

Projective tests are designed to tap the unconscious feelings (page 47) – These tests are used to study the feelings and emotions that people are not aware that they have. Different from objective tests.

Do you feel you have reached a dead end at work? (page 48) – This is an example of a test question that is asking if you feel like you won't be promoted at work or if you think your job is boring.

When the survey is a touchy topic (page 49) – Sometimes questions on a survey asks very personal questions and people may not answer them truthfully.

Illuminating information (page 54) – This refers to the large number of things learned by studying the nature of descriptive results, like correlations.

Fuhgeddaboudit (page 69) – Also, "forget about it," referring to the idea that you cannot look at the results of a study that did not use a control group for comparison.

Checks and balances (page 70) – Scientific results are examined by other scientists to make sure that the study was done properly.

PRACTICE TEST 1 - Multiple Choice

1. Introductory psychology students study research methodology to
   A. find proof for our existing beliefs so we can argue against those who disagree.
   B. be able to critically evaluate psychological findings.
   C. be able to manipulate statistics to our advantage.
   D. be able to use our own experiences as scientific proofs.

2. Which of the following is <u>NOT</u> a characteristic of scientific research?
   A. reliance on common sense   B. precision
   C. scepticism   D. openness

3. An organized system of assumptions and principles that purports to explain a specified set of phenomena is called a(n)
   A. hypothesis.   B. operational definition.
   C. theory.   D. risky prediction.

4. Which of the following is an example of a hypothesis?
   A. Alcohol decreases reaction time.
   B. Studying improves grades.
   C. Employees perform better in a supportive climate.
   D. All of the above are examples of hypotheses.

5. Defining a term in ways that can be observed and measured is known as
   A. an operational definition.   B. a theory.
   C. common sense.   D. scepticism.

6. Scores on a depression test, changes in time spent sleeping, and food intake might be
   A. hypotheses.   B. theories of depression.
   C. operational definitions of depression.   D. empirical evidence.

7. Which of the following violates the principle of falsifiability?
   A. Lack of evidence for a phenomenon is described as predictable since destroying evidence is an alleged characteristic of the phenomenon under study.
   B. Participants in a study do not represent the larger population being described.
   C. A study uses only volunteer participants who differ from nonvolunteers.
   D. An experimenter's expectations subtly influence the outcome of a study.

8. Descriptive research methods
   A. explain behaviour by identifying the causes of the behaviour.
   B. allow the researcher to describe and predict behaviour.
   C. include the experimental study.
   D. all of the above.

9. Bruno Bettelheim based his theory on studying a small number of particular individuals in great detail. This research method is called a(n)
    A. survey.   B. experiment.
    C. naturalistic observation.   D. case study.

10. One disadvantage of the research method used by Bettelheim is that
    A. it relies on memories, which can be inaccurate.
    B. it is difficult to interpret.
    C. it cannot be used to generalize about human behaviour.
    D. all of the above are disadvantages.

11. Naturalistic observations involve
    A. giving participants a series of psychological tests.
    B. assigning research participants to experimental and control groups.
    C. observing participants in the natural environment.
    D. asking people a series of questions.

12. In the area of test construction, standardization refers to
    A. the use of uniform procedures in the administration and scoring of a test.
    B. the establishment of standards of performance.
    C. getting the same results over time.
    D. the condition that a test measures what it set out to.

13. _____ validity indicates that the test questions represent fully the trait being measured.
    A. test–retest   B. content
    C. criterion   D. alternate forms

14. Validity is to reliability as
    A. consistency is to accuracy.   B. accuracy is to consistency.
    C. criterion is to content.   D. objective is to projective.

15. You take an intelligence test on Monday and receive a high score. You repeat it on Tuesday and receive a low score. This test apparently lacks
    A. content validity.   B. criterion validity.
    C. test–retest reliability.   D. alternate-forms reliability.

16. A problem with surveys is that
    A. their results can by weakened by volunteer bias.
    B. respondents may lie, forget, or remember incorrectly.
    C. biases or ambiguities in the wording of questions may exist.
    D. all of the above are potential problems with surveys.

17. To conduct research on attitudes toward abortion, Dr. Kim distributes surveys to people leaving church after a service. One problem with this survey is that
    A. people are likely to lie or forget.
    B. the questions are unclear.
    C. the sample is nonrepresentative.
    D. the procedures are not the same.

18. Correlations
    A. determine the causes of behaviour.
    B. determine whether two or more phenomena are related, and if so, how strongly.
    C. can be expressed on a numeric scale from 1 to 10.
    D. require research participants to be observed in a laboratory.

19. The more David studies, the more his test scores improve. This is an example of
    A. a naturalistic observation.
    B. a positive correlation.
    C. a negative correlation.
    D. proof of causation.

20. Dr. Takahashi is studying the relationship between hair colour and shoe size. She is likely to find
    A. a negative correlation.
    B. a positive correlation.
    C. zero correlation.
    D. it is impossible to say.

21. Based on a correlational study showing that those who exercise regularly experience lower rates of depression, which of the following conclusions can be reached?
    A. Exercise causes a reduction in depression.
    B. People who are depressed stop exercising.
    C. There is a relationship between exercise and depression.
    D. Self-esteem influences both exercise and depression levels.

22. Experimentation is
    A. a type of observational study.
    B. the only research method that looks for the causes of behaviour.
    C. one of the descriptive research methods.
    D. more limited in its conclusions than the other types of methodologies.

23. The independent variable is the variable that
    A. is manipulated by the researcher.
    B. the researcher tries to predict.
    C. is defined in a way that can be observed and measured.
    D. cannot be controlled.

24. Dr. MacLean is conducting research on the effects of alcohol on reaction time. She assigns students to two groups. One group receives three ounces of alcohol and the other group receives an alcohol-free beverage that looks, smells, and tastes like alcohol. After the participants drink the beverage, the reaction time of participants in both groups is tested. Which of the variables is the dependent variable?
   A.   alcohol
   B.   control group
   C.   alcohol-free beverage
   D.   reaction time

25. In the above study, the group of research participants that receives the alcohol-free beverage is called
   A.   the independent variable.
   B.   the control group.
   C.   the experimental group.
   D.   the random group.

26. In the study described in question 24, neither Dr. MacLean nor the research participants knew whether they were in the experimental or control group. This type of study is called a
   A.   single-blind study.
   B.   longitudinal study.
   C.   double-blind study.
   D.   case study.

27. The purpose of single- and double-blind studies is to
   A.   control for the effects of volunteer participants.
   B.   equate participants in the experimental and control groups.
   C.   utilize a placebo.
   D.   control for the expectations of participants in a single-blind study and the expectations of both participants and experimenter in a double-blind study.

28. The arithmetic mean and standard deviation are
   A.   types of descriptive statistics.
   B.   inferential statistics.
   C.   examples of meta-analyses.
   D.   statistically significant.

29. Inferential statistics
   A.   summarize individual data into group data.
   B.   combine data from many studies.
   C.   study abilities across the lifespan.
   D.   tell the researcher the likelihood that the result of the study occurred by chance.

30. In an experiment on teaching methods, participants in the experimental group received a mean score of 84, and participants in the control group received a mean score of 77. Before the experimenters can say whether the new technique was superior in this study, they must
   A.   calculate the statistical significance of the results to evaluate the probability that this result could have happened by chance.
   B.   conduct a meta-analysis.
   C.   calculate the statistical significance to determine the real-world importance.
   D.   conduct a longitudinal study to see if the improved learning lasts.

31. Cross-sectional studies differ from longitudinal studies in that
    A. cross-sectional studies compare different groups at one time, whereas longitudinal studies examine abilities across the lifespan.
    B. cross-sectional studies examine groups in the laboratory, whereas longitudinal studies examine behaviour in the natural environment.
    C. cross-sectional studies examine abilities across the lifespan, whereas longitudinal studies compare different groups at one time.
    D. cross-sectional studies cannot establish cause and effect, whereas longitudinal studies can.

32. Meta-analyses are helpful in the interpretation of research findings because they
    A. determine which studies are accurate and which are not.
    B. combine data from many studies.
    C. establish whether the findings have any real-world importance.
    D. establish the statistical significance of studies.

33. For ethical purposes, researchers must show they have considered alternative procedures and that they plan to debrief participants in order to use
    A. animals.
    B. more than one experimental condition.
    C. an informed consent.
    D. deception.

34. Dr. Milner is conducting a study in which a co-researcher pretends to trip and fall in the presence of research participants who are taking a reading comprehension test. The participants have been told the study is on memory, but Dr. Milner is really studying the circumstances under which strangers provide assistance to others. According to ethical principles, Dr. Milner
    A. must demonstrate that his study's potential value justifies the use of deception.
    B. may not continue with this study no matter what he does because it is unethical to be dishonest with the participants.
    C. never needs to disclose the true purpose of the study to the participants.
    D. needs only show that no harm will come to the participants.

35. Psychologists use animals in research
    A. because sometimes practical or ethical considerations prevent the use of human beings as participants.
    B. to discover practical applications.
    C. to conduct basic research on a particular species.
    D. all of the above are reasons that animals are used in research.

36. The tendency to look for and accept evidence that supports our assumptions and beliefs is known as
    A. face validity.
    B. hypothesis testing.
    C. confirmation bias.
    D. only single-blind.

PRACTICE TEST 2 - Short Answer

1. Research methods are important to psychologists because they help separate truth from _____.

2. "Students who spend more time studying perform better in university." This is an example of a _____.

3. Dr. Bradley is conducting a study on the effects of anxiety on test performance. She is using participants' scores on a stress test as her _____ definition of anxiety.

4. Any theory that cannot in principle be refuted violates the _____.

5. Scientists must discuss ideas, testing procedures and results so their findings can be _____ to reduce fraud and error.

6. Research methods that allow psychologists to describe and predict behaviour but not to explain its causes are _____ methods.

7. A detailed description of particular individuals that is based on careful observation refers to the _____ research method.

8. Often scientists need a good description of behaviour as it occurs in the natural environment before they can explain it. This is the primary purpose of _____.

9. _____ tests measure beliefs, behaviour, and feelings of which the person is aware, whereas _____ tests are designed to tap the unconscious.

10. To be meaningful, a person's test score should be compared to established standards of performance called _____.

11. At 8:00 a.m. Hank weighs 179 pounds. He moves the scale slightly and decides to weigh himself again. Though it's only a minute later, he now weighs 177. Hank's scale lacks the test characteristic of _____.

12. A test that claims to measure personality, but actually measures verbal abilities lacks _____.

13. If a student's high school grades are able to accurately predict a student's grade point average in university, then the high school grades are demonstrating that they have _____.

14. A survey on alcohol use among university students reported that alcohol use among students had dramatically decreased. Later the study reported that the participants were female students from one prestigious university. This survey did not use a _____ sample of students.

15. Often one drawback to surveys is that those who agree to participate may differ from those who do not. A psychologist would say these surveys suffer from _____ bias.

16. A _____ is the numerical measure of the strength and direction of the relationship between two _____.

17. Height and weight are _____ correlated, however, this correlation does not show _____ between the two variables.

18. When psychologists want to look for causes of behaviour, they must use a more controlled method called the _____.

19. In an experiment on caffeine and alertness, caffeine intake would be the _____ variable and alertness would be the _____ variable.

20. In the study described in question 19, the participants who receive caffeinated coffee are in the _____ group, whereas those who receive decaffeinated coffee are in the _____ group.

21. The decaffeinated coffee is a _____ , which is used for the control group participants' _____.

22. A study is called _____-blind when the participants do not know whether they are in the experimental or the control group.

23. Numbers summarizing the data we collect from participants are called _____ statistics.

24. If the result of a study is unlikely to have happened by chance, then we say the result is statistically _____.

25. Research in which groups are all compared at the same time is called _____ ; in _____ studies, people are followed over a period of time and reassessed at periodic intervals.

26. Robert Rosenthal gave some students "maze bright" rats and some students "maze dull" rats. Though the rats actually were the same, the "maze bright" rats learned more quickly, presumably due to the expectations of the students teaching the rats. These effects are labelled _____.

27. A primary reason for the misuse of statistics is _____.

PRACTICE TEST 3 - Essay

1.   Determine which research method is best for each situation below and explain why.

    A.   Determine the favourite foods of adolescents.
    B.   Determine whether a person is introverted or extroverted.
    C.   Determine whether or not frustration causes aggression.
    D.   Determine whether level of education is associated with criminal behaviour.
    E.   Determine conversational patterns of men and women.
    F.   Determine why a violinist gave up a flourishing career in business to play in the local symphony.
    G.   Determine the parenting patterns used on a child who is having behaviour problems and whose parents cannot control him.

2.   In the following experiments identify: 1) a possible hypothesis, 2) the independent and dependent variables, 3) their operational definitions, and 4) experimental and control conditions.

    A.   A study was conducted on the effects of caffeine on studying. Experimental participants were given 32 ounces of caffeine. Participants in the control group were given a decaffeinated beverage that looked and tasted like the beverage consumed by the experimental group. After consuming the drinks, all participants were provided with a chapter of a text to read and then were tested.

    B.   A study was conducted on the effects of types of music on aggressive behaviour. There were three experimental groups: one listened to classical music, the second listened to jazz, and the third listened to heavy metal music. Participants in the control condition were exposed to a white-noise machine for the same period of time. Following exposure to the 45-minute music session, all participants were put in a situation in which they were able to engage in aggressive behaviour (punch a punching bag).

    C.   A study was conducted on the effects of exercise on relaxation. There were two experimental groups of participants. One group engaged in supervised aerobic exercise for 45 minutes. The second experimental group engaged in sit-ups and push-ups for 45 minutes. The control group engaged in a supervised study session. Following the exposure, all participants were told to wait in a room for the experimenter to return. During this period, they were hooked up to medical equipment monitoring their heart rate, muscle tension, respiration, and blood pressure.

3. Among the following examples, identify which correlations are positive, negative, or zero.

    A.   Height and weight
    B.   Smoking and health
    C.   Studying and drop-out rates
    D.   Practice and writing ability
    E.   Education level and height
    F.   Smoking and education level
    G.   Alcohol intake and reaction time
    H.   Alcohol intake and automobile accidents
    I.   Delinquency and education level
    J.   Weight and schizophrenia

4. After reviewing the ethical guidelines adopted by the Tri-Council and the Canadian Psychological Association (CPA), determine which of the following research practices are ethical or unethical and explain why:

    A.   Require psychology students to participate in a research study.
    B.   Tell participants that once they begin a study, they must continue until the research is complete.
    C.   Withhold information about the hypothesis and research purposes.
    D.   Deliberately misrepresent research purposes.
    E.   Use animals to check the side effects of a drug thought to cure depression.
    F.   Carry out a study that causes discomfort in people after securing informed consent that includes full information about possible risks.

5. Distinguish between independent and dependent variables and identify examples of each.

6. Distinguish between experimental and control groups and discuss the use of placebos.

7. Describe single-blind and double-blind studies and explain how they improve experiments.

8. Discuss the advantages and limitations of experimental research.

9. What are the key elements of an experiment? Design your own experiment and label the variables.

CHAPTER THREE

Genes, Evolution, and Environment

LEARNING OBJECTIVES

1. Describe two historical positions advanced to explain human similarities and differences.

2. Distinguish between the field of evolutionary psychology and the field of behavioural genetics.

3. Distinguish among genes, chromosomes, and DNA.

4. Describe how the basic elements of DNA affect the characteristics of the organism.

5. Describe one type of research used to search for genes associated with many physical and mental conditions.

6. Explain how natural selection accounts for many similarities among humans.

7. Distinguish between intersexual selection and intrasexual selection.

8. Explain the assumption that the mind develops as independent "modules."

9. Describe the approach of evolutionary psychologists.

10. Describe five innate human characteristics.

11. Describe the process of phenotype matching and how it relates to sharing behaviour.

12. Define language.

13. Distinguish between the surface structure and the deep structure of language.

14. Describe evidence for Chomsky's position on language acquisition as well as the evidence for the role of learning in language acquisition based on artificial neural networks.

15. Describe the field of sociobiology.

16. Explain sociobiologists' and evolutionary psychologists' views on mating and marriage.

17. Cite evidence for and against evolutionary approaches to mating and marriage.

18. Define and discuss the characteristics of heritability and describe how it is studied.

19. Define the intelligence quotient (IQ) and describe how it is computed.

20. Summarize heritability estimates for intelligence.

21. Summarize the debate and research explaining the differences in IQ between different racial and ethnic groups, including errors in the interpretation of research findings.

22. Describe environmental factors that influence intelligence.

23. Summarize the prevailing ideas about the role of nature and nurture in explaining similarities and differences among people.

24. Describe the pros and cons of genetic testing.

BRIEF CHAPTER SUMMARY

Chapter 3 examines the biological and evolutionary bases of behaviour. Evolutionary psychology emphasizes the evolutionary mechanisms that might help explain commonalities in human behaviour. Genetic operations and the principle of natural selection contribute to the understanding of commonalities among humans. Many evolutionary psychologists believe that the mind is composed of specialized mental modules, such as an attraction to novelty and a motive to explore. Language acquisition shares similar features across cultures, suggesting that this is an innate capacity of individuals to acquire language. Evolutionary psychologists (and sociobiologists) argue that certain social behaviours, such as courtship and mating, also have a biological base and serve an evolutionary function. A discussion of heritability helps explain differences among human beings. Heritability is used in an analysis of intelligence. Common misuses of heritability are discussed, along with the difficulties and complexities of behavioural-genetic research. The complexities of human behaviour do not allow for simple "either-or" explanations: heredity and environment always interact to produce our psychological and most physical traits. The chapter demonstrates the need to be able to tolerate uncertainty in the exploration of the origins of human behaviour.

PREVIEW OUTLINE

Before you read the chapter, review the preview outline for each section of the text. After you have read the chapter, close this book and try to <u>re-create</u> the outlines on a blank piece of paper.

I. **UNLOCKING THE SECRETS OF GENES**
    A.   **Explaining human similarities and differences**
        1.   Two main camps - Nativists, who emphasized genes or nature, and empiricists, who focused on experience or nurture
        2.   Current position recognizes interaction of heredity and environment
  B. Examinign the contributions of nature and nurture
  1. **Evolutionary Psychology** – emphasizes the evolutionary mechanisms that may explain commonalities in language, learning, attention, perception, memory, sexual behaviour, emotions and reasoning
  2. **Behavioural Genetics** – attempts to understand the relative contributions of heredity and environment in order to explain individual differences
    C.   **Definition and characteristics of genes**
        1.   Definition - basic units of heredity
        2.   Characteristics
            a.   Located on chromosomes, each of which contains thousands of genes; all body cells contain 23 chromosome pairs

   b. Chromosomes consist of strands of DNA; genes consist of small segments of this DNA

   c. Some genes are inherited in the same form by everyone; others vary, contributing to our individuality

D. How elements of DNA affect characteristics of the organism

  1. Each gene has four basic chemical elements of DNA (A, T, C, G)

  2. The order of arrangement helps determine the synthesis of one of the many proteins that affect every aspect of the body

E. The search for genes that contribute to specific traits

  1. It is very difficult to identify a single gene

  2. Most traits depend on more than one pair of genes, which makes tracking down the genetic contributions to a trait very difficult

  3. Linkage studies - look at genes located close together that may be inherited together across generations

  4. Researchers with the Human Genome Project are trying to map the entire human genome, which consists of three billion units of DNA

  5. Even when a gene is located, its role in physical and psychological functioning is not automatically known

Unlocking the Secrets of Genes

II. THE GENETICS OF SIMILARITY

A. Evolutionary psychologists - apply principles of evolution to human psychological qualities and behaviour

B. Evolution and natural selection - general characteristics

  1. Definition – Evolution is a change in the gene frequencies within a population over many generations

  2. Why do frequencies change?

a.   Variations arise as genes spontaneously mutate and recombine
b.   Charles Darwin's natural selection: As individuals with a genetically influenced trait become more successful at surviving and reproducing in a particular environment, their genes will become more common and may spread
3.   Approach of evolutionary psychology
a.   Asks what challenges humans faced in prehistoric past and draws inferences about behaviours that might have evolved to solve survival problems - evaluates the inferences using research
b.   Assumes the human mind evolved as a collection of specialized and independent modules to handle specific survival problems. A particular module may involve several dispersed but interconnected areas of the brain.

C.   **Innate human characteristics -** Common evolutionary history may explain universal abilities such as infant reflexes, attraction to novelty, motive to explore and manipulate objects, an impulse to play, and basic cognitive skills.

The Genetics of Similarity

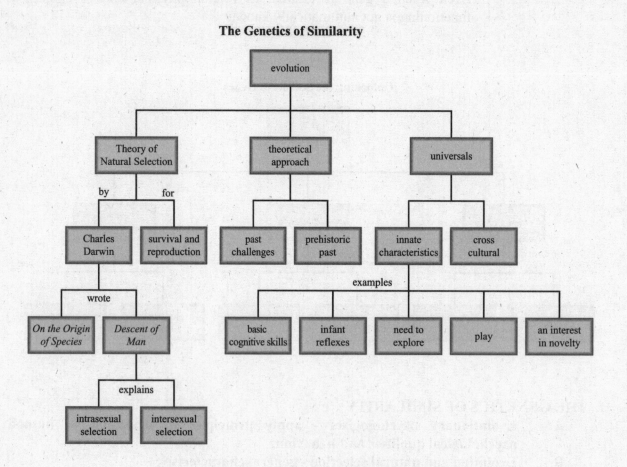

III. OUR HUMAN HERITAGE: LANGUAGE

A. **The nature of language**

1. Definition - language is a set of rules for combining elements that are in themselves meaningless into utterances that convey meaning

2. Humans seem to be the only species that acquires language naturally and that can combine sounds to produce original sentences

3. Some nonhuman animals can be taught aspects of language

B. **The innate capacity for language**

1. Noam Chomsky - changed thinking about how language is acquired

    a. Language is not learned bit by bit, but with a language acquisition device (LAD), or "mental module" in the brain

    b. Children learn surface structure - the way a sentence is spoken - and deep structure - the meaning of a sentence

    c. Though rules of grammar (syntax) aren't taught to children, they use them to transform surface structures into deep structures

    d. Psycholinguists' arguments to support Chomsky's position

        (1) Children in different cultures go through similar stages of language development - born with a universal grammar

        (2) Children make errors called overregularizations that adults would not, so they are not simply imitating

        (3) Adults do not consistently correct children's syntax, yet children learn to speak correctly

        (4) Children not exposed to adult language may invent one of their own

        (5) Infants as young as 7 months can derive simple linguistic rules from a string of sounds

2. Language may have developed as the human equivalent of mutual grooming, to facilitate the forging of social bonds

3. Researchers are trying to identify brain modules and genes involved in language acquisition

C. **Learning and language** - experience also plays a role in language

1. Infants as young as eight months are able to learn the probability that a given word will follow another, rather than infer grammatical rules

2. Parents recast or expand on children's sentences, which are then repeated

Our Human Heritage: Language

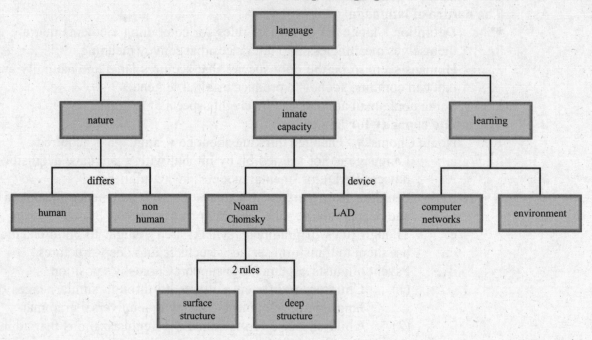

IV: OUR HUMAN HERITAGE: COURTSHIP AND MATING

A. Agreement about the role of evolution in simple behaviours, disagreement about complex social behaviours

B. Evolution and sexual strategies

1. Sociobiologists believe that gender differences in courtship and mating evolved in response to a species' survival needs

2. Males and females have faced different survival and mating problems, which has led to differences in behaviours according to sociobiologists

    a. Males compete for fertile females; females need to look for the male with the best genes since their childbearing time is limited

    b. This may explain why males are more promiscuous than females

C. Culture and the "genetic leash" – the relative power of biology and culture

1. Critics of evolutionary approach argue that

    a. Evolutionary explanations of sexual behaviours are based on stereotypes, and actual behaviours often contradict these descriptions

    b. Among humans, sexual behaviour is varied and changeable

    c. Responses on surveys are often a poor guide to their actual mating choices

    d. Similarity and proximity are best predictor for choosing a mate

2. Critics worry that evolutionary arguments will be used to justify inequalities and violence

Our Human Heritage: Courtship and Mating

V. THE GENETICS OF DIFFERENCE

A. **The meaning of heritability** - estimates of the proportion of the total variance in a trait that is attributable to genetic variation within a group

B. **Facts about heritability**

1. Heritability estimates apply only to a particular group living in a particular environment, and estimates may differ for different groups

2. Heritability estimates do <u>not</u> apply to individuals, <u>only</u> to variations within a group

3. Even highly heritable traits can be modified by the environment (i.e.height)

C. **Computing heritability**

1. Can't estimate heritability directly; must infer it by studying people whose degree of genetic similarity is known

2. Researchers study those who share either genes or environments; adopted children, identical twins reared apart, and fraternal twins

The Genetics of Difference

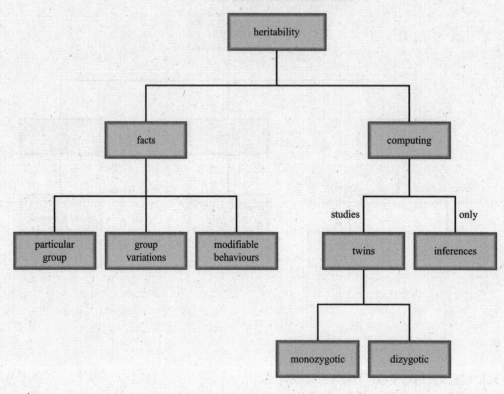

VI.   OUR HUMAN DIVERSITY: THE CASE OF INTELLIGENCE
    A.   **Genes and individual differences**
        1.   Concept of IQ is controversial and IQ tests are criticized
        2.   Intelligence that produces high IQ scores is highly heritable
        3.   Genes might affect intelligence by influencing the total amount of "gray matter"
    B.   **The question of group differences**
        1.   Focus has been on black–white differences in IQ scores
        2.   Between-group studies: problems and conclusions
            a.   Heritability estimates based on differences <u>within</u> group cannot be used to compare differences <u>between</u> groups
            b.   Black–white IQ differences are influenced by the environment
            c.   Sound methodological studies do not reveal genetic differences between blacks and whites
    C.   **The environment and intelligence**
        1.   Factors associated with reduced mental ability include poor prenatal care, malnutrition, exposure to toxins, and stressful family circumstances

2.   Healthy and stimulating environment can raise mental performance; experiences such as talking to parents, being encouraged to think things through and early lessons in the arts (e.g., music and drama) may help

V11: BEYOND NATURE VERSUS NURTURE
A. Neither nature nor nurture can entirely explain similarities or differences. Genetic and environmental influences blend and become indistinguishable in the development of any individual.

Our Human Diversity: The Case of Intelligence

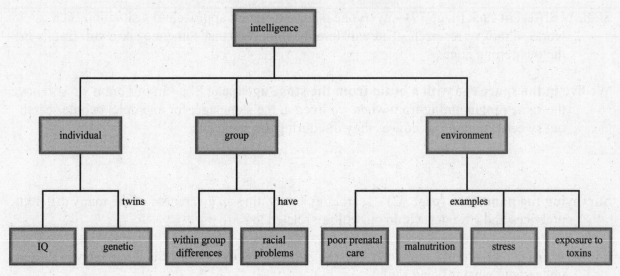

IDIOMS AND SLANGS

Street smarts (page 73) – the social skills and active ability of a person to apply common sense values to everyday life and its diverse situations. For example, being aware of personal safety on dark streets.

Blank slate of human nature (page 73) – the old western belief that man is born with a mind, free of prior information. Like a blank slate, this mind can be written on by life's experiences and learning opportunities.

Slightly different tack (page 79) – everyone takes a different approach to a situation such as work, school, or research. These different approaches that someone takes still results in the job getting done.

We live in the space age with a brain from the stone age (page 81) – In our brain we still have the same programming from when we lived in the stone age, for example, people search out sweet-tasting foods now as they did during the stone age.

Surveying the panorama (page 92) – searching, or creating an awareness of the many different practices and attitudes within our culture related to sex.

Gibberish (page 83) – rapid and incoherent talk, when you don't know the language you will not understand what is being said.

Tin ear (page 95) – lack of ability to accurately hear or distinguish musical notes and speech.

Top-notch (page 95) – first rate, excellent, high social status.

Doting (page 95) – foolishly or excessively fond. Parents who do everything for their children.

A Homer Simpson can never become an Einstein (page 104) – The textbook is trying to say that people have genetic limits, so a person of lower intelligence (Homer Simpson) can never become a highly intellectual person (Einstein).

PRACTICE TEST 1 - Multiple Choice

1. Historically, those who agree with the nature position and those who believe in the nurture approach
    A.   both agree with sociobiologists.
    B.   are both evolutionary psychologists.
    C.   disagree about the relative importance of nature and nurture in explaining human differences.
    D.   work together to develop the field of behavioural genetics.

2. Evolutionary psychology and sociobiology
    A.   are branches of behavioural genetics.
    B.   both focus on evolutionary influences on behaviours.
    C.   have very little in common.
    D.   emphasize the role of the environment.

3. Dr. Wilson is studying how evolutionary mechanisms might help explain commonalities in language learning, attention, and perception. He is a(n)
    A.   behavioural geneticist.   B.   sociobiologist.
    C.   evolutionary psychologist.   D.   empiricist.

4. Genes are
    A.   rod-shaped structures found in every cell of the body.
    B.   thread-like strands that make up chromosomes.
    C.   one of the four basic elements of DNA.
    D.   the basic units of heredity.

5. Chromosomes are
    A.   rod-shaped structures found in every cell of the body.
    B.   located on genes.
    C.   one of the four basic elements of DNA.
    D.   the basic units of heredity.

6. The full set of genes contained in each cell is the
    A.   DNA.   B.   chromosome.
    C.   genome.   D.   basis.

7. When a sperm and egg unite at conception, the fertilized egg, and all the body cells that eventually develop from it (except for sperm cells and ova) contain
    A.   46 pairs of chromosomes.   B.   23 chromosomes.
    C.   46 chromosomes in 23 pairs.   D.   23 pairs of genes.

8.	Which statement best describes the relationship between genes, chromosomes, and DNA?
   A.	Genes, the basic unit of heredity, are located on chromosomes, which consist of strands of DNA. Genes consist of small segments of DNA molecules.
   B.	Genes are composed of chromosomes and DNA.
   C.	Chromosomes, the basic unit of heredity, direct the genes and the DNA.
   D.	DNA houses both genes and chromosomes in its rod-shaped structures.

9.	Most human traits depend on
   A.	more than one pair of genes.
   B.	a single pair of genes.
   C.	one gene.
   D.	between 5 and 10 pairs of genes.

10.	Dr. Best is trying to track down the genetic contributions to eye colour. Which of the following is likely to be true?
   A.	Because it is a simple trait, probably a single pair of genes is responsible.
   B.	Most human traits, even simple ones, depend on more than one pair of genes.
   C.	She can locate the gene or genes by using a high-resolution microscope.
   D.	She will have to map the entire human genome.

11.	In search of a genetic marker for Huntington's disease, researchers studied large families in which this condition was common. This type of study is called a(n)
   A.	case study.			B.	linkage study.
   C.	evolutionary study.		D.	family research.

12.	One reason that new traits keep arising is because of genes' ability to spontaneously.
   A.	divide			B.	multiply
   C.	split			D.	mutate

13.	Within each gene, elements of DNA are arranged in a particular order, which forms a code that influences the synthesis of particular proteins. This affects every aspect of the body, from its structure to the chemicals that keep it running. This process describes
   A.	linkage studies.
   B.	how genes affect characteristics of the organism.
   C.	how genes mutate.
   D.	how natural selection occurs.

14.	As gene frequencies change within a population over generations, certain genetically influenced characteristics become more or less common. This refers to
   A.	evolution.			B.	natural selection.
   C.	sociobiology.			D.	heritability.

15. A way to explain WHY gene frequencies change is the idea that individuals with traits that are adaptive in an environment will stay alive to reproduce, and over generations their genes will become more common. This describes
    A.   evolution.   B.   natural selection.
    C.   sociobiology.   D.   heritability.

16. Psycholinguists suggest that by applying rules that make up the grammar of language, we are able to understand and produce new sentences correctly. These rules are called
    A.   surface structure.   B.   over-regularizations.
    C.   syntax.   D.   mental modules.

17. "Lee gave the ball to Lynne," and "Lynne received the ball from Lee" have
    A.   the same surface structure.
    B.   different deep structures.
    C.   the same surface and deep structures.
    D.   the same deep structure.

18. Though they are learning different languages, Lana from Morocco, Ayse from Turkey, and Paulo from Italy are going through similar stages of language development and combine words in ways that adults never would. This supports the conclusion that
    A.   language is learned in bits and pieces.
    B.   the syntax of all languages is remarkably similar.
    C.   the brain contains a language acquisition device that allows children to develop language if they are exposed to an adequate sampling of speech.
    D.   language acquisition is primarily the result of imitation of speech.

19. Chomsky's contribution to the understanding of language acquisition was the idea that
    A.   language is learned in bits, as one might learn a list of Canadian prime ministers.
    B.   there is a critical period for learning language.
    C.   children go through different stages of language development.
    D.   language is too complex to learn bit by bit, so there must be a "mental module" in the brain that allows young children to develop language.

20. Which of the following supports Chomsky's position on language acquisition?
    A.   Children everywhere go through similar stages of linguistic development.
    B.   Children combine words in ways adults never would, which rules out imitation.
    C.   Even children not exposed to language acquire language of their own.
    D.   All of the above support Chomsky's position on language acquisition.

21. Which of the following reflects the sociobiological view on mating and marriage?
    A.   Marriage and mating behaviours have been learned through reinforcements.
    B.   Males and females have faced different kinds of survival and mating problems and have evolved differently in aggressiveness and sexual strategies.
    C.   Socialization accounts for differences in mating behaviours.
    D.   None of the above reflects the sociobiological position.

22. "It is good for males to compete for access to fertile females and to try to inseminate as many females as possible, because females can give birth to only a limited number of offspring, it pays for them to be selective and look for the best mate." This reflects the position of
   A. outdated psychologists.
   B. an empiricist.
   C. sociobiology.
   D. Chomsky.

23. Critics of the evolutionary approach cite which of the following positions to support their view?
   A. Though humans and animals may engage in similar behaviours, the motives or origins of the behaviours differ.
   B. Not all animal and human behaviour conforms to the sexual stereotypes.
   C. Among human beings, sexual behaviour is extremely varied and changeable.
   D. All of the above are arguments used by critics of the evolutionary approach.

24. Heritability
   A. estimates the proportion of difference in a trait that is attributable to genetic variation within a group.
   B. is equivalent in meaning to the term "genetic."
   C. estimates the proportion of a trait that is attributable to genes in an individual.
   D. estimates the proportion of difference in a trait that is attributable to genetic variation between groups.

25. Heritability can be used to estimate
   A. IQ differences between whites and Asians.
   B. IQ differences among UBC graduates.
   C. how much of an individual's IQ is determined by heredity.
   D. exactly which genes are responsible for intelligence.

26. To study the heritability of a particular trait, which groups of people are studied?
   A. adopted children and twins   B. unrelated people
   C. biological mothers and daughters   D. husbands and wives

27. Heritability estimates of intelligence for children and adolescents
   A. are very low since IQ is shaped primarily by environmental influences.
   B. vary widely, but they have an average of .50.
   C. have an average of .90
   D. have an average of .10

28. Pete is adopting a child whose biological parents have low IQs. Pete asks whether this child is also likely to have a low IQ. Which of the following is the best response?
   A. The child is also quite likely to have a low IQ, since heritability of IQ is high.
   B. The IQs of the child's biological parents are irrelevant, since environmental influences outweigh heritability.
   C. While IQ is at least in part heritable, environmental influences can have a great impact; however, it is impossible to make predictions about any individual.
   D. Nothing is known about the heritability of IQ.

29. Which of the following is a flaw in genetic theories of black–white differences in IQ?
   A. Blacks and whites do not grow up, on average, in the same kind of environment.
   B. Because of racial discrimination and other factors, children of minorities receive less encouragement and fewer opportunities than whites.
   C. Heritability estimates based on one group (whites) are used to estimate the role heredity plays in differences between groups.
   D. All of the above are flaws.

30. Two pots of tomatoes were planted with seeds of identical quality. One pot used enriched soil and one pot used soil with few nutrients. A comparison of the plants from each of these pots is analogous to
   A. comparing the IQs of two Asian-Canadians from similar socioeconomic backgrounds, communities, and school systems.
   B. looking for a genetic explanation of IQ differences between blacks and whites.
   C. comparing the IQs of two siblings.
   D. none of the above

31. Which of the following is an environmental influence on IQ that can have a negative impact on mental ability?
   A. poor prenatal care   B. malnutrition
   C. exposure to toxins   D. all of the above

32. Specialized and independent components of the brain that handle specific survival problems, such as the need to find food, are called
   A. mental modules.
   B. heritability nodes.
   C. synapses.
   D. biological markers.

33. Your text mentioned all of the following environmental influences as contributing to intelligence EXCEPT
   A. parents reading to their children.
   B. enrichment classes.
   C. music lessons.
   D. sports.

PRACTICE TEST 2 - Short Answer

1. _genes_ are the basic units of heredity, and they are located on _chromosomes_

2. Collectively, the 25,000 or so human genes are referred to as the human _genome_

3. To find the gene responsible for Huntington's disease, researchers studied large families in which this condition was common. This approach is called a _linkage_ study.

4. _evolutionary_ psychologists try to explain commonalities in language learning, perception memory, sexuality, and many other aspects of behaviour.

5. As genes become more common or less common in the population, so do the characteristics they influence. This is referred to as _evolution_

6. Gene frequencies in a population change because genes spontaneously _mutate_.

7. The principle of _natural selection_ says that individuals with a particular genetically influenced trait tend to be more successful at staying alive long enough to produce offspring; their genes will become more and more common in the population.

8. Evolutionary psychologists believe that the human mind developed as a collection of specialized and independent _modules_ to handle specific survival problems.

9. Evolutionary psychologists believe that certain abilities, tendencies, and characteristics evolved because they were useful to our ancestors. Two of these abilities or tendencies include _language_ and _mating_.

10. Language is a set of _rules_ for combining meaningless _elements_ into utterances that convey meaning.

11. "Mary kissed John" and "John was kissed by Mary" have the same _deep_ structure but a different _surface_ structure.

12. _Chomsky_ said that language was far too complex to be learned bit by bit. Therefore, there must be an innate mental module for learning language called a language _acquisition_ device.

13. One piece of evidence that children have an innate mental module for language is that children in different cultures go through _similar stages_ of linguistic development.

14. Children are born with a(n) _universal_ grammar; their brains are sensitive to the core features of all languages.

15. _sociologists_ believe that human gender differences in courtship and mating evolved in response to our species' survival needs.

16. Evolutionary psychologists differ from sociobiologists in that they tend to argue less by _analogy_ and focus on the _common alities_ in human mating and dating practices around the world.

17. Critics of evolutionary approaches to infidelity and monogamy argue that these explanations are based on _stereo types_ of gender differences.

18. The proportion of the total variance in a trait that is attributable to genetic variation within a group is called _heritability_

19. Heritability estimates do not apply to _individuals_

20. To estimate the heritability of a trait, researchers study _adopted_ children and _identical_ twins.

21. For children and adolescents, heritability estimates of intelligence average around __.5__ and the estimates for adults are in the ___.6 to .8___ range.

22. Genetic explanations for differences in intelligence between blacks and whites are flawed because they use estimates based on a white sample to estimate the role of heredity in _group_ differences.

23. Negative environmental influences on mental ability include poor _prenatal_ care and _malnutrition, expos. toxins, stress._

24. "The police must stop drinking after midnight" has more than one possible _surface_ structure.

55

PRACTICE TEST 3 - Essay

1. A. You are working in a drug treatment program. You hear many clients in this program describe their alcoholic family backgrounds and state their belief that their alcoholism is genetic. Using information about genes, chromosomes, and DNA, give a general description of how alcoholism may be genetic.

    B. You attend a lecture in which an author of a self-help book on alcoholism says that alcoholism is 50 percent inherited and, therefore, if you have an alcoholic parent, you have a 50 percent chance of becoming an alcoholic. Discuss the problems with these statements using the facts about heritability.

    C. If you wanted to search for the genes associated with alcoholism, describe the type of study you would conduct and how you would go about collecting your data.

2. Using the approach of evolutionary psychology, expand on the idea that the following characteristics were inherited because they were useful during the history of our species (i.e., they had an evolutionary function).
    A. the feeling of disgust
    B. intuition
    C. self-concept
    D. kinship
    E. male promiscuity
    F. female selectivity

3. Compare Chomsky's position with an earlier position on the acquisition of language and use arguments to support this view.

4. A. Describe a study that you would design to evaluate the heritability of intelligence. Describe your conclusions about both hereditary and environmental influences on intelligence. What cautionary statements would you make about the heritability estimate?

    B. Based on your research findings, you are to make recommendations to a federal panel convened to develop a parental training program for low-income families to help them promote intellectual development in their children. Discuss the recommendations you would make to the panel.

CHAPTER FOUR

The Brain: Source of Mind and Self

LEARNING OBJECTIVES

1. List and describe the features and functions of the central nervous system.

2. List and describe the features and functions of the peripheral nervous system.

3. Distinguish between the somatic and autonomic nervous systems.

4. Distinguish between the sympathetic and parasympathetic nervous systems.

5. Describe the structure of a neuron and explain how impulses are transmitted from one neuron to another.

6. Summarize the structure and function of the myelin sheath. Describe its role in the disease, multiple sclerosis.

7. Describe recent research on stem cells and neurogenesis.

8. Compare the neurons in a newborn's brain to a brain at an older age. What is meant by the term plasticity?

9. Distinguish between an inhibitory and excitatory voltage shift. What is meant by the all-or-none principle?

10. What are neurotransmitters? Describe six neurotransmitters and outline some of the effects of having either too low or too high levels of some neurotransmitters.

11. Describe the structure and role of endorphins.

12. Describe the functioning of hormones, specifically those in which psychologists are especially interested.

13. List and describe techniques psychologists use to study brain functions.

14. Describe what is meant by localization of function.

15. List and describe the location and function of each of the major portions of the brain.

16. Why is the hippocampus known as the "gateway to memory"?

17. What are the four lobes of the brain, where are they located and what are their functions?

18. Summarize the functions of the brain's two hemispheres and explain their relationship.

19. Describe the procedures and results of split-brain research.

20. Describe the general position taken by neuroscientists on the self, and discuss two specific approaches advanced by scientists to explain the sense of a unified self.

21. Summarize the evidence on whether there are sex differences in the brain and how any differences might affect behaviour.

22.   Define the field of neuroethics and some of the relevant issues.

23.   Discuss the results of research looking at the relationship between diet and neurotransmitters and behaviour.

BRIEF CHAPTER SUMMARY

Chapter 4 discusses the brain and nervous system. The central nervous system is composed of the brain and spinal cord. It receives incoming messages from the senses, processes that information, and sends output to the muscles and organs. The nerves in the rest of the body are part of the peripheral nervous system. This system, in turn, is composed of the somatic nervous system, which permits sensation and voluntary actions, and the autonomic nervous system, which regulates glands, internal organs, and blood vessels. The autonomic nervous system is composed of the sympathetic nervous system, which mobilizes the body for action, and the parasympathetic nervous system, which conserves energy. The nervous system is made up of nerve cells or neurons. A neuron's key components are dendrites, the cell body, and an axon, which ends in axon terminals. A neural message goes from dendrites to axon via an electrical impulse. Neurons communicate with other neurons through chemicals called neurotransmitters. They are released by one neuron and temporarily received by another at the synapse, a tiny space between two neurons. A variety of methods for mapping the brain, such as EEG, TMS, PET scans, and MRI, are discussed. Different brain structures and their functions are explained, along with general issues about how the brain processes information. Research on split-brain patients, who have had the corpus callosum severed, provides insights into hemispheric specialization. Discussion of two challenging issues—where the self is in the brain, and whether men and women have substantially different types of brains—reveals the shortcomings of popular views on the subjects.

PREVIEW OUTLINE

Before you read the chapter, review the preview outline for each section of the text. After you have read the chapter, close this book and try to <u>re-create</u> the outlines on a blank piece of paper.

I.   **THE NERVOUS SYSTEM: A BASIC BLUEPRINT**
    A.   **The central nervous system (CNS)**
        1.   Functions - receives, processes, interprets, and stores incoming information; sends out messages to muscles, glands, internal organs
        2.   Two components - brain and spinal cord (an extension of the brain which can produce automatic reflexes without the help of the brain)
    B.   **The peripheral nervous system (PNS)** - handles the input and output of the CNS
        1.   Functions
            a.   Sensory neurons - bring input to CNS from skin, muscles, organs
            b.   Motor neurons - carry output to muscles, glands and organs

2.　　Divisions
　　　a.　　Somatic nervous system (also called skeletal nervous system) – connects to sensory receptors and skeletal muscles
　　　b.　　Autonomic nervous system - regulates blood vessels, glands, organs
　　　　　(1)　　Sympathetic nervous system - mobilizes body for action
　　　　　(2)　　Parasympathetic nervous system - slows action

The Nervous System: A Basic Blueprint

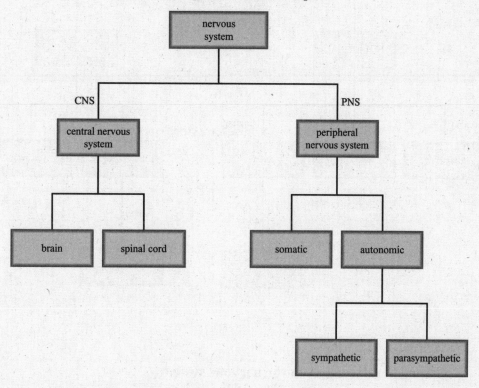

II. COMMUNICATION IN THE NERVOUS SYSTEM
A.　　**Components of the nervous system** – include both neurons and glial cells
B.　　**The structure of the neuron**
　　1.　　Dendrites - receive messages from other neurons and transmits to cell body
　　2.　　Cell body - keeps the neuron alive, determines whether neuron fires
　　3.　　Axon - transmits messages from cell body to neurons, muscles, or glands
　　4.　　Nerves - bundles of nerve fibres in the PNS
C.　　**How neurons communicate**
　　1.　　Synapse - axon terminal, synaptic cleft, membrane of receiving dendrites
　　2.　　Neural impulses - how neurons communicate
　　　a.　　Electrical impulse, or action potential
　　　b.　　Synaptic vesicles release chemical neurotransmitters
　　　c.　　They excite or inhibit the firing of the receiving neuron

d.   Neurons either fire or do not fire (all or none principle)

Communication in the Nervous System

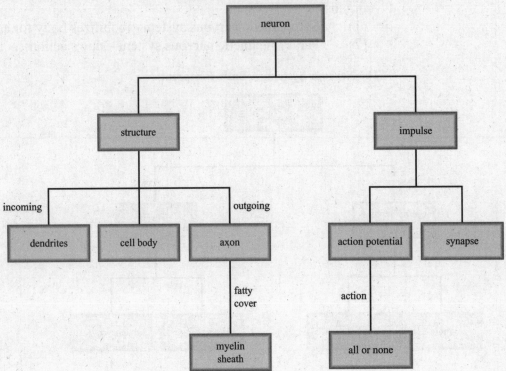

D.   Chemical messengers in the nervous system
1.   Neurotransmitters - Versatile couriers
    a.   Each neurotransmitter binds only to certain types of receptor sites
    b.   Some better understood neurotransmitters and some of their effects
        (1)   Serotonin - sleep, mood, and other behaviours
        (2)   Dopamine - movement, learning, memory, emotion
        (3)   Acetylcholine - muscle action, memory, emotion, cognition
        (4)   Norepinephrine - heart rate, learning, memory, emotion
        (5)   GABA - inhibitory neurotransmitter
(6) Glutamate – major excitatory neurotransmitter
2.   Endorphins - The brain's natural opiates (endogenous opioid peptides) reduce pain, promote pleasure as well as other behaviours
3.   Hormones - Long-distance messengers
    a.   Produced in endocrine glands and released into the bloodstream
    b.   Some may also be classified as neurotransmitters
    c.   Hormones of interest to psychologists include melatonin (regulates biological rhythms),oxytocin (enhances uterine contractions during

childbirth) adrenal hormones (related to emotion and stress), and sex hormones (androgens, estrogens, progesterone)

Chemical Messengers in the Nervous System

III. MAPPING THE BRAIN - methods for studying the brain
   A. **Lesion method** - damaging or removing section of brain in animals
   B. **Electrode methods - detect electrical activity of the neurons**
      1. Electroencephalography (EEG)
      2. Needle electrodes and microelectrodes into a single cell
   C. **Transcranial Magnetic Stimulation (TMS)**
      1. Wire coil around hand produces magnetic field
      2. Produces motor responses or inactivates an area of the brain.
   D. **Positron-Emission Tomography - PET scan**
      1. Records biochemical changes in the brain as they occur
      2. Utilizes a radioactive substance to indicate brain activity
   E. **Magnetic Resonance Imaging (MRI)**
      1. Uses magnetic fields and radio frequencies
      2. New "functional MRI" captures brain changes very quickly
   F. **Cautions about brain research**
      1. Findings are difficult to interpret and can be manipulated
      2. Results don't tell us what is happening inside the person's head
      3. Each brain, like fingerprints, is unique

Mapping the Brain

IV. A TOUR THROUGH THE BRAIN

A.   **Localization of function** - different brain parts perform different tasks

B.   **The brain stem** - rises out of spinal cord
   1.   Medulla - regulates automatic functions, such as breathing and heart rate
   2.   Pons - regulates sleeping, waking, and dreaming
   3.   Reticular activating system - network of neurons, extends upward and connects with higher brain areas; screens information, alertness

C.   **The cerebellum** – on top of the brain stem; regulates balance and coordination of muscle movement; may play a role in remembering skills, analyzing sensory information

D.   **The thalamus** - relays motor impulses out of brain, directs incoming sensory messages to higher centres

E.   **The hypothalamus and the pituitary gland**
   1.   Hypothalamus - associated with survival drives, such as hunger, thirst, emotion, sex and reproduction, body temperature
   2.   Pituitary gland - "master gland" regulated by hypothalamus

F.   **Limbic system** - loosely interconnected structures involved in emotions
   1.   Amygdala - evaluates sensory information to determine its importance
   2.   Hippocampus - allows formation and storage of new memories

G.   **Cerebrum** - site of higher forms of thinking
   1.   Divided into two halves or cerebral hemispheres that are connected by a band of fibres called the corpus callosum

      a.   Each hemisphere controls opposite side of the body

      b.   Each hemisphere has somewhat different talents (lateralization)

2.   Cerebral cortex - layers of densely packed cells covering the cerebrum

      a.   Occipital lobes - contain the visual cortex

      b.   Parietal lobes - contain somatosensory cortex

      c.   Temporal lobes - involved in memory, perception, and emotion

      d.   Frontal lobes - contain the motor cortex; responsible for making plans and thinking creatively, Broca's area (speech production)

A Tour Through the Brain

V. THE TWO HEMISPHERES OF THE BRAIN

A.   Split brains: A house divided

    1.   Normal brain - the two hemispheres communicate via the corpus callosum

    2.   Split brain refers to surgery in which the corpus callosum is severed

    3.   Daily lives of split-brain patients were not much affected, but effects on perception and memory are observable under experimental conditions

B.   The two hemispheres: Allies or Opposites

    1.   Many researchers believe the left side is dominant because cognitive skills, including language, rational, and analytic abilities, originate here

    2.   Others point to abilities of the right hemisphere: superior spatial–visual abilities, facial recognition, nonverbal sounds, and music appreciation

    3.   Differences are relative; in real life, the hemispheres co-operate

The Two Hemispheres of the Brain

VI. TWO STUBBORN ISSUES IN BRAIN RESEARCH

A. **Where is the self?**
   1. Most neuroscientists believe that the mind can be explained in physical terms as a product of the cerebral cortex
   2. One theorist suggests the brain consists of independent parts that deal with different aspects of thought; another suggests that a unified self is an illusion and that the brain is made up of independent modules working in parallel

B. **Are there "his" and "hers" brains?**
   1. Efforts to identify male–female differences have reflected biases
   2. Some evidence that male and female brains are physically different, but many conclusions can be drawn and findings often have changed
   3. Problems exist with conclusions drawn by popular writers about sex differences in the brain

VII: USING OUR BRAINS ABOUT BRAIN RESEARCH

A. **Neuroethics-** interdisciplinary specialty that focuses on the legal, ethical, and scientific implications of research

Complete this chart by identifying the function that corresponds to the brain structure listed in the left column.

BRAIN STRUCTURE	FUNCTION
BRAIN STEM	
Medulla	
Pons	
Reticular Activating System	
CEREBELLUM	
THALAMUS	
Olfactory Bulb	
HYPOTHALAMUS	
PITUITARY GLAND	
LIMBIC SYSTEM	
Amygdala	
Hippocampus	
CEREBRUM	
Left Cerebral Hemisphere	
Right Cerebral Hemisphere	
Corpus Callosum	
Cerebral Cortex	
Occipital Lobes	
Temporal Lobes	
Parietal Lobes	
Frontal Lobes	
Association Areas	

IDIOMS AND SLANGS

Bedrock (page 111) – the foundation, or basic principles, that all behaviour and mental activity are built upon.

The soul's frail dwelling house (page 112) – Shakespeare believed that the soul of a person resided in their brain.

Bridge (page 113) – the spinal cord connects the brain to other parts of the body.

Radio without a receiver (page 113) – the brain would not be able to obtain information without the peripheral nervous system acting as its receiver.

Accelerator of a car (page 113) – the sympathetic system speeds up the body when action is required.

Whirls into action (page 113) – to move rapidly, quickly.

Building blocks of the nervous system (page 115) – neurons are the units used to piece together the nervous system.

Neuron is first a catcher, then a batter (page 116) – the neuron first receives the message, then it sends it.

Got turned upside down (page 117) – what scientists had originally thought to be true was actually the opposite. For example, neurons could regrow, when previously believed they could not be regrown.

Hotly debated (page 117) – strong opposing opinions on an issue, often resulting in media attention.

Pruned away (page 119) – removing or getting rid of unnecessary connections.

Rewired (page 119) – the brain's neural connections are similar to electrical wires, which are able to reconnect themselves when damaged.

Plastic (page 119) – the brain is capable of being molded or shaped.

Nervous system "house" (page 121) – throughout this chapter the nervous system is compared to a house, where the brain is in the main room at the top.

Doors to the brain (page 127) – technology has created many new ways that allow us to observe different brain functions.

Wrong-headed (page 129) – Gall believed some opinions that were wrong, such as phrenology.

Traffic officer (page 129) – directs movement of information in the brain.

Neural alarm bells (page 132) – a signal that alerts your hippocampus of activity.

Incommunicado (page 137) – to isolate or cut off from communication.

PRACTICE TEST 1 - Multiple Choice

1.   The function of the central nervous system is
     A.   to receive, process, and interpret incoming information.
     B.   to send out messages to muscles.
     C.   to send out messages to glands and organs.
     D.   all of the above.

2.   The peripheral nervous system
     A.   is made up of the brain and spinal cord.
     B.   handles the central nervous system's input and output.
     C.   depends exclusively on sensory neurons.
     D.   depends exclusively on motor neurons.

3.   The _____ receives, processes, interprets, and stores incoming information from the senses and sends out messages destined for the muscles, glands, and internal organs. The _____ handles its input and output.
     A.   central nervous system; peripheral nervous system
     B.   peripheral nervous system; autonomic nervous system
     C.   sympathetic nervous system; parasympathetic nervous system
     D.   peripheral nervous system; central nervous system

4.   The _____ nervous system is part of the peripheral nervous system.
     A.   somatic   B.   sympathetic
     C.   autonomic   D.   all of the above

5.   One function of the somatic nervous system is to
     A.   carry information from the senses to the CNS and from the CNS to the skeletal muscles.
     B.   carry information to the glands and organs.
     C.   control the sympathetic and parasympathetic nervous systems.
     D.   process information in the brain.

6.   The autonomic nervous system is involved with
     A.   voluntary responses.
     B.   the nerves connected to the senses and skeletal muscles.
     C.   involuntary responses such as the regulation of blood vessels and glands.
     D.   only sensory nerves.

7.   The sympathetic nervous system governs _____ responses, whereas the parasympathetic nervous system governs _____ responses.
     A.   voluntary; involuntary   B.   involuntary; voluntary
     C.   arousal; relaxing   D.   sensory; motor

8. Neurons
   A. are the basic units of the nervous system.
   B. are held in place by glial cells.
   C. transmit electrical messages throughout the nervous system.
   (D.) are characterized by all of the above.

9. The three main parts of the neuron are the
   (A.) dendrites, cell body, and axon.
   B. axon, dendrites, and synapse.
   C. synapse, impulse, and cleft.
   D. myelin sheath, dendrites, and synapse.

10. The _____ receive messages from other neurons, whereas the _____ carry messages on to other neurons or to muscle or gland cells.
    A. cell bodies; dendrites
    (B.) dendrites; axons
    C. axons; dendrites
    D. myelin sheaths; cell bodies

11. Neurons are like catchers and batters in baseball. The _____ are like catchers because they receive information; the _____ are like batters because they send on the message.
    (A.) dendrites; axons   B. cell bodies; axons
    C. axons; dendrites   D. dendrites; glials

12. The cell body
    (A.) determines whether the neuron should fire.
    B. receives incoming impulses from other neurons.
    C. speeds the conduction of the neural impulse.
    D. connects with the synapse.

13. When a neural impulse reaches the tip of the axon terminal,
    A. the neuron fires.
    (B.) synaptic vesicles in the synaptic end bulb release neurotransmitters that cross the synaptic cleft and lock into receptor sites on the post-synaptic neuron.
    C. the synaptic end bulb sends an electrical current into the dendrites of the next neuron.
    D. the synaptic end bulb locks into the receptor sites on the post-synaptic dendrites.

14. During Dr. Wall's hospital rounds, he meets with patients who are suffering with Alzheimer's disease, Parkinson's disease, and severe depression. To understand these disorders better, he looks to the role of
    A. hormones.   B. endorphins.
    (C.) neurotransmitters.   D. melatonin.

15. How do neurotransmitters affect the post-synaptic neuron?
    A. They cause a change in the electrical potential, exciting the neuron and causing it to fire.
    B. They cause a change in the electrical potential, either exciting or inhibiting the next neuron.
    C. They cause a change in the electrical potential, inhibiting the neuron and stopping it from firing.
    D. They do not make contact with the next neuron; they stay in the synapse.

16. Serotonin, dopamine, acetylcholine, and norepinephrine are
    A. adrenal hormones.   B. endorphins.
    C. sex hormones.   D. neurotransmitters.

17. Mood, memory, well-being, Alzheimer's disease, depression, sleep, appetite, pain, and temperature regulation are all influenced by
    A. dopamine.   B. neurotransmitters.
    C. endorphins.   D. all of the above.

18. During a dangerous situation, pain sensations are reduced. This reduction of pain is due to an increase in
    A. testosterone levels.
    B. endorphin levels.
    C. androgen levels.
    D. insulin levels.

19. _____ are chemicals that are released directly into the bloodstream, which then carries them to organs and cells that may be far from their point of origin.
    A. neurotransmitters   B. endorphins
    C. hormones   D. neuromodulators

20. Androgen, estrogen, and progesterone are three types of
    A. sex hormones.   B. neurotransmitters.
    C. neurons.   D. neuromodulators.

21. The _____ is a method for analyzing biochemical activity in the brain that uses injections containing a harmless radioactive element.
    A. MRI (magnetic resonance imaging)
    B. PET scan (positron-emission tomography)
    C. EEG (electroencephalography)
    D. TMS (Transcranial Magnetic Stimulation)

22. Brain stem is to _____ as cerebrum is to _____.
    A. emotions; vital functions
    B. vital functions; emotions
    C. higher forms of thinking; vital functions
    D. vital functions; higher forms of thinking

23. The limbic system includes the
    A. cortex and corpus callosum.
    B. spinal cord and brain.
    C. cerebellum and brain stem.
    D. amygdala and hippocampus.

24. The _____ has deep crevasses and wrinkles that enable it to contain billions of neurons without requiring people to have much larger heads.
    A. corpus callosum   B. cerebral cortex
    C. cerebellum   D. hypothalamus

25. The four distinct lobes of the cortex are the
    A. occipital, parietal, temporal, and frontal lobes.
    B. sensory, auditory, visual, and motor lobes.
    C. hind, mid, fore, and association lobes.
    D. front, back, side, and top lobes.

26. Which of the following summarizes the different hemispheric functions?
    A. The left brain is more active in logic and the right brain is associated with spatial–visual ability.
    B. The left brain is more active in artistic and intuitive tasks, and the right brain is more involved in emotional and expressive abilities.
    C. The left brain has spatial–visual ability, while the right brain is more involved in artistic and creative activities.
    D. The right brain is more dominant and the left brain is more subordinate.

27. If Lucy is like most people, her _____ is most involved when she calculates a math problem and her _____ is most active when she reads a map.
    A. right brain; left brain   B. left brain; right brain
    C. corpus callosum; cerebellum   D. amygdala; thalamus

28. Localization of function refers to the fact that
    A. personality traits are reflected in different areas of the brain.
    B. information is distributed across large areas of the brain.
    C. different brain parts perform different jobs and store different sorts of information.
    D. brain processes are like holography.

29. The issue of whether there are sex differences in the brain is controversial because
   A.   evidence of anatomical sex differences in humans is contradictory.
   B.   findings are always changing as a result of the biases of the observers.
   C.   even if anatomical differences exist, we do not know what they mean.
   D.   all of the above reasons.

30. Throughout life, new learning results in the establishment of new synaptic connections in the brain, with stimulating environments producing the greatest changes. Conversely, some unused synaptic connections are lost as cells or their branches die and are not replaced. This indicates that the brain
   A.   is more lateralized than scientists once thought.
   B.   continues to develop and change in response to the environment.
   C.   develops new brain cells on a regular and ongoing basis.
   D.   is more holistic than scientists once thought.

72

PRACTICE TEST 2 - Short Answer

1. The nervous system is divided into two main parts: the _C_ nervous system, which receives, processes, interprets, and stores incoming information, and the _P_ nervous system, which contains all parts of the nervous system outside the brain and spinal cord.

2. The peripheral nervous system is divided into the _somatic_ nervous system, which controls the skeletal muscles and permits voluntary action, and the _autonomi_ nervous system, which regulates blood vessels, glands, and internal organs and works more or less without a person's conscious control.

3. The autonomic nervous system is divided into the _sympathetic_ nervous system, which mobilizes the body for action and increases energy, and the _parasymp_ nervous system, which conserves and stores energy.

4. Neurons have three main parts. The _cell body_ contains the biochemical machinery for keeping the neuron alive.

5. The _dentrite_ of a neuron receive messages from other nerve cells and transmit them toward the cell body. The _axon_ transmits messages away from the cell body to other cells.

6. Most neurons are insulated by a layer of fatty tissue called the _myelin sheath_ that prevents signals from adjacent cells from interfering with each other and speeds up the conduction of neural impulses.

7. Individual neurons are separated by tiny gaps called the _synapse_.

8. When an electrical impulse reaches the _axon_ of a neuron, chemical substances called _neurotransmitters_ are released into the synapse. Once across the synapse, the molecules fit into sites on the receiving neuron, changing the membrane of the receiving cell.

9. What any given neuron does at any given moment depends on the net effect of all the messages being received from other neurons. The message that reaches a final destination depends on the rate at which individual neurons are firing, how many are firing, what types are firing, and where they are located. It does NOT depend on how strongly neurons are firing because the firing of a neuron is an _all or none_ event.

73

10. *endorphins* are chemical messengers that reduce pain and promote pleasure. Dopamine, serotonin, and norepinephrine are examples of another type of chemical messenger called *neurotransmitters*

11. Hormones originate primarily in the *endocrine* glands, which deposit them into the bloodstream where they are carried to organs and cells.

12. Neurotransmitters affect a variety of behaviours. Low levels of _____ and _____ may be implicated in severe depression; _____ affects memory, and the loss of cells producing this neurotransmitter may help account for some of the symptoms of Alzheimer's disease.

13. The three main types of sex hormones that occur in both sexes (though in differing amounts) are _____, _____, and _____.

14. Living brains can be studied by probing them with electrodes. The procedure for obtaining brain wave recordings is called a(n) _____.

15. Other methods of investigating living brains are PET scans, which record biochemical changes in the brain as they are happening, and _____ which utilize magnetic fields and radio frequencies to explore the "inner space" of the brain.

16. This dense network of neurons, which extends above the brain stem into the centre of the brain and has connections with higher areas, screens incoming information and arouses the higher centres when something happens that demands their attention. Without the _____ system, we could not be alert or perhaps even conscious.

17. The structures of the brain stem include the _____ that is responsible for sleeping, waking, and dreaming, and the _____, that is responsible for bodily functions like breathing and heart rate. Standing on top of the brain stem, the _____ contributes to a sense of balance and muscle coordination.

18. The _____ is a busy traffic officer that directs sensory messages from the spinal cord to higher brain centres.

19. The _____ sits beneath the thalamus and is involved with drives vital for survival, such as hunger, thirst, emotion, sex, and reproduction.

20. The _____ system is heavily involved in emotions.

21. Oxytocin is secreted by the _____ _____ and enhances
    _____.

22. The cerebral cortex, the layer of cells that covers the cerebrum, is divided into four
    distinct lobes. The _____ lobes contain the visual cortex, the _____
    lobes contain the somatosensory cortex, the _____ contain the auditory cortex, and
    the _____ lobes contain the motor cortex.

23. A large bundle of nerve fibres called the _____ connects the two cerebral
    hemispheres. The left and right sides of the brain seem to have somewhat different tasks
    and talents, a phenomenon known as _____.

24. There are two main language areas in the brain. _____ area is involved in language
    comprehension and is located in the _____ lobe, and _____ area is involved
    in speech production and is located in the _____ lobe.

25. To examine the issue of sex differences, we need to ask two separate questions: Do
    physical differences actually exist in male and female brains, and if so, what do they have
    to do with _____?

26. The colour scales used in _____ can be manipulated in various ways,
    suggesting that even such an "objective" brain-mapping test can be interpreted
    differently.

27. A new interdisciplinary specialty that addresses the legal, ethical, and scientific
    implications of brain research is known as _____.

PRACTICE TEST 3 - Essay

1. You are sitting at your desk trying to study for a test you are very nervous about, and all you can focus on is the stereo playing in the other room. You get up, go to the other room, and turn down the stereo. Beginning with the external stimuli (the sound) and ending with your movement to the other room, describe:
    A. from the standpoint of a single neuron
    B. the brain structures that are involved, in sequence, and
    C. the nervous system involvement

2. For each scenario, indicate the brain structure(s) most likely to be involved in the behaviour that is described.
    A. Dr. Smith inserts an electrode into a structure within the brain. As this electrode is activated, the person sweats and shivers, feels hungry and thirsty, and sometimes even seems angry and sexually aroused.
    B. A computer-enhanced image has enabled a research team to observe the flow of information within the nervous system. While watching this flow, the researchers notice that incoming sensory messages are relayed through this centre before finally reaching their destination in the cerebral hemispheres.
    C. As a result of a serious automobile accident, Fred's ability to make plans and show initiative were seriously impaired.
    D. Bill's great grandmother has had a serious stroke. As a result, she is unable to speak, though she appears to understand and respond nonverbally to what is being said.
    E. Tiffany's elderly neighbour is showing signs of memory loss.
    F. Mary has been unable to continue as a gymnast since the lower rear area of her brain was damaged in a car accident. All tasks requiring balance or coordinated movements are beyond Mary's capacities.

3. As a result of mixing tranquilizers and alcohol, Helen has become what is called "brain dead," and though she does not respond to people, she continues to live without any life-sustaining equipment. Which parts of her brain have been damaged and which parts continue to function?

4. In the descriptions that follow, cortical functions are disrupted in various ways. From the descriptions identify the cortical structures and state their functions.
    A. Removing a tumour from an area just behind her forehead has dramatically altered Denise's personality. Previously outgoing and warm, she is now hostile and needs prodding to get anything done.
    B. Lately Ralph has been experiencing tingling sensations in various body parts and he sometimes "forgets" where his hands and fingers are. Tests reveal a growth near the surface of the brain just under the centre of his head.
    C. Philip has a large blind spot in his visual field, and doctors have eliminated the possibility of eye and optic nerve problems.

5. In the examples below, identify whether the phenomena are primarily related to the functioning of the right hemisphere, the left hemisphere, or both.
   A.   Ken is being tested for school placement. Part of the test involves putting puzzle pieces together so they form geometric shapes. Ken performs well.
   B.   Another portion of the test involves reading simple sentences aloud. Ken garbles the words and says them in an improper sequence.
   C.   A third portion of the test requires Ken to respond to sets of photographs, each set containing five pictures of a person posed identically except for facial expression.
   D.   The last portion of the test assesses manual dexterity in the nondominant arm and hand. Because Ken is left-handed, he is required to perform all sorts of mechanical tasks with his right hand. He fails this part of the test.
   E.   What overall conclusion might be reached about Ken's hemispheric functioning?

6. What is the field of neuroethics? What do you think about the issue of taking drugs designed for disorders for cognitive "enhancement" purposes?

CHAPTER FIVE

Body Rhythms and Mental States

LEARNING OBJECTIVES

1. Define consciousness and the biological rhythms often associated with states of consciousness.

2. Describe circadian rhythms, including how they are studied and how they may be desynchronized.

3. Describe the role of the superchiasmatic nucleus (SCN) and the hormone melatonin in the maintenance of circadian rhythms.

4. Summarize the research evidence surrounding Seasonal Affective Disorder.

5. Summarize the research evidence on Premenstrual Syndrome (PMS) and discuss whether emotional symptoms associated with PMS are tied to the menstrual cycle.

6. Distinguish between rapid eye movement (REM) and non-REM periods in sleep and describe the four stages of non-REM sleep.

7. Why is REM sleep known as paradoxical sleep? Review the purpose of REM sleep.

8. Summarize theories about why we sleep.

9. Review the mental consequences of sleeplessness.

10. Describe two sleep disorders—sleep apnea and narcolepsy.

11. Summarize the principles of the psychoanalytic theory of dreaming. Distinguish between the manifest and latent content of dreams.

12. Summarize the problem-focused approach to dreaming. How is it similar and how does it differ from the cognitive approach to dreaming?

13. Summarize the activation-synthesis theory of dreaming.

14. Evaluate the four theories of dreaming.

15. Define hypnosis and summarize its characteristics.

16. Describe the dissociation and sociocognitive theories of hypnosis.

17. Discuss historical approaches to altering states of consciousness. Define what is meant by a psychoactive drug.

18. List the types of psychoactive drugs and describe their physical and behavioural effects.

19. List and explain the factors that influence the effects of psychoactive drugs.

20. Summarize the debate regarding the criminalization and decriminalization of certain drugs.

21.   Describe some of the alternatives suggested by sleep researchers in order to get a better
        night's sleep.

BRIEF CHAPTER SUMMARY

Chapter 5 examines biological rhythms and states of consciousness. Circadian rhythms are biological rhythms that have an approximately 24- hour cycle. The effects of internal desynchronization and hormones are discussed.

During the sleep cycle, four stages of non-rapid eye movement (NREM) sleep alternate with rapid eye movement sleep (REM) approximately every 90 minutes during the night. Dreaming is more likely to happen during REM sleep. Although the purpose of dreams is not conclusively known, psychologists have proposed several explanations, such as dreams that reflect the unconscious (Freud), the problem-focused explanation, the cognitive explanation and the activation–synthesis theory.

The characteristics of hypnosis are discussed, as are the two principle theories of hypnosis: the dissociative theories (and the hidden observer) and the sociocognitive approach. Several myths about hypnosis (e.g., that hypnosis has enormous effects on memory) are refuted.

Classes of consciousness-altering drugs include stimulants, depressants, opiates, and psychedelics. Their effects on functioning are discussed.

PREVIEW OUTLINE

Before you read the chapter, review the preview outline for each section of the text. After you have read the chapter, close this book and try to <u>re-create</u> the outlines on a blank piece of paper.

I. **BIOLOGICAL RHYTHMS: THE TIDES OF EXPERIENCE**
    A.   **Definitions**
            1.   Consciousness - awareness of oneself and the environment
            2.   Biological rhythms - regular fluctuations in biological systems
            3.   Entrainment - synchronization of rhythms with external events
            4.   Endogenous rhythms - occur in absence of external cues

    B.   **Circadian rhythms** –occur roughly every 24 hours; exist in plants, animals, insects, and humans
            1.   The body's clock
                    a.   Controlled by the suprachiasmatic nucleus (SCN)
                    b.   SCN regulates neurotransmitters and hormones (e.g., melatonin)
            2.   When the clock is out of sync or not working properly
                    a.   Change in routine may cause internal desynchronization
                    b.   Cycles are affected by environmental and individual factors

    C.   **Moods and long-term rhythms**
            1.   Does the season affect moods? Seasonal affective disorder (SAD); less prevalent than originally thought

2.   Does the menstrual cycle affect moods?
      a.   Clear support for emotional symptoms of premenstrual syndrome (PMS) is lacking
b. Research on hormonal (testosterone) influences on men is lacking
      c.   Conclusion - few people of either sex are likely to undergo personality shifts because of hormones

II. THE RHYTHMS OF SLEEP

A.   **The realms of sleep** - sleep is not an unbroken state of rest
    1.   Cycle (series of stages) occurs, on average, every 90 minutes
      (a)   Four non-REM stages, each deeper than the previous
          1 - small, irregular brain waves; light sleep
          2 - high-peaking waves called sleep spindles
          3 - delta waves begin; slow with high peaks
          4 - mostly delta waves and deep sleep
      (b)   REM sleep (also called paradoxical sleep) is characterized by active brain waves, increased heart rate and blood pressure, limp muscles, and dreaming
(c) REM and non REM sleep alternates throughout the night, with REM sleep getting longer and closer together, and deeper sleep (stages 3 and 4) getting shorter
B.   **Why do we sleep?** Some theories:
a. Sleep is recuperative for the body
b. Sleep is necessary for normal mental functioning
c. Causes of daytime sleepiness include sleep apnea, narcolepsy and not getting enough sleep
d. Mental benefits of sleep include consolidation and problem solving

Biological Rhythms: The Tides of Experience

80

III. EXPLORING THE DREAM WORLD

A.   **Characteristics of dreams** – inward focus of attention, lucid dreams

B.   **Theories of dreams** - every culture has its theories about dreams

    1.   Dreams as unconscious wishes (Freud)

        a.   Manifest content - what we experience and remember

        b.   Latent content - hidden, symbolic; unconscious wishes

    2.   Dreams as efforts to deal with problems (problem-focused)

        a.   Reflect ongoing, conscious concerns of waking life

        b.   Some believe dreams provide an opportunity for resolving problems

    3.   4.   Dreams as thinking (cognitive approach.)

        a.   Brain does similar work as when awake, but more unfocused.

    5.   Dreams as interpreted brain activity (Activation–synthesis theory)

        a.   Dreams are the result of neurons firing spontaneously (activation) in the lower brain (in the pons) that are sent to the cortex

        b.   Signals from pons have no meaning, but the cortex tries to make sense of (synthesize), them

Exploring the Dream World

IV THE RIDDLE OF HYPNOSIS

A.   **Definition - procedure in which the practitioner suggests changes in the sensations, perceptions, thoughts, feelings, or behaviour of the participant**

B.   **The nature of hypnosis** - researchers agree on the following:

    1.   Responsiveness depends more on the person being hypnotized than hypnotist's skill

2. Participants cannot be forced to do things against their will; hypnotic inductions increase suggestibility but only to a modest degree

3. Feats performed under hypnosis can be performed by motivated people without hypnosis

4. Hypnosis does not increase the accuracy of memory; it can increase amount of information remembered, but it also increases errors

5. Does not produce a literal re-experiencing of long-ago events

6. Hypnosis has been effective for medical and psychological purposes

C. **Theories of hypnosis** - two competing theories predominate

1. Dissociation theories - a split in consciousness in which one part of the mind operates independently of the rest of consciousness; hidden observer

2. The sociocognitive approach

   a. The effects are a result of the interaction between the hypnotist and the abilities, beliefs, and expectations of the participant

   b. People are playing the role of a hypnotized person without faking

V. CONSCIOUSNESS-ALTERING DRUGS

A. **Altering mood and consciousness**

1. Efforts to alter mood and consciousness appear to be universal

2. During the 1960s, people sought to produce altered states of consciousness

B. **Classifying drugs**

1. Psychoactive drug - substance affecting perception, mood, thinking, memory, or behaviour by changing the body's biochemistry

2. Classified according to the drug's effects on central nervous system

   a. Stimulants - speed up activity in central nervous system; include cocaine, amphetamines, nicotine, and caffeine

   b. Depressants (sedatives) - slow down activity in central nervous system; include alcohol, tranquilizers, and barbiturates

   c. Opiates - mimic endorphins; include opium, morphine, heroin, methadone

   d. Psychedelics - alter normal thought and sometimes produce hallucinations; include LSD, mescaline, and psilocybin

   e. Anabolic steroids and marijuana - don't fit other classifications

C. **The physiology of drug effects**

1. Effects produced by acting on neurotransmitters in a variety of ways

2. Some drugs lead to tolerance and withdrawal

D. **The psychology of drug effects** - effects depend on a person's physical condition, experience with the drug, environmental setting, and "mental set"

E. **The drug debate** It is often difficult to distinguish drug use from drug abuse, to differentiate between heavy use and light and moderate use and to separate issues of a drug's legality or illegality from the drug's potential dangers and benefits

Consciousness Altering Drugs

The Riddle of Hypnosis

IDIOMS AND SLANGS

Space out (page 151) – to be physically present in the room but to be absent mentally. Distracted, not paying attention to the present moment.

Master pacemaker (page 154) – leading the way, sets the pace for other bodily rhythms.

Controversy has also raged (page 157) – lengthy discussions, aggressive arguments, involving strong emotion, and enthusiasm on opposing views.

Land of Nod (page 161) – the imaginary world of sleep and dreams one drifts deeply into.

Children of an idle brain (page 170) – to be inactive or lazy. Whereas dreams come from an active mind.

Saturday night binge (page 184) – drinking excessively on one occasion can be more harmful than drinking small amounts daily.

Came into force (page 187) – rules were developed to control the use of marijuana for medical purposes.

Totally absorbed (page 173) – focused on one particular activity to the point of not noticing anything else.

Runs counter (page 175) – a theory that presents information from the opposite perspective.

PRACTICE TEST 1 - Multiple Choice

1. Jim likes to get drunk and smoke marijuana because this enables him to see himself and the world differently. This motive is consistent with which one of the following statements about consciousness?
   A. Consciousness is awareness of one's bodily changes or rhythms.
   B. Consciousness is awareness of oneself and the environment.
   C. Consciousness is directly related to changes in brain-wave patterns.
   D. Consciousness is a philosophical issue that cannot be defined.

2. As part of a research study, Bob is living in a comfortable room with a VCR and stereo, but there are no windows, clocks, or sounds coming in from outside. He is told to eat, sleep, and work whenever he feels like doing so. This type of study is used to
   A. examine sensory deprivation.
   B. examine the affect of daylight on depression.
   C. explore endogenous circadian rhythms.
   D. explore intrinsic motivation

3. Which of the following can desynchronize circadian rhythms?
   A. an overseas trip
   B. switching shifts at work
   C. going on daylight savings time
   D. all of the above

8. Menstrual cycle research on hormones and mood shifts suggests that
   A. for most people, hormones are reliably and strongly correlated with mood.
   B. hormonal shifts cause mood shifts.
   C. mood changes cause hormonal shifts.
   D. no causal relationship has been established between hormonal shifts and moods.

9. Which of the following conclusions reflects the findings on premenstrual symptoms?
   A. The idea of mood swings as a premenstrual symptom has been questioned since men and women don't differ in the number of mood swings they experience in a month.
   B. For most women, the relationship between cycle stage and symptoms is weak.
   C. There is no reliable relationship between cycle stage and work efficiency.
   D. All of the above have been found.

10. Sleep is necessary
    A. because of its recuperative properties.
    B. because the brain requires sleep.
    C. to repair cells and remove waste products from the muscles.
    D. for all of the above reasons.

11. The brain waves that occur when you first go to bed and relax are called
    A. alpha waves.
    B. delta waves.
    C. beta waves.
    D. gamma waves.

12. Joe is a participant in a sleep study. When his brain emits occasional short bursts of rapid, high-peaking waves called sleep spindles, he is in which stage of sleep?
    A.   Stage 1   B.   Stage 3
    C.   Stage 2   D.   Stage 4

13. REM sleep is called paradoxical sleep because
    A.   dreams are often paradoxical and they occur most often in REM sleep.
    B.   the brain is extremely active but the body is devoid of muscle tone.
    C.   people are easily awakened, even though it is a deep sleep.
    D.   the brain is very calm and inactive, but the body is quite active.

14. After the first 30 to 45 minutes of sleep, you have progressed from Stage 1 sleep to Stage 4 sleep. After this, you most likely
    A.   go into a prolonged non-REM period.
    B.   enter REM sleep.
    C.   progress back up the ladder from Stage 4 to Stage 3 to Stage 2 to Stage 1.
    D.   go back to Stage 1 and continue through the four stages all night.

15. The most vivid dreams occur during
    A.   the menstrual cycle.   B.   REM sleep.
    C.   Stage 1 sleep.   D.   non-REM sleep.

16. When Ruth dreams, she is in the dream, but also observing the dream and controlling what happens in it. Ruth is experiencing
    A.   nightmares.   B.   manifest dreams.
    C.   lucid dreams.   D.   REM dreams.

17. According to the _____ hypothesis, dreams express our unconscious desires.
    A.   cognitive   B.   psychoanalytic
    C.   activation–synthesis D.   problem-solving

18. Which hypothesis suggests that dreams result from cortical attempts to interpret spontaneous neural activity?
    A.   cognitive   B.   psychoanalytic
    C.   activation–synthesis   D.   problem solving

19. Psychoactive drugs work primarily by affecting
    A.   brain structures.   B.   bodily rhythms.
    C.   neurotransmitters.   D.   blood flow to the brain.

20. Which of the following are psychoactive drugs?
    A.   tobacco   B.   opium
    C.   caffeine   D.   all of the above

21. Though cocaine is a(n) _____, heroin is a(n) _____, and marijuana is a(n) _____, they can all produce euphoria.
    A. stimulant; psychedelic; depressant
    B. amphetamine; opiate; psychedelic
    C. psychedelic; stimulant; unclear category
    D. stimulant; opiate; unclear category

22. Alcohol, tranquilizers, and sedatives are examples of
    A. opiates.
    B. depressants.
    C. psychedelics.
    D. stimulants.

23. When Mickey began using drugs, he used only a small amount. After six months, he required more and more to achieve the same effect. Mickey experienced
    A. withdrawal.
    B. brain damage.
    C. tolerance.
    D. mental set.

24. Hank and Bill both used the same amount of cocaine, but they each had different reactions. Which of the following differences between them might account for this?
    A. physical condition
    B. expectations for the drug
    C. prior experience with cocaine
    D. all of the above

25. Which of the following statements describes the effect of hypnosis on memory?
    A. "Age regression" allows one to remember childhood experiences accurately.
    B. Under hypnosis, people can accurately recall events from earlier lives.
    C. Memories recalled under hypnosis are often vivid but inaccurate.
    D. Memory errors decrease under hypnosis.

26. Which evidence argues against the credibility of age regression?
    A. Participants who were age-regressed as part of a study could not accurately recall their favourite comforting object from age three.
    B. Participants in a study did not know basic facts about the time period in which they were supposed to have lived in a previous life.
    C. When people are regressed to an earlier age, brain-wave patterns do not resemble those of children.
    D. all of the above

27. Those who believe that hypnotic state differs from normal consciousness believe
    A. that hypnosis involves dissociation.
    B. the powers of hypnosis are exaggerated.
    C. that suggestion alone can produce the same results.
    D. all of the above.

28. Those who say hypnosis is a(n) _____ believe that hypnosis involves role-playing.
    A. altered state
    B. deliberate deception
    C. sociocognitive process
    D. none of the above

87

29. Susan, who is normally very modest, is removing some of her clothes under hypnosis. How might this be explained, according to the theory that hypnosis is a social-cognitive process?
   A. She is in an altered state.
   B. She has dissociated.
   C. She is playing the role of a hypnotized person.
   D. She has relinquished control to the hypnotist.

30. Entrainment is
   A. the roughly 24-hour biological rhythm cycle.
   B. increased tolerance of a psychoactive drug.
   C. a sleep disorder involving sudden daytime attacks of sleepiness.
   D. the synchronization of biological rhythms with external cues.

31. When individuals are unaware of the actual time, their "day" cycle typically averages
   A. exactly 24 hours.   B. about 28 hours.
   C. slightly more than 24 hours.   D. only 12 hours.

32. Circadian rhythms are controlled by a biological clock located in the
   A. suprachiasmatic nucleus.   B. frontal lobes.
   C. pons.   D. amygdala.

33. The hormone involved in circadian rhythms is
   A. testosterone.   B. serotonin.
   C. melatonin.   D. progesterone.

34. A sleep disorder in which breathing periodically stops, often hundreds of times a night, is known as
   A. narcolepsy.   B. sleep apnea.
   C. consolidation.   D. interrupted sleep disorder.

PRACTICE TEST 2 - Short Answer

1.   _____ is defined as the awareness of oneself and the environment.

2.   The sleep cycle is an example of a(n) _____ rhythm.

3.   Circadian rhythms are controlled by a biological clock called the _____.

4.   A periodic, more or less regular fluctuation in a biologicalsystem is known as a
      . _____.

5.   Internal _____ occurs when your normal routine changes, such as when you must take a long airplane flight over many time zones.

6.   Few people of either sex are likely to undergo personality shifts solely as a result of _____.

7.   The majority of vivid dreams occurs during _____.

8.   The short bursts of rapid, high-peaking waves that occur during Stage 2 sleep are known as sleep _____.

9.   REM sleep is called paradoxical sleep because the body is _____ while the brain is _____.

10.   _____ dreaming occurs when people are aware that they are dreaming.

11.   Psychoanalytic theory suggests that we must distinguish the obvious, or _____, content of a dream from the hidden, or _____, content that reveals the true meaning of the dream.

12.   The _____ approach to dreaming asserts that dreams reflect the ongoing conscious preoccupations of waking life.

13.   The _____ hypothesis suggests that dreams are the result of spontaneous neural firing.

14.   _____ drugs affect perception, mood, thinking, memory, or behaviour.

15.   Drugs are classified according to their effects on the _____.

16.   Amphetamines, cocaine, caffeine, and nicotine are all examples of _____.

17.   Some drugs, such as heroin and tranquilizers can lead to _____, a state in which larger and larger doses are needed to produce the same effect.

18.   The psychoactive drugs exert effects by influencing _____ levels.

19.   Several factors influence the way a particular individual reacts to the use of a drug. Two of those factors are _____ and _____.

20.   Some suggest that alcohol can provide an excuse for belligerent behaviour. This is called the _____ phenomenon.

21.   Hilgard suggests that only one part of consciousness goes along with hypnotic suggestions. The other part is like a _____, watching but not participating.

22.   Some people report that hypnosis has helped them recall long-ago events. These memories are likely to be _____.

23.   The _____ explanation of hypnosis suggests that during hypnosis a split in consciousness occurs.

24.   Hypnosis has been used effectively for _____ purposes.

25.   The _____ explanation regards hypnosis as a form of role-playing.

26.   A periodic, more or less regular fluctuation in a biological system is known as a _____.

27.   A sleep disorder involving sudden and unpredictable daytime attacks of sleepiness or lapses into REM sleep is known as _____.

PRACTICE TEST 3 - Essay

1.   Dr. Irving is conducting a survey on premenstrual syndrome (PMS). Of the 100 participants who responded to the survey, 70 percent indicated that they experience PMS on a regular basis. Compare these findings to the research in the text that argues against PMS and answer the following questions:

A.   How was PMS defined? What symptoms were included and why is this important?

B.   What are some of the problems with the self-reporting of PMS symptoms?

C.   Describe possible influences of expectations and attitudes about menstruation on the results of the survey.

D.   Describe the results of research findings from studies that did not reveal their true purpose.

2.   For the ninth grade science project, Megan kept a detailed diary of her sleep experiences during a one-month interval. The information obtained and her conclusions are submitted below. Using actual evidence related to sleep, comment on each of these claims:

A.   During the period of the study, I awakened myself once during each night at different times. Each time I woke up, I felt the same as when I usually wake up in the morning. This indicates that sleep actually is the same kind of thing all through the night.

B.   I was allowed to stay up all night twice. It was really hard to keep my eyes open at around 4:00 a.m., but by 6:00 a.m. I felt wide-awake. This suggests that the loss of sleep is invigorating.

C.   After missing sleep two nights in a row, I felt like going to bed extra early the next day. This indicates that we need to catch up on our rest.

D.   Even though I felt O.K. after missing sleep for two nights, I got a "D" on an exam at school. This suggests that maybe sleep loss has more effects than I thought!

E.   During the time of the study, I had two dreams and my sister had five. This indicates that we only dream several times a month.

3.   Anne had a dream that she and her husband had gone horseback riding. He was far ahead of her and, though she was riding as fast as she could, she was unable to catch up. Eventually she lost her way and was unsure where she was going. She dismounted her horse and found that she was in a beautiful valley, and she stopped there and felt very peaceful. Identify which theory would give each of the following interpretations of this dream:

A.   This dream has little significance or meaning. It represents the attempt of the cortex to make sense of random neuronal firing in the brain stem.

B.   This dream has little significance. It represents the brain's mental housekeeping. It is sorting, scanning, and sifting new information into "wanted" and "unwanted" categories.

C.   The dream has great significance. It is likely a dream about Anne's unresolved relationship with her father. She has always felt abandoned by him and could never win his attention or affection, which she has always deeply desired.

D.   The dream has to do with Anne's concern that she cannot keep up with her husband's pace. He always has more energy than she does and although she tries, what she would most like to do is "get off the merry-go-round," relax, and take life easier.

4.   For each type of drug listed below, indicate the following: 1) the type of drug, 2) the common effects of the drug, and 3) the result of abusing the drug.

     A.   alcohol
     B.   tranquilizers
     C.   morphine
     D.   amphetamines
     E.   cocaine
     F.   LSD
     G.   marijuana

5.   You and your friends see a hypnotist at a show. Afterward, your friends ask various questions about hypnosis. Can you be forced to do things against your will under hypnosis? Can you remember long-forgotten memories under hypnosis? Is hypnosis ever used in practical situations, outside of entertainment? Based on your study of hypnosis, what are your answers to your friends' questions?

CHAPTER SIX

Sensation and Perception

LEARNING OBJECTIVES

1. Distinguish between sensation and perception.

2. Describe the doctrine of specific nerve energies.

3. Describe the rare condition known as synesthesia.

4. Distinguish between anatomical and functional codes in the nervous system.

5. Define psychophysics, absolute and difference thresholds, and signal-detection theory.

6. Explain sensory adaptation, sensory deprivation and sensory overload.

7. Explain selective attention and inattentional blindness.

8. List the characteristics of light waves and their correspondence to the visual experience.

9. Identify the parts of the eye and describe how they convert light to vision.

10. Explain why the visual system should not be compared to a camera.

11. Discuss two theories of colour vision and their connection to stages of processing.

12. Explain how form perception occurs and describe five Gestalt principles.

13. Explain how distance and depth perception occurs, describing various monocular and binocular cues.

14. List and explain visual constancies and distinguish them from visual illusions.

15. Describe how sound wave characteristics correspond to loudness, pitch, and timbre.

16. Identify the parts of the ear, describe how they convert sound to hearing, and discuss the role of perceptual processes in making sound meaningful.

17. List and explain the factors that affect gestation.

18. List and explain the factors that affect olfaction.

19. List the four skin senses.

20. Describe the gate-control theory of pain and the updated version of this theory.

21. Describe the internal senses of kinesthesis and equilibrium.

22. Summarize the evidence for innate abilities in perception and describe the psychological and cultural influences on perception.

23. Discuss the evidence on the effectiveness of "subliminal perception" tapes and the existence of extrasensory perception (ESP).

24. Outline and describe the strategies that many pain treatment programs encourage.

BRIEF CHAPTER SUMMARY

Chapter 6 examines the processes of sensation and perception for the various senses and the relationship between them. Receptors in the senses change physical energy into neural energy. The physical characteristics of the stimuli correspond to psychological dimensions of our sensory experience. Psychophysics (how the physical properties of stimuli are linked to psychological experiences), signal-detection theory, sensory adaptation, and sensory overload are discussed. The general processes of vision, hearing, taste, smell, pain, equilibrium, and kinesthesis are reviewed. For each of these senses, the chapter examines the relevant biological structures processes (e.g., rods and cones) as well as the relevant theories that explain perception (e.g., trichromatic theory and opponent-process theory to explain how we see colour). Once sensation has occurred, the process of organizing and interpreting the sensory information, or perception, begins. Perceptual strategies, including depth and distance strategies, visual constancies, and form perception strategies, are described. Some perceptual abilities appear to be inborn, whereas others are influenced by psychological, environmental, and cultural factors. The gate-control theory of pain and a newer, modified version of this theory are reviewed. Conscious and nonconscious processes are examined, and extrasensory perception (ESP) is critically evaluated.

PREVIEW OUTLINE AND REVIEW QUESTIONS

Before you read the chapter, review the preview outline for each section of the text. After you have read the chapter, close this book and try to <u>re-create</u> the outlines on a blank piece of paper.

I. **OUR SENSATIONAL SENSES**
    A. **Definitions**
        1. Sensation – the detection of physical energy emitted or reflected by physical objects by cells (receptors)
        2. Perception – organizing sensory impulses into meaningful patterns
    B. **The riddle of separate sensations** – how can we explain separate sensations?
        1. There are five widely known senses and other lesser-known senses; all of them evolved to help us survive
        2. Sense receptors (cells in sense organs) detect a stimulus and convert the energy into electrical impulses that travel along nerves to the brain
        3. The nervous system encodes the neural messages using anatomical codes and functional codes (doctrine of specific nerve energies)
    C. **Measuring the senses**
        1. Psychophysics – how the physical properties of stimuli are related to our psychological experience of them
        2. Absolute threshold – the smallest amount of energy a person can detect reliably (50 percent of the time)

3.   Difference thresholds - the smallest difference in stimulation that a person can detect reliably; also called just noticeable difference (jnd)

4.   Signal-detection theory

       a.   Accounts for response bias (tendency to say yes or no to a signal)

       b.   Separates sensory processes (the intensity of the stimulus) from the decision process (influenced by observer's response bias)

D.   Sensory adaptation

1.   Senses designed to respond to change and contrast in the environment

2.   Decline in sensory responsiveness occurs when a stimulus is unchanging; nerve cells temporarily get "tired" and fire less frequently

3.   Sensory deprivation studies - participants became edgy, disoriented, confused

E.   Sensing without perceiving

1.   "Cocktail party phenomenon" - blocking out unimportant sensations

2.   Selective attention - protects us from being overwhelmed with sensations

3.   Inattentional blindness - failing to consciously register objects that we are looking straight at

Our Sensational Senses

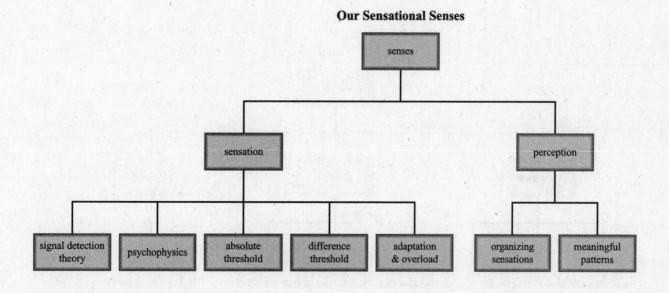

II. VISION

A.   What we see

1.   Psychological dimensions of visual world - hue, brightness, saturation

2.   Physical properties of light - wavelength, intensity, complexity

B.   An eye on the world - parts of the eye

1.   Parts of the eye include cornea, lens (focuses light), iris (controls amount of light that gets into eye) and pupil (dilates to let light in)

2.   Retina - in the back of the eye where the visual receptors are located

       a.   Rods - sensitive to light, not to colour

       b.   Cones - see colour, but needs more light to respond

C. **Why the visual system is not a camera**
1. Eyes are not a passive recorder of external world; neurons build picture
2. Visual system cells have response specialties (feature detectors in animals)
3. Controversy over specialized "face modules" in the brain

D. **How we see colours**
1. Trichromatic theory – first level of processing – three types of cones
2. Opponent-process theory – second stage of processing (ganglion cells)

E. **Constructing the visual world**
1. Visual perception - the mind interprets the retinal image and constructs the world using information from the senses
2. Form perception - Gestalt descriptions of how we build perceptual units include: figure and ground, proximity, closure, similarity, continuity
3. Depth and distance perception - binocular cues and monocular cues
4. Visual constancies - when seeing is believing
   a. Perceptual constancy - perception of objects as unchanging though the sensory patterns they produce are constantly shifting
   b. Shape, location, brightness, colour, and size constancies

III. HEARING

   A.   **What we hear**
   1. Stimulus for sound is a wave of pressure created when an object vibrates, which causes molecules in a transmitting substance (usually air) to move
   2. Characteristics of sound
      a. Loudness - intensity (amplitude) of a wave's pressure; decibels
      b. Pitch - frequency (and intensity) of wave; measured in hertz
      c. Timbre - complexity of sound wave; the distinguishing quality of a sound

   B.   **An ear on the world - the process of hearing**
   1. Sound wave passes into the outer ear through a canal to strike the eardrum
   2. Eardrum vibrates at the same frequency and amplitude as the wave
   3. The wave vibrates three small bones, then to the cochlea
   4. Organ of Corti in the cochlea contains the receptor cells called cilia, or hair cells, which are imbedded in the basilar membrane
   5. The hair cells initiate a signal to the auditory nerve, which carries the message to the brain

   C.   **Constructing the auditory world**
   1. Perception is used to organize patterns of sounds to construct meaning
   2. Strategies include figure and ground, proximity, continuity, similarity, closure
   3. Loudness is a distance cue; using both ears helps estimate direction

Hearing

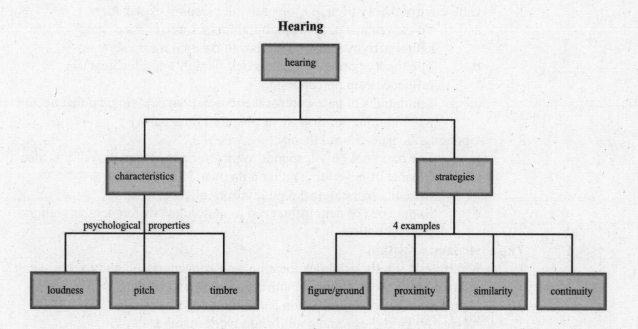

IV. OTHER SENSES

A. **Taste: Savoury sensations**
1. Chemicals stimulate receptors on tongue, throat, and roof of mouth
   a. Papillae - bumps on tongue - contain taste buds
   b. Replaced every 10 days - number declines with age
2. Four basic tastes: salty, sour, bitter, sweet – and a new one (umami)
   a. Each taste produced by a different type of chemical
   b. Flavours are a combination of the four, but it is unclear how this occurs
   c. Taste is heavily influenced by smell, temperature, and texture of food, culture, and individual differences

B. **Smell: The sense of scents**
1. Receptors are specialized neurons (5 million) in a mucous membrane in upper part of nasal passage that respond to chemical molecules in the air
2. Signals travel from receptors to the brain's olfactory bulb by the olfactory nerve to the higher regions of the brain
3. The psychological impact of odours may be because olfactory centres in the brain are linked to areas that process memories and emotions

C. **Senses of the skin**
1. Skin protects what is inside, it helps identify objects, it is involved in intimacy, and it serves as a boundary
2. Skin senses include - touch, warmth, cold, and pain

D. **The mystery of pain**
1. Pain differs from other senses in that the removal of the stimulus doesn't always terminate the sensation
2. Gate-control theory of pain - for years, the leading explanation
   a. To experience pain sensation, impulses must pass a "gate" of neural activity that sometimes blocks pain messages
   b. The theory correctly predicts that thoughts and feelings can influence pain perception
   c. Limitations of gate-control theory - cannot explain pain that occurs without injury or disease or phantom limb pain
3. Updating the gate-control theory
   a. The brain not only responds to incoming pain signals, but it is also capable of generating pain on its own
   b. Chronic, pathological pain involves glial cells
   c. Experience of pain influenced by individual differences as well as cultural beliefs

E. **The environment within**
1. Kinesthesis - tells us about location and movement of body parts using pain and pressure receptors in muscles, joints, and tendons
2. Equilibrium - gives information about the body as a whole
3. Normally, kinesthesis and equilibrium work together

Other Senses

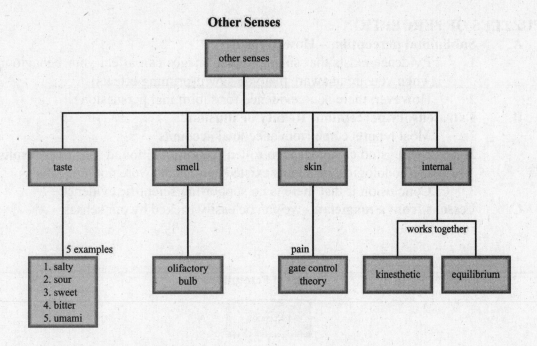

V. PERCEPTUAL POWERS: ORIGINS AND INFLUENCES
A. Inborn abilities
Research concludes that infants are born with many perceptual abilities
B. Critical periods – exist in various senses(sight, hearing, smell)
C. Psychological and cultural influences on perception
1. Perceptions affected by needs, beliefs, emotions, and expectations
2. Culture and experience also influence perception

Perceptual Powers: Origins & Influences

VI. PUZZLES OF PERCEPTION
    A.   **Subliminal perception – How persuasive?**
        1.   Evidence exists that simple visual images can affect your behaviour even when you are unaware that you saw it(priming effects)
        2.   However, there is no evidence for subliminal persuasion
    B.   **Extrasensory perception: Reality or illusion?**
        1.   Most reports come from anecdotal accounts
        2.   Some studies under controlled conditions found positive results, but methodological problems existed and results were not replicated
        3.   Conclusion is that there is no supporting scientific evidence
    C.   **Lessons from a magician** - we can be easily tricked by our senses

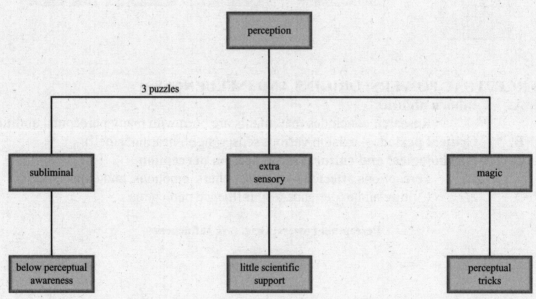

Puzzles of Perception

IDIOMS AND SLANGS

Some of us scoff at them (page 193) – making fun of and not taking it seriously.

Variety, they say is the spice of life (page 198) – having the opportunity to experience a wide selection of experiences leads to a rewarding and enriched life.

Grist for the mill of the mind (page 206) – provides information for the mind to build or create a visual picture of the world.

Snail shells (page 218) – if you look at Figure 6.10 in the text, you will see that the cochlea resembles a snail shell.

As Goldilocks found (page 221) – Goldilocks is a girl from a western fairy tale who goes into the bear's house when they are not home and eats their porridge (oatmeal). This refers to the idea that the texture of cold porridge in the mouth is not as nice when compared to hot porridge.

Senses as pipelines (page 225) – a means by which information is brought into the body.

Primed to evaluate (page 230) – biased or influenced.

PRACTICE TEST 1 - Multiple Choice

1.   The detection of physical energy by receptors in the sense organs is known as
    A.   perception.   B.   sensory overload.
    C.   sensation.   D.   sensory adaptation.

2.   The eyes, ears, tongue, nose, skin, and internal body tissues all contain
    A.   anatomical codes.   B.   functional codes.
    C.   sense receptors.   D.   sense organs.

3.   Perception differs from sensation in that
    A.   perception allows us to organize and interpret sensations.
    B.   perception is the raw data coming in from the senses.
    C.   sensation is an organizing and interpretive process; perception is not.
    D.   perception can be measured; sensations cannot.

4.   Which theory argues that light and sound produce different sensations because they stimulate different regions of the brain?
    A.   signal-detection theory   B.   trichromatic theory
    C.   doctrine of specific nerve energies   D.   opponent-process theory

5.   Which of the following best accounts for the fact that light and sound produce different sensations due to the specific cells that are firing, how many are firing, the rate at which they are firing, and the patterning of each cell's firing?
    A.   anatomical codes   B.   functional codes
    C.   doctrine of specific nerve energies   D.   feature detectors

6.   _____ stimulate different nerve pathways, which go to different places in the brain, whereas focusing on the number, rate, and pattern of the firing of particular cells in response to certain stimuli describes _____.
    A.   anatomical codes; functional codes   B.   neural codes; cellular codes
    C.   functional codes; anatomical codes   D.   psychophysics; transduction

7.   Signal-detection theory takes into account
    A.   observers' response tendencies.
    B.   sensory differences among species.
    C.   the role of feature detectors.
    D.   which cells are firing, how many cells are firing, and the rate at which they fire.

8.   As a research participant, Betsy is asked to compare lights within several pairs of lights and indicate whether one is brighter than the other. Betsy is being asked to detect
    A.   the absolute threshold.   B.   the jnd
    C.   the difference threshold.   D.   Weber's Law.

9.	Researchers have found that sensory deprivation may
	A.	lead to confusion and grouchiness.
	B.	produce a restless, disoriented feeling.
	C.	cause hallucinations.
	D.	cause all of the above.

10.	Mary enjoys the wonderful smells from the kitchen when she first arrives at her mother's house, but she no longer notices them after a while. What accounts for this?
	A.	sensory adaptation				B.	selective attention
	C.	absolute thresholds				D.	difference thresholds

11.	In class, Jonah is completely focused on the professor's words, though there are noises and distractions all around him. This is best explained by
	A.	sensory adaptation.				B.	selective attention.
	C.	sensory deprivation.				D.	sensory overload.

12.	Humans experience the wavelength of light as
	A.	hue or colour.					B.	brightness.
	C.	saturation or colourfulness.			D.	wave complexity.

13.	The fovea contains
	A.	only rods.					B.	only cones.
	C.	an equal number of rods and cones.		D.	more rods than cones.

14.	Rods are to cones as
	A.	bright light is to dim light.			B.	the iris is to the pupil.
	C.	black and white vision is to colour vision.	D.	none of the above.

15.	The visual receptors are located in the
	A.	cornea.						B.	pupil.
	C.	lens.						D.	retina.

16.	The optic nerve connects
	A.	rods and cones.					B.	the cornea with the brain.
	C.	the pupil and the lens.				D.	the retina with the brain.

17.	Which theory of colour vision suggests that one type of cone responds to blue, another type of cone to green, and a third to red?
	A.	doctrine of specific nerve energies		B.	opponent-process theory
	C.	trichromatic theory				D.	feature-detector theory

18.	Which theory of colour vision best explains negative afterimages?
	A.	trichromatic theory				B.	opponent-process theory
	C.	doctrine of specific nerve energies		D.	Weber's Law

19. Which Gestalt strategy would explain why you see $$$AAA### as three groups of figures instead of nine separate figures?
    A. closure
    B. figure-ground
    C. continuity
    D. similarity

20. The slight difference in sideways separation between two objects as seen by the left eye and the right eye is called
    A. a binocular cue.
    B. a depth cue.
    C. retinal disparity.
    D. all of the above.

21. As you watch a door opening, its image changes from rectangular to trapezoidal, yet you continue to think of the door as rectangular. What explains this phenomenon?
    A. perceptual constancy
    B. retinal disparity
    C. monocular depth cues
    D. selective attention

22. Pitch is the dimension of sound related to the
    A. amplitude of a pressure wave.
    B. frequency of a pressure wave.
    C. distinguishing quality of a sound.
    D. complexity of a pressure wave.

23. The part of the ear that plays the same role in hearing as the retina plays in vision is called the
    A. cochlea.
    B. eardrum.
    C. organ of Corti.
    D. auditory nerve.

24. Rods and cones are to vision as the _____ is/are to hearing.
    A. cilia or hair cells
    B. eardrum
    C. basilar membrane
    D. cochlea

25. The cilia are imbedded in the _____ of the _____.
    A. cochlea; auditory nerve
    B. basilar membrane; cochlea
    C. eardrum; cochlea
    D. cochlea; basilar membrane

26. When you bite into a piece of bread or an orange, the taste is a result of
    A. a combination of the four basic tastes: salty, sour, bitter, and sweet.
    B. a combination of the four basic tastes: salty, smooth, pungent, and sweet.
    C. the activation of specific taste receptors.
    D. the taste receptors located in a specific part of the tongue.

27. How does the sense of smell differ from the sense of vision and taste?
    A. Smell does not have receptor cells.
    B. Although vision and taste have limited numbers of basic cell types, smell may have as many as a thousand.
    C. Smell uses anatomical coding and not functional coding, whereas vision and taste use both.
    D. There are fewer basic smells than basic tastes or colours.

28. The skin senses are
    A. tickle, temperature, touch, and pain.
    B. tickle, itch, tingle, and burn.
    C. touch, warmth, cold, and pain.
    D. warmth, heat, cool, and cold.

29. Phantom pain
    A. does not exist.
    B. is strictly psychological.
    C. may occur because a matrix of neurons in the brain is generating pain signals.
    D. is a result of the increase in pain fibres.

30. Carrie is trying to balance on her left leg while holding her right foot with her left hand. Her ability to balance relies on the sense of _____, and her ability to grab her foot relies on the sense of _____.
    A. equilibrium; kinesthesis
    B. kinesthesis; equilibrium
    C. touch; equilibrium
    D. coordination: touch

31. Tina can touch her finger to her nose with her eyes shut. What allows her to do this?
    A. the olfactory sense   B. kinesthesis
    C. equilibrium   D. ESP

32. Which group is studied to evaluate whether perceptual abilities are inborn?
    A. cats
    B. people who first gained sensation as an adult
    C. babies and infants
    D. all of the above

33. Shinsaku has a rare condition in which colours sometimes evoke smells for him, such as the colour blue smelling like oregano. This condition is known as
    A. transduction.   B. anatomical codes.
    C. synesthesia.   D. opponent-process theory.

34. The concept of priming is
    A. the subliminal or explicit exposure to information, and then assessing if memory or performance is affected by this information.
    B. the experiencing of one sensation (such as the sound of a bee) with different sense (such as a particular smell).
    C. a habitual way of perceiving, based on expectations.
    D. the focus of attention on some stimuli at the expense of others.

PRACTICE TEST 2 - Short Answer

1.   _____ is the process by which sensory impulses are organized and interpreted.

2.   The two basic kinds of code used by the nervous system to convey sensations are _____ and _____ codes.

3.   Researchers in the field of _____ study the relationships between physical properties of stimuli and our psychological experience of them.

4.   The smallest amount of energy that a person can detect reliably is known as the _____ threshold.

5.   The smallest difference between two stimuli that a person can reliably detect is the _____ .

6.   Signal-detection theory holds that responses in a detection task consist of both a _____ process and a _____ process.

7.   When a stimulus is unchanging or repetitious, receptors may stop firing so that we no longer notice it. This process is referred to as sensory _____ .

8.   The amount or intensity of light emitted or reflected by an object determines its _____ .

9.   Although located in the eye, the structure known as the _____ is actually part of the brain.

10.   The visual receptors sensitive to low levels of light are called _____; receptors sensitive to colour are called _____ .

11.   _____ cells are responsive to specific patterns, such as horizontal versus vertical lines.

12.   Humans almost always organize the visual field into figure and _____ .

13.   The Gestalt principle of _____ suggests that the brain tends to fill in gaps in order to perceive complete forms.

14.   Our tendency to perceive objects as stable and unchanging even when the sensory patterns they produce are changing is referred to as perceptual _____ .

15. An opponent-process cell that fired in response to red would turn _____ in response to green.

16. The receptors for hearing are hair cells embedded in the _____, in the interior of the _____.

17. The physical properties that correspond to the loudness of a sound is the _____ of the pressure waves in the air.

18. The four basic tastes are _____, _____, _____, and _____. A possible fifth basic taste is _____.

19. People's responses to particular odours are affected by both _____ and individual differences.

20. The skin senses include _____, _____, _____, and _____.

21. The _____ theory of pain holds that pain depends on whether neural impulses get past a point in the spinal cord and reach the brain.

22. _____ tells us where our body parts are located, and _____ tells us the orientation of the body as a whole.

23. A widely used procedure for studying depth perception in children is the _____ procedure.

24. Certain psychological influences affect perception. These include needs, beliefs, _____, and _____.

25. _____ refers to telepathy, clairvoyance, precognition, and out-of-body experiences.

26. New evidence on pain suggests that chronic pain also involves _____ cells.

27. _____ is the term for when people don't "see" or register a particular object even though it is right in front of them.

PRACTICE TEST 3 - Essay

1. Explain the phenomena listed below in terms of the concept listed after it.

   A. Roberta is shopping at a flea market and has just refused to buy a scarf because the salesperson is charging $10 and she saw it at another stall for $8.00. Later that week, she is shopping for a new car and does not think anything about spending an extra $2.00 for a car. Discuss this as an analogy of Weber's Law.

   B. A nurse notices that patients perform more poorly on auditory tests - tests of auditory thresholds - when they are tired as a result of losing sleep. Analyze the effects of their performance using signal-detection theory.

   C. John is looking all over for his glasses when his wife points them out at the top of his head. Explain this behaviour using principles of sensory adaptation.

   D. Malcolm is studying for a test in psychology while the TV is blaring and his roommate is on the phone in the same room. Discuss this in relation to sensory overload.

2. Describe the process of vision, starting from a light wave and going to the eye and then to the brain, including all relevant structures.

3. Assume that you are developing a colour-generating device that will reproduce the colours in the human colour spectrum. Explain which colours you need and why, according to the two theories of colour vision listed below.

   A. Trichromatic theory
   B. Opponent-process theory

4. You are watching a monitor that depicts sound waves. Describe what changes in the sound would accompany the modifications indicated below.

   A. The sound waves remain constant except for their height, which is increasing.
   B. The wave frequency is changing.
   C. Waves of different types are being increasingly mixed together.

5. In each of the examples below, identify and describe the Gestalt principle involved.

   A. People scattered on a beach appear to be in clusters.
   B. A sequence of dots on a canvas appears to form a face.
   C. People crowded on a soccer field appear to be two different teams and referees.
   D. A wall seems to be continuous even though vines block sections from view.

6. Psychological factors can influence what we perceive and how we perceive it. Identify the psychological factors that could influence the following perceptions.

    A. You had an argument with your sister. As you are walking home from school, she drives past you. You saw her look at you but figured that she did not stop because she is angry with you.

    B. You think that your neighbour is an unethical character. One day you see him entering his house during the day and you are certain that he is sneaking around so that no one will see him.

    C. You are expecting your best friend to come visit you and you are very excited. Every time you hear something, you run to the door, certain that there was a knock.

CHAPTER SEVEN

Learning and Conditioning

LEARNING OBJECTIVES

1.   Define learning.

2.   Distinguish between the schools of behaviourism and social-cognitive learning.

3.   Identify the two types of conditioning shown by behaviourists to explain human behaviour.

4.   Describe the process of classical conditioning and define and give examples of an unconditioned stimulus (US), an unconditioned response (UR), a conditioned stimulus (CS) and a conditioned response (CR).

5.   List and explain the four features of classical conditioning, including extinction, higher-order conditioning, stimulus generalization and discrimination.

6.   Compare the traditional and recent views of how associations are formed between unconditioned and conditioned stimuli.

7.   Describe both the impact of classical conditioning on everyday life and the therapeutic technique of counterconditioning.

8.   Describe how classical conditioning can also be used to explain food preferences and taste aversion, as well as reactions to medical treatments.

9.   Compare and contrast the principles of operant and classical conditioning.

10. List and explain the three types of consequences a response can lead to.

11. Distinguish between positive and negative reinforcement and positive and negative punishment.

12. Distinguish between primary and secondary reinforcement and primary and secondary punishment.

13. Describe extinction, stimulus generalization, and stimulus discrimination in operant conditioning.

14. Distinguish between continuous and intermittent schedules of reinforcement and describe the four types of intermittent reinforcement schedules.

15. Describe the function and procedures used in shaping.

16. Describe the real world application of operant conditioning known as behaviour modification.

17. Describe why punishment works.

18. List and discuss six limitations of punishment as a way of controlling behaviour and state a more effective strategy.

19. Distinguish between intrinsic and extrinsic reinforcers, and discuss the effects of extrinsic reinforcers on motivation. Describe how extrinsic reinforcers should be used.

20. Explain latent learning.

21. Explain social-cognitive theories and compare them to conditioning models of learning.

22. Describe the results of studies on the effects of media violence.

23. Describe strategies that can be used to modify behaviour and to become a better student. Give examples.

BRIEF CHAPTER SUMMARY

Chapter 7 explores how we learn to make permanent changes in our behaviours due to experience. Two broad types of learning are explored: conditioning models and social-cognitive models. Both conditioning models suggest that learning is acquired through simple stimulus-response associations without the involvement of mental processes. Classical conditioning explains how we learn involuntary behaviours, such as fears and preferences. Operant conditioning explains how we learn complex behaviours as a result of favourable or unfavourable consequences of our actions. These consequences can take the form of positive reinforcement, negative reinforcement, or punishment. In addition, when reinforcement is not continuous (intermittent), the schedules of reinforcement may vary (i.e., fixed ratio, variable ratio, fixed interval, variable interval) and learning is more long-lasting. Biological limitations to conditioning also are discussed. Social-cognitive theories expand behavioural principles to recognize the role that mental processes play in the acquisition of new behaviours. Observational learning and latent learning are two social-cognitive theories of learning.

PREVIEW OUTLINE

Before you read the chapter, review the preview outline for each section of the text. After you have read the chapter, close this book and try to <u>re-create</u> the outlines on a blank piece of paper.

I.   **INTRODUCTION TO LEARNING**
 A.   **Definitions**
  1.   Learning - any relatively permanent change in behaviour that occurs because of experience
  2.   Behaviourism - the school of psychology that accounts for behaviour in terms of observable events, without reference to mental entities
  3.   Conditioning - a basic kind of learning that involves associations between environmental stimuli and responses
 B.   **Types of learning:** Classical and Operant conditioning; Social-cognitive learning theories
II.   **CLASSICAL CONDITIONING -** began with the research of Ivan Pavlov

A. **New reflexes from old - terminology**
  1. Unconditioned stimulus (US) - thing that elicits an automatic response
  2. Unconditioned response (UR) - response that is automatically produced
  3. Conditioned stimulus (CS) - when an initially neutral stimulus comes to elicit a conditioned response after being paired with a US
  4. Conditioned response (CR) - response that is elicited by a CS
  5. Classical conditioning - procedure by which a neutral stimulus is regularly paired with a US and the neutral stimulus becomes a CS, which elicits a CR that is similar to the original, unlearned one

B. **Principles of classical conditioning**
  1. Extinction - repeating the conditioned stimulus without the unconditioned stimulus, and the conditioned response disappears
  2. Spontaneous recovery – the reappearance of an extinguished response
  3. Higher-order conditioning - a neutral stimulus can become a conditioned stimulus by being paired with an already established conditioned stimulus
  4. Stimulus generalization - after a stimulus becomes a conditioned stimulus for some response, other, similar stimuli may produce the same reaction
  5. Stimulus discrimination - different responses are triggered by stimuli that resemble the conditioned stimulus in some way

C. **What is actually learned in classical conditioning?**
  1. The stimulus to be conditioned should precede the unconditioned stimulus because the CS serves as a signal for the US
  2. Many psychologists say that the learner learns information that is more than an association between two stimuli, that the CS predicts the US
  3. Rescorla introduced cognitive concepts; organism as information seeker to form a representation of the world

Classical Conditioning

112

III. CLASSICAL CONDITIONING IN REAL LIFE - recognized early by John B. Watson

    A.   Learning to like - conditioning positive emotions (e.g., used in advertising)

    B.   Learning to fear - conditioning negative emotions

         1.   Humans biologically primed to learn some fears and tastes more easily than others

         2.   Phobias (irrational fears) can be learned through conditioning (e.g., Little Albert) and unlearned through counterconditioning

    C.   Accounting for taste – taste aversions may be learned through an association of illness and foods (Garcia effect)

    D.   Reacting to medical treatments may generalize to a range of other stimuli

Classical Conditioning in Real Life

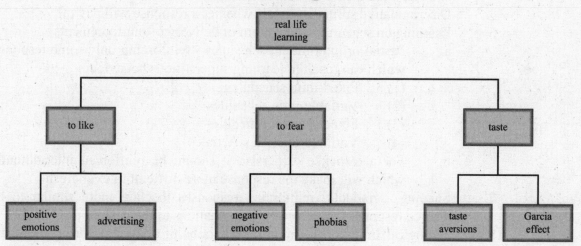

IV. OPERANT CONDITIONING

    A.   **Introduction to operant conditioning**

         1.   Behaviour becomes more or less likely, depending on its consequences; emphasis is on environmental consequences

         2.   Whereas classical conditioning involves reflexive responses, operant conditioning shapes complex, voluntary responses

    B.   **The birth of radical behaviourism - Thorndike and Skinner**

    C.   **The consequences of behaviour**

1. A neutral consequence neither increases nor decreases the probability that the response will occur.

2. Reinforcement makes a response more likely to occur.

3. Punishment makes a response less likely to occur.l   1.   The sooner a consequence follows a response, the greater its effect

         2.   Primary and secondary reinforcers and punishers - can be very powerful

            a.   Primary reinforcers satisfy physiological needs

            b.   Primary punishers are inherently unpleasant

    c. Secondary reinforcers (and punishers) are reinforcing (and punishing) through association with other (primary) reinforcers

  3. Positive and negative reinforcers and punishers

    a. Positive reinforcement - something pleasant follows a response; negative reinforcement - something unpleasant is removed

    b. Positive punishment - something unpleasant occurs; negative punishment - something pleasant is removed

D. Principles of operant conditioning

  1. Extinction - learned response weakens when the reinforcer is removed

  2. Spontaneous recovery - the return of a response that has been extinguished

  3. Stimulus generalization - a response occurs to stimuli that resemble the stimuli present during the original learning

  4. Stimulus discrimination - the ability to distinguish between similar stimuli and responding only to the one that results in the reinforcer

  5. Discriminative stimulus signals whether a response will pay off

  6. Learning on schedule - the pattern of delivery of reinforcements

    a. Partial or intermittent schedules - reinforcing only some responses which can result in learning superstitious behaviours

      (1) Fixed-ratio schedules

      (2) Variable-ratio schedules

      (3) Fixed-interval schedules

      (4) Variable-interval schedules

    b. For a response to persist, it should be reinforced intermittently, which will make the response more difficult to extinguish

  7. Shaping - gradually reinforcing responses that are more similar to the desired response (successive approximations to the desired response)

  8. Biological limits on learning - limitations of genetic predispositions and physical characteristics, instinctive drift

E. Skinner: The man and the myth

  1. Did not deny the existence of consciousness; said that it cannot explain behaviour, and that aspects of consciousness are learned behaviours

  2. Controversial idea that free will is an illusion (determinism)

Operant Conditioning

V.   **OPERANT CONDITIONING IN REAL LIFE**
   A.   **General problems** - if reinforcers, punishers, and discriminative stimuli in life remain the same, it is difficult to change behaviours
   B.   **Behaviour modification** – operant-conditioning programs used in real life
   C.   **The pros and cons of punishment**
      1.   When punishment works - for behaviours that can't be ignored or rewarded; with some criminals (consistency matters more than severity)
      2.   When punishment fails:
         a.   Punishment is often administered inappropriately or mindlessly
         b.   The recipient often responds with anxiety, fear, or rage
         c.   Effects can be temporary; may depend on punisher being present
         d.   Most misbehaviour is hard to punish immediately
         e.   Punishment conveys little information about desired behaviour
         f.   A punishment may be reinforcing because it brings attention
      3.   Alternatives to punishment - avoid abuse, give information about desirable behaviour, try extinction, and reinforce the alternative behaviours

D.   **The problems with reward**
  1.   Misuse of reward - rewards must be tied to the desired behaviour
  2.   Why rewards can backfire - people work for intrinsic as well as extrinsic reinforcers, and extrinsic reinforcers can interfere with intrinsic motivation

Operant Conditioning in Real Life

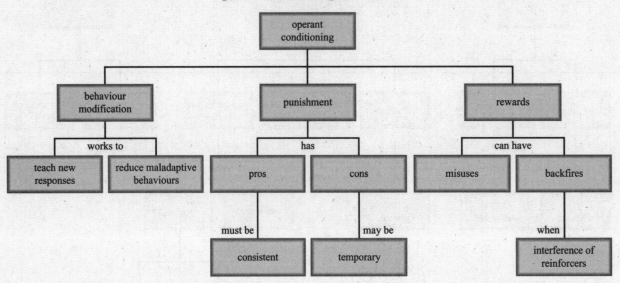

VI.   **LEARNING AND THE MIND**
  A.   **Latent learning**
    1.   Tolman and Honzik's experiment with latent learning
    2.   Learning can occur even when there is no immediate response and when there is no obvious reinforcement
  B.   **Introduction to social-cognitive theories**
    1.   Added higher-level cognitive processes to the idea of how people learn
    2.   Humans have attitudes, beliefs, and expectations that affect how they acquire information, make decisions, and reason
  C.   **Learning by observing** - called observational learning
    1.   Vicarious conditioning occurs from observing a model
    2.   Supported by Bandura's studies with children learning social behaviours
    3.   **The case of media violence**
    1.Some people become more aggressive after exposure to violent images in the media but most do not
    2. Aggressive individuals tend to be drawn to violent images and are more affected by them

Learning and the Mind

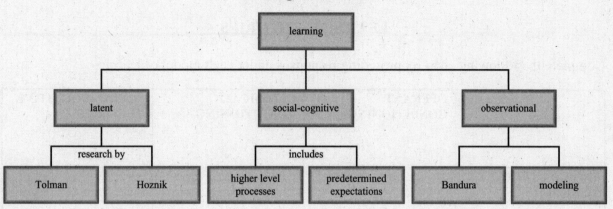

LEARNING THEORIES

Complete the following chart by providing responses under each model of learning.

	OPERANT CONDITIONING	CLASSICAL CONDITIONING	SOCIAL-COGNITIVE THEORIES
INDICATE WHAT IS LEARNED			
EXAMPLES			
IDENTIFY KEY FIGURES			
LIST KEY TERMS			
LIST PRINCIPLES			

IDIOMS AND SLANGS

Mend their ways (page 230 – to make improvements, to fix. For example, commit to practise better health routines.

Mouth-watering (page 240) – the increase of saliva in a person's mouth at the sight of certain foods.

Whole array of human emotion (page 245) – the diversity and abundance of human emotion.

Sentimental feelings sweep over us (page 245) – remembering memories with strong positive emotional attachment.

Fell for the bait (page 248) – drawn in, or enticed by, the object left to attract or trap.

Stamped in (page 251) – learning or being programmed for a behaviour.

Stamped out (page 251) – unlearning or not repeating a behaviour again.

Roughly (page 252) – approximately the same or resembles the original.

Hard-work behaviour (page 252) – diligent, industrious effort.

Drawbacks (page 253) – disadvantages, less than ideal.

Egghead (page 254) – a name to distinguish someone as an intellectual through ridicule.

Go hand in hand (page 254) – one follows the other. They are separate yet connected or related.

Spurt of responding (page 256) – increased activity, more frequent responses.

Groundbreaking work (page 259) – pioneering, or the first to research an area of information.

Cold-blooded (page 259) – portrayed as a person who is unkind, cruel to others.

Practised what he preached (page 260) – followed his own instructions and teachings, was not a hypocrite.

In the limelight (page 264) – to attract attention to a person, an obvious position before the public.

Crazy about reading (page 266) – very interested in the activity, spend a lot of time reading for pleasure.

City is laid out (page 269) – knowing your way around a city, the map of the city. Knowing the correct direction to go.

On the other hand (page 274) – the other side of the argument or position being presented.

Gushing (page 274) – overenthusiastic praise.

PRACTICE TEST 1 - Multiple Choice

1.   Learning is defined as
      A.   memorization of information.
      B.   acquisition of practical skills.
      C.   any relatively permanent change in behaviour that occurs because of experience.
      D.   any relatively permanent change in behaviour.

2.   A neutral stimulus becomes a conditioned stimulus by
      A.   preceding it with an unconditioned stimulus.
      B.   following it with an unconditioned stimulus.
      C.   pairing it with a conditioned response.
      D.   reinforcing it.

3.   Once a neutral stimulus becomes a conditioned stimulus, it
      A.   can elicit a conditioned response.
      B.   can elicit an unconditioned response.
      C.   elicits a voluntary response.
      D.   elicits none of the above.

4.   A loud, sudden clap behind a child causes the child to cry. The child's tears are called the
      A.   conditioned stimulus.   B.   unconditioned stimulus.
      C.   conditioned response.   D.   unconditioned response.

5.   Every time I open any can of food, my cat Luna, comes running. The food is
      A.   an unconditioned stimulus.   B.   an unconditioned response.
      C.   a conditioned stimulus.   D.   a conditioned response.

6.   In the above question, the can opener is
      A.   an unconditioned stimulus.   B.   an unconditioned response.
      C.   a conditioned stimulus.   D.   a conditioned response.

7.   When Olympia threw tantrums, her father ignored this behaviour and eventually it decreased. Ignoring her behaviour is an example of
      A.   extinction.   B.   stimulus generalization.
      C.   stimulus discrimination.   D.   spontaneous recovery.

8.   If the CS is repeatedly presented without the US, what will happen?
      A.   extinction   B.   stimulus discrimination
      C.   stimulus generalization   D.   higher-order conditioning

121

9. If a stimulus similar to the conditioned stimulus is repeatedly presented without being followed by the unconditioned stimulus, it will stop evoking the conditioned response. The differential responses to the conditioned stimulus and the similar stimulus demonstrate

   A.   extinction.   B.   stimulus discrimination.
   C.   stimulus generalization.   D.   higher-order conditioning.

10. _____ views state that a CR is learned simply because the CS and US occur close together in time, whereas _____ views suggest that information is conveyed by one stimulus about another.

    A.   Recent; traditional   B.   Social learning; traditional
    C.   Traditional; recent   D.   Classical; operant

11. Tastes and fears are examples of behaviours learned through

    A.   operant conditioning.   B.   social learning.
    C.   imitation.   D.   classical conditioning.

12. Peter was afraid of rabbits. John Watson and Mary Cover Jones presented a rabbit to Peter along with milk and crackers and eventually Peter could play with the rabbit. This technique is called

    A.   operant conditioning.   B.   counterconditioning.
    C.   spontaneous recovery.   D.   higher-order conditioning.

13. Classical is to operant as

    A.   learning is to instinct.   B.   voluntary is to involuntary.
    C.   involuntary is to voluntary.   D.   unlearned is to instinct.

14. A difference between classical and operant conditioning is that

    A.   classical conditioning does not involve consequences.
    B.   classical conditioning involves reflexive responses.
    C.   operant conditioning involves more complex responses than classical conditioning.
    D.   all of the above are differences.

15. In operant conditioning, a response may lead to one of three types of consequences. One consequence strengthens or increases the probability of the response that it follows. This consequence is known as

    A.   neutral.   B.   reinforcement.
    C.   punishment.   D.   higher-order conditioning.

16. "Because you took out the garbage, you don't have to do the dishes." Which learning principle does this represent?

    A.   positive reinforcement   B.   punishment
    C.   negative reinforcement   D.   primary reinforcement

17 "Because you got all As, you get to go on vacation." This represents
    A.   positive reinforcement.   B.   punishment.
    C.   negative reinforcement.   D.   primary reinforcement.

18. When a stimulus or event that follows a response weakens it or makes it less likely to
    recur, it is called
    A.   negative reinforcement.   B.   positive reinforcement.
    C.   punishment.   D.   secondary reinforcement.

19. _____ is a primary reinforcement, whereas _____ is/are a secondary reinforcement.
    A.   Food; money   B.   Food; water
    C.   Money; grades   D.   Applause; food

20. Cindy's teacher tells her parents, "Cindy's misbehaviour is just for attention. You should
    just ignore her and it should stop." Cindy's teacher is using what principle?
    A.   primary reinforcement   B.   extinction
    C.   stimulus generalization   D.   stimulus discrimination

21. Extinction, stimulus generalization, and stimulus discrimination are principles of
    A.   classical conditioning only.   B.   operant conditioning only.
    C.   classical and operant conditioning. D.   counterconditioning.

22. When Tracey throws a tantrum in the supermarket, her father tries to talk to her calmly or
    to ignore her behaviour. Sometimes, he does not have the patience to be calm and he just
    gives her a cookie to quiet her down. He has put her on
    A.   a partial reinforcement schedule.   B.   a variable schedule.
    C.   an intermittent reinforcement schedule. D.   all of the above.

23. One time Hiro got an extra $20 from a money machine. Though it has never happened
    since, Hiro keeps going to that machine whenever possible just in case the error is
    repeated. He is on a
    A.   continuous reinforcement schedule.   B.   variable-interval schedule.
    C.   variable-ratio schedule.   D.   fixed-ratio schedule.

24. Receiving your paycheque every Friday represents what type of reinforcement schedule?
    A.   fixed-interval   B.   fixed-ratio
    C.   variable-interval   D.   variable-ratio

25. You take a quiz on every chapter in psychology. Some chapters are covered in one class
    and some chapters require two classes. This is a _____ reinforcement schedule?
    A.   fixed-interval   B.   fixed-ratio
    C.   variable-interval   D.   variable-ratio

26. A prison has instituted a program to teach inmates problem-solving skills, life-coping skills, and career training. This program addresses which problem related to punishment?
   A.   The effects of punishment may depend on the presence of the punisher.
   B.   Punishment may be reinforcing misbehaviour because of the attention received.
   C.   Punishment conveys little information about how to behave differently.
   D.   Those who are punished often respond with anxiety, fear, or rage.

27. One disadvantage of punishment is
   A.   the effects of punishment are enduring.
   B.   punishment conveys a great deal of information, sometimes too much to absorb.
   C.   most behaviour is too difficult to punish immediately.
   D.   all of the above.

28. Nick is a struggling artist who loves his work. He becomes well-known and people are now commissioning him to paint. He finds that his passion for his work has decreased. What has happened?
   A.   Intrinsic reinforcers have interfered with extrinsic reinforcers.
   B.   He has been put on a token economy and does not like it.
   C.   Extrinsic reinforcers have interfered with intrinsic motivation.
   D.   His love for his work has been extinguished through the absence of reinforcers.

29. Tolman's experiments demonstrating latent learning showed that
   A.   learning can occur even though it may not be immediately expressed.
   B.   rats are capable of insight.
   C.   extrinsic reinforcement can reduce intrinsic motivation.
   D.   personality characteristics interact with environmental influences.

30. Social-cognitive theories differ from conditioning models of learning in that
   A.   proponents study higher-level cognitive processes as well as environmental influences.
   B.   social learning theories do not utilize discrimination and generalization.
   C.   they are more scientific than conditioning models of learning.
   D.   they focus almost exclusively on the use of primary reinforcers.

31. Maggie is 16 years old and learning to drive. Though she has never driven before, she is able to put the key in the ignition, turn the starter, and put the car into gear. Which of the following best explains these abilities?
   A.   Maggie's intelligence
   B.   observational learning
   C.   cognitive maps
   D.   the ABCs of learning

32. Bandura's study with children who watched the short film of two men playing with toys demonstrated which of the following?
   A. Children must be rewarded to imitate models.
   B. Children were likely to imitate the aggressive behaviours of adults in the film.
   C. Children will only imitate other children, not adults.
   D. Aggression cannot be learned through imitation.

33. Classical conditioning research involving functional MRI associated certain images with pleasant smells like peanut butter. Exposure to these images revealed increased activity in which two brain areas linked to motivation and emotion?
   A. amygdala and orbitofrontal cortex
   B. hippocampus and prefrontal cortex
   C. corpus callosum and Broca's area
   D. thalamus and occipital lobes

PRACTICE TEST 2 - Short Answer

1.   Any relatively permanent change in behaviour that occurs because of experience is _____.

2.   When a neutral stimulus is paired with an unconditioned stimulus that elicits some reflexive unconditioned response, the neutral stimulus comes to elicit a similar or related response. The neutral stimulus is then called a _____.

3.   If a conditioned stimulus is repeatedly presented without the unconditioned stimulus, the conditioned response eventually disappears. This is called _____.

4.   The process by which a neutral stimulus becomes a conditioned stimulus by being paired with an already established conditioned stimulus is known as _____ conditioning.

5.   Julia developed a conditioned fear response to the cocker spaniel that bit her. She is now afraid of all dogs. This is called stimulus _____.

6.   In stimulus _____, different responses are made to stimuli that resemble the conditioned stimulus in some way.

7.   Many theorists believe that the conditioned stimulus (CS) elicits a conditioned response (CR) because the CS _____ the US, not simply because they are associated with one another.

8.   Responses such as fear are often acquired through conditioning, and can be extinguished in the same way. One method for eliminating such fear responses is _____, which pairs a feared object with another object that elicits responses incompatible with fear.

9.   In _____ conditioning, behaviour becomes more or less likely to occur depending on its _____.

10.   A response may be strengthened or may be more likely to occur again as a result of a stimulus known as a _____.

11.   In classical conditioning, _____ responses are learned whereas in operant conditioning, more _____ responses are likely to be learned.

12. Pain, cold, and food are considered _____ reinforcers, whereas money, praise, and smiles are considered _____ reinforcers.

13. In _____ reinforcement or punishment, something is given following a desired or undesired response; in _____ reinforcement or punishment, something is taken away or withdrawn following a desired or undesired behaviour.

14. Frequently, people confuse _____ reinforcement with _____ because both involve unpleasant stimuli.

15. Punishment _____ the likelihood of a response, whereas negative reinforcement _____ the likelihood of a response.

16. Responses are more resistant to extinction when they are not always followed by a reinforcer. Such schedules are called _____ schedules of reinforcement.

17. Real estate agents are paid when they sell a home, regardless of how long it takes for them to sell one. This is a _____ schedule of reinforcement.

18. In many occupations, employees are paid every two weeks. This is a _____ schedule of reinforcement.

19. In _____, you initially reinforce a tendency in the right direction, then gradually require responses that are more and more similar to the final, desired response.

20. An alternative to punishment is a combination of _____ and _____.

21. _____ reinforcers are not inherently related to the activity being reinforced but _____ reinforcers are.

22. Regardless of the strength of the reinforcer, human beings cannot be taught to live underwater without a life support system. This fact demonstrates the _____ limits on learning.

23. Learning that is not immediately displayed in an overt response is called _____.

24. In _____ learning, the learner observes a model making certain responses and experiencing the consequences.

25. The _____ theories focus on the role played by beliefs, interpretations of events, and other cognitions.

26. Recent classical conditioning experiments involving functional MRI have helped to explain why we may feel full after eating but may find a surge in motivation to eat more when presented with a different type of food. This phenomenon is known as the _____.

PRACTICE TEST 3 - Essay

1. In the following examples, identify the unconditioned stimulus, unconditioned response, conditioned stimulus, and conditioned response.

    A.   When your father is angry with you, he calls you by both your first and middle names. Every time you hear him call you that way, you become anxious.

    B.   You keep your dog's leash in the front closet. Every time you go to get something out of the closet, Fido comes running excitedly and waits to go out.

    C.   Your true love wears a certain perfume. Every time you smell that perfume, you feel happy inside.

    D.   You had a terrifying car accident at the corner of Park Place and Main Street. Now every time you approach that corner, you feel anxious.

2. In the following examples identify the principles of classical conditioning, such as stimulus discrimination, stimulus generalization, extinction, etc.

    A.   While caring for your friend's dog, you notice that it displays a cowering posture as you roll up a newspaper. You try this several more times with magazines or stacks of notebook paper and the dog displays the same behaviour. You become convinced that this dog is generally afraid of rolled-up paper.

    B.   Joan, a dog breeder, has been phobic about Doberman pinschers since one attacked her. After the attack, she felt tense and apprehensive whenever she walked by a Doberman, even if the dog was in a cage or on a leash, though she was never uncomfortable with any other type of dog. Recently she has been experiencing a change in her feelings toward Dobermans. She was given four Doberman puppies to sell and since being around them for several months, she is no longer fearful of Dobermans.

    C.   At a red light, Bob and Fred automatically tensed and felt chills when they heard the screech of tires behind them. Later, while watching a car race, Bob remarked that the screeching of tires was having little effect on them then.

    D.   After Bill got food poisoning from roast chicken, he vowed he would never return to that restaurant nor would he ever eat chicken again. All he wanted was to go home and eat his mother's cooking. As he entered the kitchen, he became very ill when he saw the turkey sitting on the table.

3. Identify whether the consequences in the following examples are positive or negative reinforcement, or positive or negative punishment. Indicate the probable effects of the consequences, according to operant theories of learning.

    A. A buzzer sound continues until a seat belt is fastened.
    B. Whenever Joe picks up a cigarette, his roommate complains and insults him.
    C. Whenever Warren does the dishes, his girlfriend compliments and kisses him.
    D. Whenever Fred skis down the most difficult slopes, he always has a bad fall.

4. Identify the problem or problems in the following examples and, using principles of learning theories, suggest the changes needed.

    A. Ten-year-old Sara is expected to keep her room clean. Her parents check her room weekly and in the past year, her room was clean on 20 occasions. Sara's parents praised her lavishly on 10 of those occasions that her room was clean and on the other 10 occasions, Sara received no reinforcement. This technique has not been working well since on any given day, the room is likely to be a mess.
    B. Baby Ari is not yet sleeping through the night. Every time the baby cries, one of his parents picks him up. His parents decide that after checking to make sure the baby is O.K., they will just let him cry. Ari cries and cries for five nights in a row. On the first four nights, his parents kept to their agreement, but on the fifth night, they couldn't stand it any longer and picked him up. Now Ari is crying more than ever.
    C. Sue is always in trouble in class. Her teacher has tried everything he knows to make her behave: talking to her privately, having her stay after class, and scolding her in public. Regardless of what he does, her misbehaviour continues.

5. Below is an application of punishment. Identify the problems demonstrated in this example and suggest a more effective approach.

A parent discovers crayon marks and scribbling on a recently painted wall. Tommy, 18-months-old, is angrily pulled from the playpen, brought before the wall, and harshly told, "No! No! No!" and given a sharp slap on the back of his hand. He is still crying when placed in the crib for a nap. Things become quiet for a time, and then the sound of movement is heard. A quick check shows Tommy is not in his crib. A search locates Tommy in the office room. He has doodled in various places with pens and pencils from the desk.

6. Identify the schedule of reinforcement that is being used in each example.

   A. Pop quizzes
   B. Quizzes after every chapter
   C. Quizzes every Monday
   D. $10 for every A

7. Describe similarities and differences between social-cognitive and behavioural models of learning.

8. Do you procrastinate on school assignments? Describe how you can use operant conditioning (and possibly classical conditioning as well) to improve your study habits. From a conditioning perspective, why is one's bed a poor place to study?

CHAPTER EIGHT

Behaviour in Social and Cultural Context

LEARNING OBJECTIVES

1. Discuss the focus of the field of social psychology and cultural psychology.

2. Distinguish between social roles and social norms.

3. Define culture.

4. Describe Stanley Milgram's obedience study, its findings and criticisms.

5. Describe Philip Zimbardo's prison study, its findings and criticisms.

6. Discuss how the obedience and prison study demonstrate the influence of roles on behaviour.

7. List and explain the reasons why people obey authority and when they may disobey.

8. Describe the field of social cognition and social cognitive neuroscience.

9. Summarize the principles of attribution theory. Distinguish between situational and dispositional attributions.

10. Describe the fundamental attribution error, the self-serving bias, the group-serving bias and the just-world hypothesis.

11. Define attitudes and review the origins of attitudes.

12. Describe the relationship between attitudes and behaviour, specifically noting the influence of cognitive dissonance.

13. Distinguish between friendly and coercive persuasion as techniques of attitude change.

14. Define conformity and discuss some reasons for conforming to social pressure in a group.

15. Define groupthink and describe 4 symptoms of its presence.

16. Define diffusion of responsibility, bystander apathy, social loafing, and deindividuation. Discuss the conditions under which each of these is most likely to occur and the consequences of each process.

17. Discuss the steps involved in dissent, and altruistic action.

18. Distinguish between personal and social identities.

19. Distinguish between ethnic identity and the process of acculturation.

20. Describe the four ways of balancing ethnic identity and acculturation.

21. Define ethnocentrism and explain its consequences.

22. Describe some of the effects of competition and co-operation.

23. Describe ways that stereotypes are useful and three ways that they distort reality.

24. Define prejudice and the psychological, social, and economic functions that perpetuate it.

25. Describe some of the difficulties with defining and measuring prejudice.

26. Discuss approaches for reducing prejudice and conflict between groups.

27. Discuss some of the suggestions based upon psychological research on bridging the cultural divide.

BRIEF CHAPTER SUMMARY

Chapter 8 examines some of the main topic areas in the fields of social psychology and cultural psychology, which study the individual in the social and cultural context. The influence of the social context begins with norms or rules that people are expected to follow. Each of us fills many social roles that are governed by norms about how a person in that position should behave. The roles we fill and the rules that govern those roles heavily influence our behaviour, as demonstrated by two classic studies (Milgram's investigation of obedience and Zimbardo's prison study). These studies show how roles can override our own beliefs and values. The social context also influences our thought processes. Attitudes are fundamental concepts.Attempts to change our attitudes are all around us. To resist unwanted persuasion, one must think critically about information from all sources. Attributions—the way we explain why events happen—influence our responses to the world. Certain types of attributional errors and tendencies can occur that may cause misinterpretations of events (e.g., fundamental attribution error, self-serving bias). Behaviours such as groupthink, conformity, deindividuation, and social loafing can occur as a result of the presence and influence of other group members. The chapter examines the factors that influence independent action, particularly altruism and dissent. The importance of group identity and interactions among groups are discussed. Stereotypes help us organize new information, but they also distort reality (e.g., the tendency to exaggerate differences between groups). The origins of prejudice and efforts to reduce prejudice are discussed. Finally, the chapter raises the question of human nature and its influence on behaviour. Studying individuals in a social context helps to identify the normal social influences that contribute to behaviours that we often mistakenly think result from individual or personality factors.

PREVIEW OUTLINE

Before you read the chapter, review the preview outline for each section of the text. After you have read the chapter, close this book and try to re-create the outlines on a blank piece of paper.

I. **ROLES AND RULES**
    A. **Definitions**
        1. Social psychology and cultural psychology - fields that examine the influence of social and cultural environment on individuals and groups
        2. Norms – unspoken rules about how we are supposed to act

3. Roles - positions in society that are regulated by norms about how people in those positions should behave

B. The obedience study by Milgram
1. Subjects thought they were in an experiment about learning and were instructed to shock another participant when an error was made
2. All participants gave some shock; two-thirds obeyed the experimenter and went to the highest shock level ("severe shock")
3. Subsequent studies found disobedience occurs when the experimenter left the room, the victim was right there in the room, etc.
4. Conclusion - Obedience is a function of the situation, not of personalities
5. Evaluating the obedience study: some considered the study unethical, but the Milgram study highlighted the danger of unquestioning obedience

C. The prison study by Zimbardo
1. When university students were randomly assigned to be prisoners or guards, prisoners became passive and panicky, while some guards became abusive
2. Behaviour depends on social roles, which can overrule personality or values

D. Why people behave
1. People obey because they believe in the authority's legitimacy and to avoid negative outcomes and gain positive ones
2. Why do people obey when it's not in their interest or violates their values?
    a. Investing the authority, not themselves, with responsibility
    b. Routinization - defining the activity as routine; normalizing it
    c. Rules of good manners - people lack the words to disobey
    d. Entrapment - commitment to course of action is escalated

Roles and Rules

II. SOCIAL INFLUENCES ON BELIEFS

    A.   **Social cognition -** how the social environment influences thoughts, beliefs, etc.

    B.   **Attributions -** explanations we make for behaviour

            1.   Types of attributions and biases

                  a.   Situational attributions - identify the cause of an action as something in the environment or situation

                  b.   Dispositional attributions - identify the cause of an action as something in the person, such as a trait or motive

                  c.   Fundamental attribution error - tendency to overestimate dispositional factors and underestimate the influence of the situation when explaining someone else's behaviour

                  d.   Self-serving bias – tendency to take credit for good actions and rationalize mistakes when explaining one's own behaviour

                  e.   Just-world hypothesis - the need to believe the world is fair and that good people are rewarded and bad people are punished

    C.   **Attitudes -** beliefs that may be explicit or implicit

            1.   Not always based on reason; can be based on conformity, habit, rationalization, economic self-interest, and generational events

            2.   Attitudes can change to achieve consistency or to reduce cognitive dissonance (when two attitudes or an attitude and a behaviour conflict)

3.Recent research suggests a possible role of genetics in attitude formation.

            4.   Attitudes are also influenced by other people trying to persuade us

                  a.   Friendly persuasion – enhanced by familiarity, repetition (validity effect), argument by admired person, linking message to good feelings

                  b.   Coercive persuasion (brainwashing) suppresses ability to reason, to think critically, and to make good choices; a person's access to information is severely controlled, often by a powerful leader

Social Influences on Beliefs

III. INDIVIDUALS IN GROUPS
   A.   **Conformity**
      1.   Asch's conformity study - comparing line segments
      2.   Conformity varies with cultural norms
      3.   People conform for a variety of reasons including identification with group members, popularity, self-interest, and to avoid punishment
      4.   Conformity has good and bad sides, but it can suppress critical thinking

B.Groupthink – the tendency for all members of the group to think alike and suppress disagreement; often results in faulty or even disastrous decisions

1. Occurs when a group's need for total agreement overwhelms its need to make the wisest decision

2. Groupthink more likely when group has illusion of invulnerability, biased information seeking, self censorship, pressures on dissenters to conform, and an illusion of unanimity

3. Groupthink can be countracted if doubt and dissent are encouraged and if decisions are made by a majority rather than by unanimity

   C.   **The anonymous crowd**
      1.   Diffusion of responsibility
         a.   The more people who are around when a problem occurs, the less likely one of them will offer assistance
         b.   Individuals fail to act because they believe someone else will do so
         c.   May explain why crowds of people fail to respond to an emergency
      2.   Social loafing - diffusion of responsibility in work groups; individuals work less and let others work harder
         a.   More likely to occur when members not accountable, when workers feel that others are getting a "free ride," when the work itself is uninteresting, and when working harder duplicates efforts
         c.   Social loafing declines when the challenge of a job is increased and when each member has a different job
      3.   Deindividuation - losing all awareness of individuality and sense of self; people more likely to conform to the norms of the specific group situation
         a.   Increases willingness to do harm, break the law (e.g., riots)
         b.   Can also increase friendliness and self-disclosure
   D.   **Altruism and dissent**
      1.   Altruism - the willingness to take selfless or dangerous action for others
      2.   Reasons for altruistic action include a combination of personal convictions and situational influences
      3.   Steps involved in disobedience, dissent, and altruism
         a.   The individual perceives the need for intervention or help
         b.   The situation affects decisions to take responsibility
         c.   Cultural norms encourage you to take action
         d.   The costs of doing nothing outweigh the costs of getting involved
         e.   The individual has an ally

f.   The individual becomes entrapped; once initial steps have been taken, most people will increase their commitment

Individuals in Groups

IV. US VERSUS THEM: GROUP IDENTITY AND CONFLICT

A. Social Identities – part of a person's self concept that is based on identification with a nation, ethnic group, gender or other affiliations

B. Ethnic Identity
1. Ethnic Identity - close identification with a religious or ethnic group
2. Acculturation - identification with the dominant culture
3. Four ways of balancing ethnic identity and acculturation (bicultural, assimilation, ethnic separatism, marginal)

C. Ethnocentrism
1. Ethnocentrism - the belief that one's own culture is superior to others
2. Influence of social identities
   a. Social identities create "us" or in-group, versus "them" or out-group categories
   b. Us–them identities are strengthened when the groups compete
   c. Competition can have positive results (e.g., better inventions) and negative results (e.g., reduced motivation)
   d. Interdependence in reaching mutual goals (co-operation) can reduce competitiveness and hostility

D. Stereotypes
1. Summary impression of a group in which all members of that group are viewed as sharing common traits that may be positive, negative, or neutral

2. Stereotypes help us process new information, retrieve memories, organize experience, make sense of differences, and predict how people will behave

3. Stereotypes can distort reality (e.g., exaggerate differences <u>between</u> groups, underestimate differences <u>within</u> other groups)

V. GROUP CONFLICT AND PREJUDICE

    A. **Prejudice** - a negative stereotype and a strong, unreasonable dislike or hatred of a group or its individual members

        1. Resists rational argument and evidence; resistant to change

        2. Prejudice may serve psychological, social, cultural, & economic functions

        3. Though studies show prejudice in North America is decreasing, there is disagreement about how to accurately measure prejudice

        4. Implicit or unconscious prejudice may be more pervasive than explicit prejudice; it can be measured via symbolic measures of racism, behavioural measures, measures of physiological changes in the brain, or measures of unconscious associations with the target group

        5. Conditions that must be met in order to reduce prejudice or group conflict:

           a. Both sides must have equal legal status, economic opportunities, and power

           b. The larger culture must endorse egalitarian norms and provide moral support and legitimacy for both sides

           c. Both sides must have opportunities to work and socialize together, formally and informally

           d. Both sides must co-operate; work together for common goal

VI. THE QUESTION OF HUMAN NATURE

Under certain conditions, good people often can be induced to do bad things and everyone is affected by the rules of their culture

Group Conflict and Prejudice

137

IDIOMS AND SLANGS

Enshrined in law (page 281) – included in the laws of our society.

Top of your lungs (page 281) – to sing as loud as possible.

Uneasy (page 282) – not comfortable with the situation.

Turned out (page 283) – the results provided different information than first expected.

Backed down (page 283) – gave up their position.

Kept in the dark (page 284) – not revealing important information to participants in a study.

Rock the boat (page 286) – to upset the flow or routine of the experiment.

Language of the tea table (page 286) – polite discussions, formal or proper language, no slang or derogatory comments used.

A chilling study (page 287) – upsetting or disturbing to read.

Pressured me into it (page 289) – forced or coerced into a decision by someone else.

It's another ball game (page 291) – a different set of rules or beliefs. Some people hold strong beliefs, while others appear not to care about the same belief.

To beat the hell (page 295) – to act violently and viciously attack another person, inflicting damage and harm.

Hazing (page 296) – rituals of ridicule and mild torture to initiate a new member into a special group.

Society runs more smoothly (page 297) – works efficiently, more effective when people follow the same the rules.

In sync (page 298) – in synchronicity, to follow the same routine as the group you're a part of.

Free ride (page 299) – to take advantage of other peoples generosity, not doing as much work as the rest of the group members.

Hand themselves over (page 300) – give control and responsibility of your actions to the group.

Speak up for (page 302) – to give support, to create awareness of an opinion.

Whistle-blower (page 302) – a person who reveals information that is hidden from others.

Like loose marbles rolling around in an unconnected universe (page 304) – social identities provide us with a sense of ourselves and how we relate and interact with the rest of society. They keep us directed and connected.

Pooling their resources (page 307) – bringing together information and resources to achieve a common goal.

Slippery nature of prejudice (page 309) – subject to change, not reliable, deceitful, an unreasonable bias. A judgment or opinion held in disregard of facts that contradict it.

Scapegoat (page 309) – a person, group, or thing who is held responsible for the mistakes or crimes of others. Takes the blame for someone else.

Prejudice is a tonic for low self-esteem (page 309) - people will use discrimination and prejudice to lift, or raise, their low self-esteem. This means that people may say mean things about someone else to make them feel better about themselves.

Deep-seated (page 310) – originating far beneath the surface, deeply rooted.

Mindlessly (page 310) – not using intellectual abilities, senseless, no thought.

Flip side of ethnocentrism (page 310) – the less popular side.

Isn't cool to admit prejudice (page 314) – not popular, looked down upon. People will hide their feelings of prejudice to avoid being unpopular.

Spur behind efforts (page 316) – stimulates into action, incites, or urges efforts to happen.

PRACTICE TEST 1 - Multiple choice

1. Rules that regulate "correct" behaviours for a manager or an employee are called
    A.   norms.   B.   occupational roles.
    C.   social rules.   D.   depersonalization.

2. In the obedience experiments, Milgram found that people were more likely to disobey the experimenter and refuse to administer shock when
    A.   the experimenter stayed in the room.
    B.   the subject administered shocks directly to the victim in the same room.
    C.   authority figures, rather than "ordinary" people, ordered subjects to continue.
    D.   the subject worked with a peer who also administered shocks.

3. In Milgram's obedience studies, the person most likely to disobey would be a subject who
    A.   felt very upset about administering shocks to another person.
    B.   worked with peers who refused to go further.
    C.   had strong moral and religious principles.
    D.   had a very passive personality.

4. In the obedience experiments, what percentage of the subjects administered the maximum amount of shock to the victim?
    A.   only 1 to 2 percent   B.   approximately two-thirds
    C.   30 percent   D.   all of the subjects

5. The major point of the Zimbardo prison study was
    A.   to demonstrate that certain personality types should not be in positions of authority.
    B.   that people's behaviour depends largely on the roles they are asked to play.
    C.   that students are very suggestible and are not good research subjects.
    D.   how quickly people are corrupted by power.

6. Which conclusion is shared by the prison study and the obedience study?
    A.   The roles people played influenced their behaviour more than their personalities.
    B.   What people did depended on the role they were assigned.
    C.   Social roles and obligations have a powerful influence on behaviour.
    D.   All of the above

7. Which of the following causes people to obey when they really would rather not?
    A.   entrapment   B.   good manners
    C.   routinization   D.   all of the above

8. When Ashley's husband forgot to run an errand, she attributed his forgetting to his selfishness. When Andy's wife forgot to run an errand, he attributed her forgetting to her being preoccupied with problems at work. Ashley made a(n) _____ attribution, whereas Andy made a(n) _____ attribution.
    A. dispositional; situational
    B. situational; dispositional
    C. self-serving; external
    D. internal; dispositional

9. "Sally rides her bike to school because she is athletic" is an example of
    A. a dispositional attribution.
    B. the self-serving bias.
    C. the fundamental attribution error.
    D. situational attribution.

10. "Jennifer rides her bike to school because she can't get a ride" is an example of
    A. a dispositional attribution.
    B. the self-serving bias.
    C. the fundamental attribution error.
    D. situational attribution.

11. In attributing causes to other people's behaviours, the tendency to overestimate the effects of personality factors and underestimate the effects of situational factors is called
    A. a dispositional attribution.
    B. the just-world hypothesis.
    C. the fundamental attribution error.
    D. the self-serving bias.

12. I believe that I got an A in geometry because I'm a hard worker, but I got a D in biology because the teacher doesn't like me. This demonstrates
    A. the just-world hypothesis.
    B. the self-serving bias.
    C. the fundamental attribution error.
    D. blaming the victim.

13. "People get what they deserve" is an example of
    A. the just-world hypothesis.
    B. situational attribution.
    C. the fundamental attribution error.
    D. the self-serving bias.

14. When Hortense was diagnosed with cancer, she believed that she must have done something wrong to have deserved such an illness. Her belief is an example of
    A. a situational attribution.
    B. guilt.
    C. the just-world hypothesis.
    D. an internal attribution.

15. Attitudes are affected by
    A. thinking.
    B. conformity.
    C. habit.
    D. all of the above.

16. Students were asked to publicly advocate the importance of safe sex, and then list the reasons for their own past failure to use condoms. Afterwards, they experienced
    A. friendly persuasion.
    B. cognitive dissonance.
    C. coercive persuasion.
    D. insight.

17. Following their confrontation with the discrepancy between their attitudes and their behaviours, what would the students in the previous question be most likely to do?
    A. increase their use of condoms
    B. make no change in their behaviour
    C. decrease their use of condoms
    D. none of the above

18. That repetition increases the perception that familiar statements are true demonstrates
    A. cognitive dissonance.
    B. generational identity.
    C. the validity effect.
    D. coercive persuasion.

19. One of the techniques that facilitates coercive persuasion is
    A. repeating a piece of information over and over.
    B. exposing people to arguments from someone they admire.
    C. defining a person's problems in simplistic terms, and offering simple answers.
    D. offering people food while listening to an argument.

20. People are likely to conform
    A. in order to keep their jobs, win promotions, or win votes.
    B. if they wish to be liked.
    C. if they want to avoid being unpopular.
    D. for all the reasons listed above.

21. In the discussion of attitudes and behavioural genetics, your textbook mentions all of the following traits as being highly heritable EXCEPT
    A. religiosity.
    B. political conservatism.
    C. openness to experience.
    D. preference for cognitive consistency.

22. Your text mentions all of the following as situational factors involved in deciding to dissent or act courageously EXCEPT
    A. cultural norms encourage you to take action.
    B. you do not become entrapped.
    C. the cost-benefit ratio supports getting involved.
    D. you have an ally.

23. A woman was stabbed and none of the numerous onlookers called for help. What accounts for this?
    A. social loafing
    B. conformity
    C. diffusion of responsibility
    D. deindividuation

24. The willingness to take selfless or dangerous action on behalf of others is called
    A. interdependence.
    B. individuation.
    C. altruism.
    D. all of the above.

25. Which of the following is <u>NOT</u> one of the factors that predicts altruism?
    A.   an altruistic personality   B.   an ally
    C.   perceiving the need for help   D.   entrapment

26. The belief that one's own culture or ethnic group is superior to all others is called
    A.   ethnic separatism.   B.   prejudice.
    B.   social norms.   D.   ethnocentrism.

27. A stereotype
    A.   may be positive.   B.   may be negative or neutral.
    C.   helps us to organize the world.   D.   includes all of the above.

28. Stereotypes can be helpful because they help us
    A.   increase the accuracy of our opinions about particular individuals.
    B.   see the differences between groups.
    C.   rapidly process new information and organize experience.
    D.   do all of the above.

29. Students are shown a slide of a white male committing a crime against a black male. Later, when they are asked what they saw, most reported seeing a black male committing a crime against a white male. This error is a result of the fact that stereotypes
    A.   produce selective perception.
    B.   accentuate differences between groups.
    C.   underestimate differences within other groups.
    D.   help us process new information.

30. Stereotypes distort reality by
    A.   accentuating differences between groups.
    B.   producing selective perceptions.
    C.   underestimating differences within other groups.
    D.   propagating all of the above.

31. An unreasonable negative feeling toward a category of people is called
    A.   ethnocentrism.   B.   a stereotype.
    B.   prejudice.   D.   social identity.

32. Which characteristic is most likely to lead to evil actions?
    A.   adherence to roles, obedience to authority, conformity, entrapment
    B.   lack of developed conscience
    C.   mental illness
    D.   an evil nature

33. In close knit groups, members tend to think alike and suppress dissent. This is called
a) group polarization
b) validity effect

c) diffusion of responsibility
d) group think

34.Gerry's boss likes to be right and to be the expert on any topic. Whenever their work team meets, he becomes irritated with whoever disagrees with him. If anyone tries to challenge him, others in the group quickly change the subject. What is occurring in this situation?
a) groupthink
b) diffusion of responsibility
c) social loafing
d) deindividuation

35. All of the following are features of groupthink EXCEPT
a) pressure on dissenters to conform
b) an illusion of invulnerability
c) diffusion of responsibility
d) self censorship

PRACTICE TEST 2 - Short Answer

1.   _____ are positions in society regulated by norms that describe how people in those positions should behave.

2.   In the obedience study by Milgram, psychologists were surprised to find that _____ of the subjects gave all the shocks.

3.   In the prison study, the "prisoners" became panicky and helpless and some of the guards became tyrannical and cruel. Their behaviour probably depended on the _____they were asked to play.

4.   The obedience studies and the prison study demonstrate the power of social roles to influence behaviour. Some of the reasons that people obey authority, even when it's not in their own interest or may violate their own values, are the rules of good _____ and _____, which occurs when commitment to a course of action is escalated.

5.   How the social environment influences thoughts, beliefs, and memories and how people's perceptions of themselves and others affect their relationships is the subject matter of social _____.

6.   A _____ attribution identifies the cause of an action as something in the environment.

7.   The tendency to overestimate _____ factors and underestimate the influence of the _____ when explaining someone else's behaviour describes the _____ attribution error.

8.   The _____ occurs when people take credit for positive actions and attribute the bad ones to the situation.

9.   The need to believe that the world is fair, and that good people are rewarded and bad people are punished, is called the _____.

10.   A relatively stable opinion is a(n) _____.

11.   The more a statement is repeated, the more people will believe that it is true. This is known as the _____ effect.

12. _____ persuasion techniques suppress people's ability to reason, to think critically, and to make good choices.

13. _____ refers to a behaviour performed when carrying out an order from someone in authority. In contrast, _____ refers to behaviour or attitudes that occur as a result of real or imagined group pressure.

14. According to research on behavioural genetics, some core attitudes stem from personality traits that are highly heritable, such as the personality trait _____.

15. Rather than bystander apathy, _____ may account for why individuals in crowds fail to respond to an emergency.

16. One reason for social loafing in a work group may be that the work is _____.

17. _____ increases a person's willingness to do harm to someone else, to cheat, and to break the law. It may also be a primary reason for mob violence.

18. _____, or the willingness to take risks or dangerous action for others, may be a result of a combination of both conscience and situational influences.

19. People have _____ identities based on their nationality, ethnic heritage, occupation, and social roles.

20. "We" are good, noble, and humane; "they" are bad, stupid, and cruel. Such beliefs reflect _____.

21. Believing that all "Wispians" are good in math, is a(n) _____. Disliking and refusing to live next to a Wispian is an example of _____.

22. One way stereotypes distort reality is that they _____ differences between groups and _____ differences within other groups.

23. Prejudice is the _____ of ethnocentrism.

24. Social and cultural psychologists suggest that human behaviour depends more on _____ organization than on human nature.

25. Identification with the dominant culture is known as _____.

26. Certain historical decisions have been made by strong leaders who discouraged disagreement, preferred unanimous decisions, and did not get opinions from people outside of the group. These decisions were a result of _____.

PRACTICE TEST 3 - Essay

1. Identify the influences and effects of roles and norms in the Zimbardo prison study and the obedience study.

2. A group of students were asked to explain the source of a person's grades. They provided the explanations below. Examine each explanation and identify the explanatory device it relies upon.

    A. Grades result from a person's intelligence and self-discipline. When these are high, grades are good and vice versa.
    B. Grades depend on doing the right things. A person should earn good grades for reading instructions, meeting deadlines, and turning in assignments. If a person does not do these things, he or she deserves bad grades.
    C. Grades depend on quality teaching and educational materials. If the teacher is good, students should be motivated and do well.
    D. Grades depend on luck. Sometimes it doesn't matter whether a person has studied or not if the test is tricky.

3. You need to get a B in all of your classes to get the scholarship you need. You are right on the border between a B and a C in your French class. Using information on persuasion, discuss how you might approach your French teacher to attempt to persuade him to give you the benefit of the doubt.

4. Dr. Wong requires a group project in her sociology class. She wants each group to design a federally funded project to reduce the number of homeless and provide appropriate services for those who remain homeless. She is aware of all the principles of group behaviour and she wants to reduce the likelihood of social loafing, diffusion of responsibility, groupthink, deindividuation, group polarization, and competition. She wants to increase co-operation and independent action. Develop a set of instructions she should use to meet all of her goals for this assignment.

5. Jan and her sister are having a debate about the Agyflops, people from a country located in the Pacific Ocean. Jan's sister does not like the Agyflops and is explaining why to Jan. Most of her reasons are based on stereotypes. For each statement Jan's sister makes, indicate which problem with stereotypes it exemplifies.

    A. "When I visited Agyflopia, everyone was so unfriendly. No one smiled."

    B. "They are so different from us. Canadians are so direct, but you never know what the Agyflops are thinking."

    C. "I guess that there are many Agyflops in school with us, but they never seem to speak correctly and they always seem so stupid."

6. Why is prejudice so hard to eliminate? You are the principal of a school with students from many different backgrounds. Design a program that attempts to improve relationships and reduce prejudice.

7. Suppose that you are going to help first-year college students learn about—and avoid falling victim to—coercive persuasion by dangerous groups. List some characteristics of coercive persuasion or brainwashing. To help you remember the characteristics, try applying them to a particular group that you know uses the techniques.

CHAPTER NINE

Thinking and Intelligence

LEARNING OBJECTIVES

1. Define thinking.

2. Define and distinguish among concepts (including basic concepts and prototypes), propositions and cognitive schemas.

3. Briefly describe Whorf's theory relating to language and cognition.

4. Define a mental image. How are mental images, cognitive schemas, propositions and concepts connected?

5. Distinguish among subconscious processes, nonconscious processes and mindlessness.

6. Define reasoning and distinguish between formal and informal reasoning problems.

7. Distinguish between an algorithm and a heuristic.

8. Distinguish between inductive and deductive reasoning.

9. Define reflective judgment and identify the seven cognitive stages of reflective judgment.

10. Discuss the various types of cognitive bias that can influence reasoning.

11. Describe the research results and implications of the work of behavioural economists.

12. Describe the theory of cognitive dissonance.

13. Describe the conditions under which people are most likely to try to reduce dissonance.

14. Define intelligence, noting the results of studies using factor analysis. What is the g factor?

15. Distinguish between the psychometric approach and cognitive approaches to intelligence.

16. Describe Binet's contribution to the field of intelligence testing.

17. Define IQ and illustrate the computation of the original IQ.

18. Review the contributions of Terman and Wechsler to the development of IQ tests and the computation of IQ.

19. Discuss the objectives, uses, and criticisms of IQ tests, specifically noting the effects of culture on IQ.

20. Describe the results of the research examining the effects of expectations and stereotypes on IQ scores.

21. Describe the components of Sternberg's triarchic theory of intelligence and discuss whether these components are measured on most intelligence tests.

22. Describe Gardner's theory of domains of intelligence.

23. Describe the relationship between motivation, hard work and intellectual success.

24. Discuss the concept of the theory of mind. What evidence is there that animals have the capacity for higher order thinking?

25. Define language, noting the four properties that must be present in order for a system of communication to be deemed to be a language (meaningfulness, displacement, grammar and productivity).

26. Using these criteria, review the research regarding animals and language.

27. Distinguish between anthropomorphism and anthropodenial.

28. According to your textbook, what makes the human species unique?

29. Distinguish between divergent and convergent thinking. Review the personality characteristics and circumstances that affect creative thinking.

BRIEF CHAPTER SUMMARY

Chapter 9 examines the elements and processes of thinking. Concepts, propositions, schemas, and images are all elements of thought. Deductive and inductive reasoning are types of formal reasoning that are useful for well-specified problems that have a single correct answer. Dialectical reasoning and reflective judgment are types of informal reasoning that are useful for more complex problems that require critical thinking. Several cognitive biases affect rational thinking and cause cognitive errors and distortions. Examples include the affect heuristic, the availability heuristic, the fairness bias, the hindsight bias, and the confirmation bias. Intelligence is a characteristic that is difficult to define but is related to one's ability to think. Theorists examine intelligence using two approaches: the psychometric approach, which attempts to measure intelligence through tests, and the cognitive approach, which examines the aspects or domains of intelligence. Sternberg's triarchic theory is described. Intellectual achievement as measured by test scores is heavily influenced by such factors as motivation and hard work. Finally, psychologists also are interested in the cognitive abilities of nonhumans. Whether animals have the cognitive capacity for language has been studied and debated.

PREVIEW OUTLINE

Before you read the chapter, review the preview outline for each section of the text. After you have read the chapter, close this book and try to <u>re-create</u> the outlines on a blank piece of paper.

I. **THOUGHT: USING WHAT WE KNOW**
   A.   **The elements of cognition**
       1.   Thinking - mental manipulation of internal representations of objects, activities, and situations

2.   Concepts - a mental category that groups objects, relations, activities, abstractions, or qualities having common properties

        a.   Basic concepts - those with a moderate number of instances

        b.   Prototype - most representative example of a concept

c. Whorf's theory: language molds thought

      3.   Proposition - units of meaning made of concepts that express unitary idea

      4.   Cognitive schemas - mental network of knowledge, beliefs, and expectations

      5.   Mental images - mental representations, often visual

B.   **How conscious is thought?**

      1.   Subconscious processes - outside of awareness but can be made conscious

      2.   Nonconscious processes - remain outside of awareness

      3.   Implicit learning - learning without the conscious intention to do so

      4.   Mindlessness - inflexibly acting, speaking, making decisions out of habit

Thought: Using What We Know

II. REASONING RATIONALLY

    A.   **Reasoning** - mental activity that involves operating on information in order to reach conclusions; drawing inferences from observations or facts

    B.   **Formal reasoning: algorithms and logic**

        1.   Algorithms - procedures guaranteed to produce a solution (a recipe)

        2.   Deductive reasoning - if the premises are true, the conclusion must be true

        3.   Inductive reasoning - the conclusion probably follows from the premises, but could conceivably be false

    C.   **Informal reasoning: heuristics and dialectical thinking**

        1.   Heuristics - rules of thumb that don't guarantee an optimal solution

        2.   Dialectical reasoning - comparing different views to resolve differences

    D.   **Reflective judgment** - critical thinking; the ability to evaluate and integrate evidence, relate evidence to theory or opinion, and reach conclusions

Reasoning Rationally

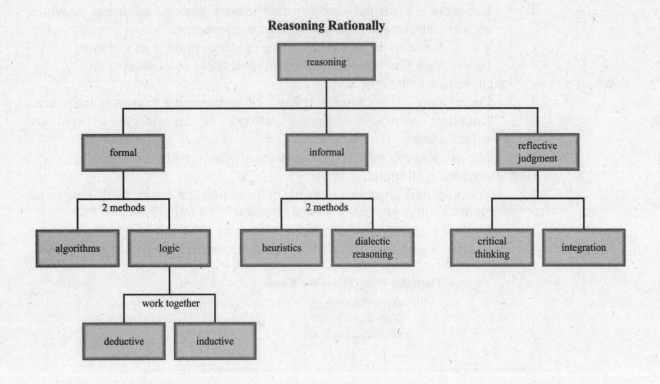

III. BARRIERS TO REASONING RATIONALLY

A. **Exaggerating the improbable and minimizing the probable (availability heuristic) -** judging the probability of an event by how easy it is to think of examples; **(affect heuristic)** – the tendency to consult emotions instead of being objective

B. **Avoiding loss -** making decisions based on avoiding loss

C. **Fairness bias-** avoiding loss and economic rationality

D. **Mental sets -** trying to solve problems by using rules that worked in the past

E. **Hindsight bias -** believing that an outcome was known all along

F. **Confirmation bias -** paying attention to what confirms our beliefs

G. **Cognitive consistency -** motivation to reduce cognitive dissonance that occurs when a person simultaneously holds two cognitions that are inconsistent or holds a belief that is inconsistent with the person's behaviour. Attempts to reduce dissonance are especially high under the following conditions:
    1. Need to justify a choice (postdecision dissonance)
    2. Need to justify behaviour that conflicts with your view of yourself
    3. Need to justify your efforts

H. **Overcoming biases:** biases are not always bad; biases usually diminish when decisions have serious consequences, and knowledge can reduce its impact

Barriers to Reasoning Rationally

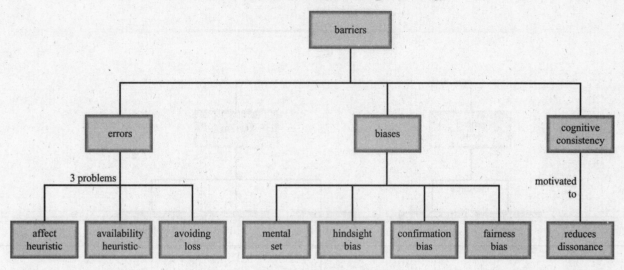

IV. MEASURING INTELLIGENCE: THE PSYCHOMETRIC APPROACH

Defined as the ability to profit from experience, acquire knowledge, think abstractly, act purposefully, or adapt to changes in the environment

A. **Factor analysis – statistical method for analyzing the intercorrelations among various measures or test scores**

B. **g factor** - Many believe in a general ability that underlies all other abilities

C. **The psychometric approach** - traditional approach that focuses on how well people perform on standardized mental tests

    1. Researchers use statistical technique known as factor analysis

    2. g factor debated

D. **The invention of IQ tests**

    1. Binet measured children's mental age (MA) - intellectual development relative to other children's

    2. Wechsler developed test for adults (WAIS) and children (WISC)

    3. Culture-free tests (nonverbal tests) and culture-fair tests (used items common to many cultures) are unable to eliminate bias

    4. Scores are influenced by expectations, which shape stereotypes and can affect scores by creating a doubt called stereotype threat

    5. Tests have value (they do predict school performance), but educators must recognize the limits of the tests and use them better

Measuring Intelligence: The Psychometric Approach

V. DISSECTING INTELLIGENCE: THE COGNITIVE APPROACH

A. **The triarchic theory of intelligence** - Robert Sternberg identifies three aspects
   1. Componential intelligence – includes meta-cognition
   2. Experiential intelligence – includes creativity in new situations
   3. Contextual intelligence – includes tacit knowledge (practical knowledge)

B. **The theory of multiple intelligences**
   1. Gardner's theory of multiple intelligences
   2. Emotional intelligence – understanding your own and others' emotions

C. **Thinking critically about intelligence(s)**
   1. There is disagreement about the idea of new intelligences
   2. Some say some of Gardner's domains are personality traits or talents

D. **Motivation, hard work and intellectual success**
   1. Terman study showed motivation was a determining factor in life success
   2. Stevenson study found that Asian students far outperformed North American students on math tests, and the gap is increasing
      a. Differences could not be accounted for by educational resources or intellectual abilities
      b. North American parents had lower standards for their children's performance and were more likely than Asian parents to believe math ability was innate
      c. North American students did not value education as much

Dissecting Intelligence: The Cognitive Approach

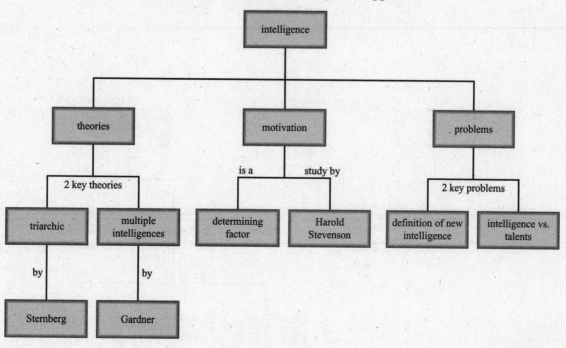

VI. ANIMAL MINDS

A. **Animal intelligence** - subject of study in cognitive ethology
   1. Cognitive ethologists say animals anticipate future events, make plans, and coordinate their activities with others of their species
   2. Even complex actions may involve pre-wired behaviour, not cognition
   3. Some behaviours do demonstrate cognitive abilities

B. **Animals and language**
   1. Primary ingredient in human cognition is language
   2. Criteria for language
       a. Meaningfulness - adequate ability to refer to things, ideas, feelings
       b. Displacement - permits communication about objects not present
       c. Productivity - ability to produce and comprehend new utterances
       d. Grammar
   3. By these criteria, animals communicate but do not have language
   4. Early efforts to teach language had success which was followed by skepticism and recognition of methodological problems in the research
   5. Newer research better controlled; has found that with training animals can use symbols, signs, understand some words, and learn without formal training
   6. Some evidence nonprimates can acquire aspects of language

Animal Minds

IDIOMS AND SLANGS

Bumbling (page 325) – to stumble and make mistakes.

Mental toolbox (page 331) – a collection of mental skills that assist in solving problems and discovering information.

Makes it a more complex soup to try to strain out (page 335) – many different motives make it hard to understand the real reason why people conduct certain research and discover particular answers to publish.

Smacks us in the face (page 342) – makes itself apparent or obvious and we cannot avoid the information.

Muddling along (page 342) – managing to succeed in spite of apparent mistakes and confusion.

Dilemma at the heart (page 350) – a choice between two equally unfavourable or disagreeable alternatives at the core or depth of intelligence testing.

Backtracking (page 352) – to review or reread, to return to the same area to search for more information.

Long-winded account (page 354) – describing at great with often boring detail.

Drifting into (page 356) – gradual, slow movement in a direction.

Broad battery (page 357) – a general series of tests for a wide range of abilities.

Last bastion of human uniqueness (page 361) – the most unique characteristic, the defining aspect of humans, because we are the only animals thought to possess language.

Crowning accomplishment (page 364) – high achievement or top level of success.

Tried-and-true path (page 365) – tested and proven to be a successful route.

PRACTICE TEST 1 - Multiple Choice

1.   The ability to think
     A.   is defined as the physical manipulation of the environment.
     B.   confines us to the immediate present.
     C.   allows for the mental manipulation of internal representations of objects, activities, and situations.
     D.   incorporates all of the above.

2.   A mental category that groups things that have common properties is called a
     A.   concept.   B.   symbol.
     C.   proposition.   D.   schema.

3.   Relationships between concepts are expressed by
     A.   super concepts.   B.   symbols.
     C.   propositions.   D.   schemas.

4.   Propositions are
     A.   complicated networks of knowledge.   B.   prototypes.
     C.   units of meaning made up of concepts. D.   composed of schemas.

5.   Processes that are automated, such as typing or driving, are called _____, whereas making decisions without stopping to analyze what we are doing makes use of

     _____.
     A.   subconscious processes; nonconscious processes
     B.   mindlessness; subconscious processes
     C.   nonconscious processes; mindlessness
     D.   subconscious processes; mindlessness

6.   Nonconscious processes refer to
     A.   processes that can be brought into consciousness when necessary.
     B.   decisions that are made without thinking very hard.
     C.   processes that are outside awareness but affect behaviour.
     D.   the practice of operating on information in order to reach conclusions.

7.   "All cats have fur. This animal is a cat. Therefore, it has fur." This is an example of
     A.   deductive reasoning.   B.   dialectical reasoning.
     C.   inductive reasoning.   D.   divergent thinking.

8. Inductive reasoning
   A. is used when the premises provide support for the conclusion, but the conclusion still could be false.
   B. is often used in scientific thinking.
   C. allows for a specific conclusion.
   D. incorporates all of the above.

9. When information is incomplete or many viewpoints compete, it is necessary to use
   A. informal reasoning.
   B. formal reasoning.
   C. inductive reasoning.
   D. deductive reasoning.

10. For complicated problems in real life, it is best to use
    A. dialectical reasoning.
    B. informal reasoning.
    C. reflective judgment.
    D. all of the above.

11. When asked about his views on abortion, Carl responds, "That's what I was brought up to believe." According to Kitchener and King, he is in the _____ stage of reflective thought.
    A. quasi-reflective
    B. prereflective
    C. reflective judgment
    D. none of the above

12. People are more likely to take risks
    A. for a potentially more rewarding solution than for a smaller sure gain.
    B. if the risks are perceived as a way to avoid loss.
    C. when the results are explained in terms of lives saved, not lives lost.
    D. none of the above.

13. Which of the following helps to explain the popularity of lotteries and why people buy earthquake insurance?
    A. confirmation bias
    B. loss aversion
    C. availability heuristic
    D. hindsight bias

14. Unless your coursework is totally determined for you, you probably use _____ to decide what courses to take.
    A. an algorithm
    B. a heuristic
    C. deductive reasoning
    D. hindsight

15. Though Allison lives comfortably in a city with a high crime rate, she is afraid to visit Vancouver because of a potential earthquake. Which cognitive bias does this represent?
    A. loss aversion
    B. availability heuristic
    C. cognitive dissonance
    D. confirmation bias

16. Harry and Larry are in a very boring class. It is a required course for Harry, but Larry chose to take this course, and it is too late to withdraw. What is likely to happen?
    A. Harry is likely to try to reduce dissonance by saying he likes the class.
    B. Larry is likely to try to reduce dissonance by saying he likes the class.
    C. Larry is not likely to experience any dissonance.
    D. Both are likely to experience dissonance.

17. The g factor refers to
    A. a general ability that underlies all specific abilities.
    B. a technique using factor analysis.
    C. the psychometric approach to intelligence.
    D. all of the above.

18. The psychometric approach to intelligence focuses on
    A. culture-free and culture-fair tests.
    B. how well people perform on standardized mental tests.
    C. those with learning disabilities.
    D. strategies people use when problem solving.

19. Dr. Bell is more interested in how students arrive at their answers on IQ tests than in their scores. This represents
    A. the psychometric approach to intelligence.   B. the triarchic theory.
    C. the cognitive approach to intelligence.   D. practical intelligence.

20. Componential, experiential, and contextual refer to
    A. Gardner's domains of intelligence.   B. aspects of meta-cognition.
    C. the triarchic theory of intelligence. D. divergent thinking.

21. Though Emily has never travelled overseas before, she is coping well with and adapting well to new situations on her trip to Europe. Which type of intelligence is involved?
    A. componential   B. contextual
    C. experiential   D. meta-cognitive

22. Which of the following are measured on most intelligence tests?
    A. experiential intelligence   B. componential intelligence
    C. contextual intelligence   D. all of the above

23. Based on the studies comparing Asian and American school children, which of the following contributes to achievement?
    A. whether skills are seen as innate or learned
    B. standards for performance
    C. expectation for involvement in outside activities
    D. all of the above

24. Jacob's IQ score is in the upper one percent of the distribution, yet he continues to get Cs in school. What might explain this?
   A. low contextual intelligence
   B. poor practical intelligence
   C. low motivation
   D. mild brain damage

25. Cognitive ethology refers to the study of cognitive processes in
   A. humans.
   B. children.
   C. the elderly.
   D. nonhumans.

26. Which of the following summarizes the current thinking on language ability in nonhumans?
   A. Nonhumans are able to use the basics of language.
   B. Though animals have greater cognitive abilities than is often thought, scientists are divided on this issue.
   C. Animals do not demonstrate any of the aspects of human language.
   D. Only primates (chimpanzees and gorillas) have shown any type of language abilities.

27. Kanzi can use a sign to represent food that is not present in the room. This represents which feature of language?
   A. meaningfulness
   B. productivity
   C. displacement
   D. creativity

28. According to Kitchener and King, quasi-reflective judgment is characterized by
   A. the assumption that a correct answer always exists.
   B. emphasizing the reception of truth through the senses or authorities.
   C. the understanding that some judgments are more valid than others.
   D. paying attention only to evidence that fits what someone already believes.

29. The statistical method that identifies clusters of correlated items that seem to measure some common ability is known as
   A. factor analysis.
   B. psychometric analysis.
   C. g factor.
   D. triarchic logic.

PRACTICE TEST 2 - Short Answer

1. Thinking can be defined most simply as the _____ manipulation of information.

2. One unit of thought is the _____, a mental category grouping objects, relations, activities, abstractions, or qualities that share certain properties.

3. Horse, shoe, chair are all examples of _____ concepts that have a moderate number of instances.

4. "Psychology is interesting" is an example of a(n) _____, while "Psychology is an interesting subject and it is one of the most popular majors. Psychologists work with people, but they also conduct research and engage in consultation" is an example of a(n) _____.

5. While nonconscious processes remain outside of awareness, _____ processes can be brought into consciousness when necessary.

6. "Intuition" and "insight" are thought to be a result of _____ processes.

7. In deductive reasoning, if the premises are true, the conclusion _____ be true; in inductive reasoning, if the premises are true, the conclusion _____ be true.

8. Inductive reasoning and deductive reasoning are types of _____ reasoning. Problems requiring this type of reasoning can be solved by applying a(n) _____, a set of procedures guaranteed to produce a solution.

9. Juries must weigh opposing viewpoints. They would be most likely to use _____ to reach a verdict in a case.

10. Critical thinking requires that people ask questions, analyze assumptions, tolerate uncertainty, and resist oversimplification. These abilities require _____ judgment.

11. The idea that any judgment is as good as any other and is purely subjective would be most likely to occur in the _____ stage of reflective judgment.

12. One kind of rigidity that can hamper problem solving is biases due to _____, a tendency to approach problems in a particular way due to prior experience with similar problems.

13. That a person might be more afraid of an airplane crash than something much more likely to occur, like a car accident, may be a result of the _____.

14. Cognitive _____ occurs when a person simultaneously holds two cognitions that are psychologically inconsistent or holds a belief that is inconsistent with the person's behaviour.

15. Mayumi has a great deal of knowledge about her own cognitive processes and can effectively monitor and control those processes. She would be described as being very good at _____.

16. The _____ focuses on how well people perform on standardized mental tests, while the _____ emphasizes the strategies people use to solve problems.

17. IQ tests have been criticized for being _____ in favour of certain groups. In an attempt to address this problem, psychologists developed tests that were intended to be _____ free and fair.

18. Some people believe that a(n) _____ ability underlies the many specific abilities tapped by intelligence tests, whereas others believe that there are _____ and independent intelligences.

19. According to Sternberg's _____ theory, a person who easily adapts to the demands of new environments exhibits _____ intelligence.

20. Sternberg has identified three facets of intelligence: _____, _____, and _____.

21. Intellectual achievement also depends on _____ and _____.

22. The cross-cultural study by Stevenson found that American parents had _____ standards for their children's performance and for schools than Asian parents.

23. The four criteria for language are meaningfulness, _____, grammar or syntax, and _____.

24. Attributing human emotions to certain animal behaviour is an example of _____.

25. The language theorist who proposed that language influences how people think was _____.

PRACTICE TEST 3 - Essay

1. List a prototype for each of the concepts listed below.
    A. clothing
    B. animal
    C. pet
    D. relative

2. In each of the following examples, indicate what type of reasoning is most suitable for each problem and explain why.

    A. A navigator must determine the ship's position from the knowledge of a standard formula and the position of the North Star.
    B. A psychologist must determine if nonconformity facilitates creativity.
    C. A scientist must decide whether to pursue a career in teaching or research.
    D. A couple must decide if they are going to have a child.

3. Identify the cognitive biases in each of the following situations.
    A. Richard would rather drive 1000 kilometres than fly because it is safer.
    B. Not only did you choose to go to this party 45 minutes away, but you convinced three other friends to go along. Even though no one is enjoying the party, you say you are having a good time.
    C. Jane doesn't want to get married and John does. When discussing the issue, Jane brings up only troubled relationships she knows of and cannot think of any of the happy relationships.

4. In the following examples identify what type of intelligence is being described, according to Sternberg's theory.
    A. Dr. Morris can go into a big organization and quickly identify the problem and select effective strategies for its solution.
    B. Dr. Mira works with people in psychotherapy and knows which strategies are working and when she needs to try something different.
    C. Regardless of what group of people Nicholas finds himself with, he is able to quickly adjust to the situation, handle himself appropriately, and feel comfortable with himself.

5. Do animals have cognitive abilities? Make a case for and against this question.

6. What additional domains has Howard Gardner proposed regarding intelligence? What are some criticisms of this approach?

CHAPTER TEN

Memory

LEARNING OBJECTIVES

1.   Define memory. What is the function of memory?

2.   Discuss the reconstructive nature of memory. What are flashbulb memories and how accurate are they? How is memory affected by source misattribution?

3.   Define confabulation. Describe three circumstances in which confabulation is more likely to occur.

4.   Discuss the reliability of eyewitness testimony. What factors are likely to affect the accuracy of eyewitness recollections?

5.   Describe the special case of child abuse that was alleged to have occurred in Saskatchewan in 1992. How accurate is children's testimony and what are the implications for legal cases?

6.   Discuss different measures of memory, specifically comparing recognition, recall, priming and relearning methods.

7.   Distinguish between explicit and implicit memory.

8.   Describe the "three-box model" of memory and explain its components.

9.   Describe the parallel distributed processing model of memory.

10.   Discuss the role of the sensory register.

11.   Describe the processes and limitations of short-term memory (STM). Describe the characteristics of long-term memory (LTM), and explain how information is organized.

12.   Distinguish between procedural and declarative memories.

13.   Distinguish between semantic and episodic memories.

14.   Explain the limitations of the three-box model in accounting for the serial-position effect.

15.   Review the changes that occur in your neurons when you store a long-term memory.

16.   Summarize current findings about the brain areas involved in memory.

17.   Review the research on the influence of hormones on memory.

18.   List and discuss the various strategies that are involved in effortful encoding, including rehearsal and the use of mnemonics. Discuss the theories of why forgetting occurs, including decay theory, replacement theory and interference theory.

19.   Describe various retrieval cues.

20.   Describe the repression controversy.

21.   Define childhood amnesia and describe biological and cognitive explanations of the phenomenon.

22.   Describe the relationship between a person's "life story" and actual memories.

23.   Describe the Innocence project and similar Canadian initiatives.

24.   Describe some useful strategies for improving memory.

BRIEF CHAPTER SUMMARY

Chapter 10 examines the nature of memory. Memory is not simply a taped video recording that can be replayed at a later time. Rather, our memories incorporate outside information into our recollections so that what we recall is a reconstruction of events and not necessarily a memory of them. Memory is tested using recall, retrieval, and relearning methods. There are two prominent models of memory: the information-processing model, which compares memory processes to computer processes, and the parallel distributed processing model, which states that knowledge is represented as connections among thousands of processing units operating in parallel. The three-box model, an information-processing model, suggests that there are three types of memory: sensory memory, short-term memory, and long-term memory. Psychologists are interested in knowing what kinds of brain changes take place when we store information. Research examines memory and its relationship to neurons, brain structures, and hormones. There are several different theories that explain why we forget. They include decay theory, replacement theory, interference theory, repression, cue-dependent forgetting, and theories about childhood amnesia. The implications of the reconstructive nature of memory for the criminal justice system are discussed.

PREVIEW OUTLINE

Before you read the chapter, review the preview outline for each section of the text. After you have read the chapter, close this book and try to re-create the outlines on a blank piece of paper.

I. **RECONSTRUCTING THE PAST**
    A.   **Memory** is the capacity to retain and retrieve information
    B.   **Reconstructing the past** - memory is a reconstructive process
    C.   **The fading flashbulb** - memories of dramatic (even positive) events can be inaccurate over time
    D.   **The conditions of confabulation**
            1.   The person has thought about the imagined event many times
            2.   The image of the event contains a lot of details
            3.   The event is easy to imagine

Reconstructing the Past

II. MEMORY AND THE POWER OF SUGGESTION
    A.   **The eyewitness on trial**
        1.   People fill in missing pieces from memories, which can lead to errors
        2.   Errors especially likely when ethnicity of suspect differs from witness
        3.   The power of suggestion – the way in which a question is asked, or the more often a story is told can influence what and how much is recalled
    B.   **Children's testimony** – children are most suggestible when there's pressure to conform to expectations, and when they want to please the interviewer

Memory and the Power of Suggestion

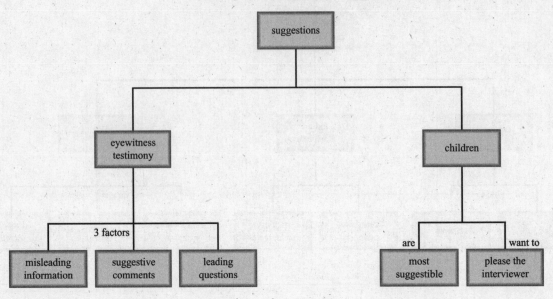

III. IN PURSUIT OF MEMORY
A.   Measuring memory
1.   Explicit memory is conscious recollection
2.   Two ways of measuring explicit memory: recall and recognition
3.   Implicit memory is unconscious retention in memory
B.   Models of memory
1.   Three-box model (information-processing)
    a.   Sensory register - retains information for a second or two
    b.   Short-term memory (STM) - holds limited amount for 30 seconds
    c.   Long-term memory (LTM) - accounts for longer storage
2.   Parallel distributed processing (connectionist) model
    a.   Information is processed simultaneously, or in parallel
    b.   Considers knowledge to be connections among thousands of units

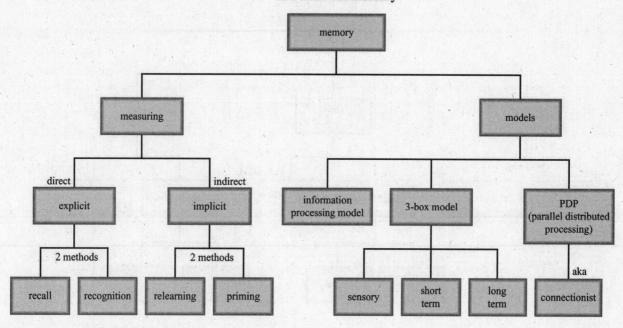

In Pursuit of Memory

IV. **THE THREE-BOX MODEL OF MEMORY**
   A.   **Sensory register: fleeting impressions**
       1.   Includes separate memory subsystems for each of the senses
       2.   Compares a stimulus to information already contained in long-term memory; it then goes to short-term memory or it vanishes
   B.   **Short-term memory: memory's scratch pad**
       1.   Holds information up to about 30 seconds as an encoded representation
       2.   Working memory - holds information retrieved from long-term memory for temporary use
       3.   The leaky bucket - holds seven (plus or minus two) chunks of information
   C.   **Long-term memory: final destination** - capacity is unlimited
       1.   Organization in long-term memory
           a.   Information is organized by semantic categories
           b.   Network models - contents is a network of interrelated concepts
       2.   The contents of long-term memory
           a.   Procedural memories - knowing how
           b.   Declarative memories - knowing that
       3.   From short-term to long-term memory - three-box model has been used to explain the serial-position effect

The Three-Box Model of Memory

V. THE BIOLOGY OF MEMORY
    A.   **Changes in neurons and synapses**
        1.   In STM, changes within neurons temporarily alter neurotransmitter release
        2.   LTM changes involve permanent structural changes in the brain
        3.   Long-term potentiation; consolidation
    B.   **Locating memories**
        1.   Areas in frontal lobes very active during short-term memory tasks
        2.   Formation of declarative memories involve hippocampus
        3.   Procedural memories involve the cerebellum
        4.   Different brain involvement for implicit and explicit memory tasks
        5.   A memory is a cluster of information distributed across areas of the brain
    C.   **Hormones and memory**
        1.   The adrenalin connection - hormones released during stress enhance memory, but high levels interfere with ordinary learning
        2.   Sweet memories - the effect of these hormones may be due to glucose

The Biology of Memory

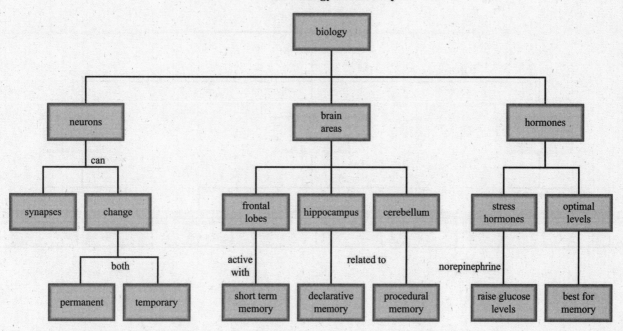

VI. HOW WE REMEMBER
    A.   **Effective encoding**
           1.   Some encoding is effortless; some is effortful
           2.   Rehearsal - review or practice of material while you are learning it
                 a.   Maintenance rehearsal - maintains information in STM only
                 b.   Elaborative rehearsal - associating new information with stored knowledge
           3.   Deep processing - processing of meaning
    B.   **Mnemonics** - strategies for encoding, storing, and retaining information

How We Remember

VII. **WHY WE FORGET**
- A. **The decay theory** - memories fade with time; doesn't apply well to LTM
- B. **Replacement** - new information wipes out old information
- C. **Interference** - retroactive interference (new information interferes with old) or proactive interference (old information interferes with new)
- D. **Cue-dependent forgetting** - forgetting due to lack of retrieval cues
- E. **Repression** - Traumatic memories are blocked from consciousness (also called psychogenic amnesia); lack of evidence to support the idea of repressed memories

Why We Forget

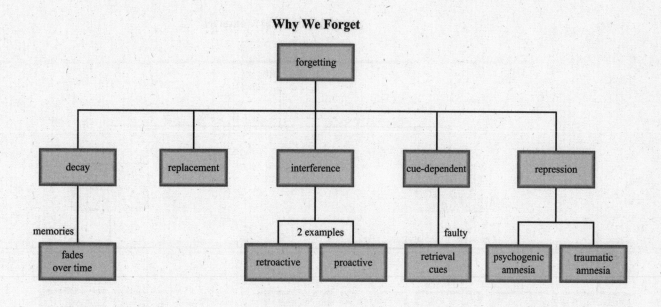

VIII. **AUTOBIOGRAPHICAL MEMORIES: THE WAY WE WERE**
  A. **Childhood amnesia: the missing years**
   1. May occur because brain areas involved in formation or storage of events are not well developed until a few years after birth
   2. Cognitive explanations have also been offered - lack of a sense of self, differences between early and later cognitive schemas, impoverished encoding, and a focus on routine
  B. **Memory and narrative: the stories of our lives**
   1. Narratives are a unifying theme to organize the events of our lives
   2. Themes serve as a cognitive schema that guides what we remember
   3. Reminiscence bump - tendency to recall certain periods and not others

Autobiographical Memories

IX. MEMORY AND MYTH
    A.   Unreliable memories are those from the first years of life, those that become increasingly unlikely, and those that result from suggestive techniques

    B.   Memories are considered most reliable when there is corroborating evidence, other signs of trauma, and they are recalled without pressure from others

C. As DNA evidence has exonerated people falsely convicted of rape, murder, and other crimes, people are becoming more aware of the limitations of eyewitness testimony and the fallibility of memory.

IDIOMS AND SLANGS

Utterly wrong (page 371) – absolutely incorrect.

Tucked away (page 371) – stored or put into an isolated area.

Frozen in time (page 372) – unchanging, always stay the same; never forget the details of the event.

Dredging up stored information (page 373) – actively searching and gathering information stored in one's memory.

Thorny problems in legal cases (page 375) – lots of obstacles, difficult, full of controversial points.

Slides of faces (page 380) – photographs of people projected on a screen or wall.

Bolstered (page 392) – to strengthen or support the information.

Smorgasbord (page 392) – a wide selection or varied assortment of findings.

Hyper (page 393) – extremely excited, high-strung.

Laid back (page 393) – relaxed, calm, easygoing.

Fasted overnight (page 393) – ate no food overnight.

It sticks (page 394) – remember the information.

Along with the diamonds of experience, he kept dredging up the pebbles (page 397) – he was able to impress people with his brilliant memory, but it also caused him to be overwhelmed with many memories.

Dropped out of her memories (page 398) – eventually forgotten details.

Wipe out old information (page 399) – remove or erase old information.

Implanted in their minds (page 374) – information added or placed falsely in a person's memory.

Lost among the stacks in the mind's library (page 401) – unable to retrieve or locate information with the belief that you still possess it.

Should hear alarm bells go off (page 403) – alerts a person to something wrong or misleading happening.

Pram (page 404) – baby carriage.

Memorable in the long run (page 405) – long-lasting memory, remains in storage, old.

Spin (page 406) – how you present an idea or information influences how it will be perceived.

Memory can be as fickle (page 407) – memory can be unstable and changing.

Fly in the face (page 410) – go against the research, opposite to what has been proven.

PRACTICE TEST 1 - Multiple Choice

1.　The reconstructive nature of memory refers to
　　A.　the alteration of remembered information to help make sense of it.
　　B.　the capacity to retain and retrieve information.
　　C.　the ability to retrieve from memory previously encountered material.
　　D.　vivid, detailed recollections of circumstances.

2.　Eyewitness testimony is influenced by
　　A.　the fact that the details of events are often inferred rather than observed.
　　B.　memory errors that increase when the races of the suspect and witness differ.
　　C.　the wording of questions.
　　D.　all of the above.

3.　Why does the tendency to reconstruct memories present a particularly serious problem in the courtrooms?
　　A.　Witnesses will lie to cover their memory errors.
　　B.　Reconstructed memories are almost always wrong.
　　C.　Witnesses who have reconstructed testimony will fail lie detector tests.
　　D.　Witnesses sometimes can't distinguish between what they actually saw and what they have reconstructed.

4.　Multiple choice is to essay as
　　A.　recall is to relearning.　　　　　　　　B.　recall is to recognition.
　　C.　priming is to recall.　　　　　　　　　D.　recognition is to recall.

5.　Unconsciously remembered material that continues to have an effect on actions is
　　A.　semantic memory.　　　　　　　　　　B.　implicit memory.
　　C.　explicit memory.　　　　　　　　　　　D.　declarative memory.

6.　Comparing the mind to a computer and speaking in terms of inputs and outputs reflects the
　　A.　parallel distributed processing model of memory.
　　B.　cognitive model of memory.
　　C.　information-processing model of memory.
　　D.　connectionist model of memory.

7.　According to the "three-box" model, which is the first step in memory?
　　A.　short-term memory　　　　　　　B.　retrieval
　　C.　storage　　　　　　　　　　　　　　D.　sensory register

8.　Which of the following is not a basic memory process?
　　A.　encoding　　　　　　　　　　　　　B.　retrieval
　　C.　storage　　　　　　　　　　　　　　D.　perception

9. Which model maintains that knowledge is represented in the brain as connections among thousands of interacting processing units that are distributed in a vast network and operate in parallel?
   A. "three box" model
   B. information-processing model
   C. parallel distributed processing model
   D. all of the above

10. Why does the parallel distributed processing model reject the computer metaphor?
    A. Unlike computers, the brain does not process information sequentially.
    B. The brain is not as complex as a computer.
    C. Unlike the brain, computers process information in a parallel manner.
    D. The brain recognizes bits of information, rather than patterns all at once.

11. Which of the following describes the function of the sensory register?
    A. It holds information that has been retrieved from LTM for temporary use.
    B. It acts as a holding bin until we select items for attention.
    C. It retains information for up to 30 seconds.
    D. It aids in the retrieval of information from short-term memory.

12. By most estimates, information can be kept in STM for _____ without rehearsal.
    A. 0.5 to 2 seconds
    B. up to 10 seconds
    C. up to 30 seconds
    D. up to 5 minutes

13. One way to increase the amount of information held in STM is to
    A. group information into chunks.
    B. form echoes and icons.
    C. reduce interference.
    D. use all of the above methods.

14. You call information and ask the number of your favourite restaurant. How long do you have to dial the number before you forget?
    A. 10 seconds
    B. up to 10 minutes
    C. up to 30 seconds
    D. 3 to 5 minutes

15. What could you do to extend the time that you remember this information?
    A. maintenance rehearsal
    B. deep processing
    C. elaborative rehearsal
    D. all of the above

16. Which of the following helps transfer information from short-term memory to long-term memory?
    A. deep processing
    B. chunking
    C. elaborative rehearsal
    D. all of the above

17. Information is stored by subject, category, and associations in
    A. the sensory register.
    B. short-term memory.
    C. the sensory memory.
    D. long-term memory.

18. You recall from the chapter on learning that B. F. Skinner was involved in the development of operant conditioning. Your ability to remember this information demonstrates which specific type of memory?
   A. declarative
   B. semantic
   C. explicit
   D. all of the above

19. Learning to type, swim, or drive is a function of which type of memory?
   A. semantic
   B. episodic
   C. procedural
   D. declarative

20. Semantic and episodic memories
   A. are types of declarative memories.
   B. are types of implicit memories.
   C. are examples of procedural memories.
   D. exhibit the primacy effect.

21. How does the "three-box" model account for the recency effect?
   A. Recent items are recalled because they have the best chance of getting into LTM.
   B. Short-term memory is empty when recent items are entered.
   C. At the time of recall, recent items are still in short-term memory and have not been dumped yet.
   D. all of the above.

22. A list of words has been read to you. You are retested on them one hour later and find that you recall more words at the end of the list. This demonstrates
   A. the primacy effect.
   B. a problem with the explanation provided by the "three-box" model of the recency effect.
   C. ways to extend the length of time information can remain in short-term memory.
   D. the effects of sensory memory.

23. Physiologically, short-term memory involves changes in _____, whereas long-term memory involves _____.
   A. the neuron's ability to release neurotransmitters; permanent structural changes in the brain
   B. permanent structural changes in the brain; changes in the neurons
   C. the hippocampus; the cortex
   D. long-term potentiation; changes in the neuron's ability to release neurotransmitters

24. Synaptic responsiveness
   A. is influenced by long-term memory.
   B. increases are known as long-term potentiation.
   C. increases during the formation of long-term memories.
   D. has all of the above characteristics.

25. Pat learned to speak French at home as a child. Now when she studies Spanish, she can recall only the French words. This is an example of
    A. retroactive interference.
    B. motivated forgetting.
    C. proactive interference.
    D. decay.

26. Decay theory does not seem to explain forgetting in long-term memory as evidenced by the fact that
    A. it is not uncommon to forget an event from years ago while remembering what happened yesterday.
    B. it is not uncommon to forget an event from yesterday while remembering what happened years ago.
    C. people who took French in high school did not do well on French tests 30 years later.
    D. people generally don't remember high school algebra by the time they go to university.

27. The idea that you will remember better if you study for a test in the same environment in which you will be tested is an example of
    A. state-dependent memory.
    B. elaborated rehearsal.
    C. cue-dependent memory.
    D. deja-vu.

28. Jocelyn is convinced that she remembers an event that occurred when she was six months old. This is impossible because
    A. parts of the brain are not well developed for some years after birth.
    B. cognitive processes are not in place at that age.
    C. at that age encoding is much less elaborate.
    D. all of the above are reasons.

29. Why is it difficult to remember events earlier than the third or fourth year of life?
    A. The brain systems involved in memory take up to three or four years to develop.
    B. Adults use different schema than children.
    C. Children use different encoding methods than adults.
    D. All of the above.

30. Which of the following best describes the relationship between a person's "life story" and actual memories?
    A. Both are quite accurate.
    B. Only memories are accurate.
    C. Both involve some reconstruction.
    D. Only life stories are accurate.

PRACTICE TEST 2 - Short Answer

1.   Research in which volunteers often eliminated or changed details of a story that did not make sense to them, and then added other details to make the story coherent, demonstrates that memory is a _____ process.

2.   In reconstructing their memories, people often draw on many sources. They may incorporate information from family stories, photographs, or videos in a new integrated account. Later they may not be able to separate the original experience from what they added after the fact. This phenomenon is called _____ amnesia.

3.   False memories can be as _____ over time as true ones.

4.   Eyewitness accounts of events are heavily influenced by _____ comments made during an interrogation.

5.   Short answer questions, such as these, rely on _____ method of measuring memory; whereas multiple-choice questions depend on _____.

6.   Conscious recollection of an event or an item of information is called_____ memory.

7.   Suppose you had read a list of words, some of which began with the letters "def." Later you are asked to complete word stems with the first word that comes to mind. You would be more likely to complete the word fragments with words from the list than you would be if you had not seen the list. This technique for measuring _____ memory is called _____.

8.   Models of memory that borrow heavily from the language of computer programming are referred to as _____ models.

9.   We _____ information when we convert it to a form that the brain can process and use. To use it in the future, we must _____ the information and be able to recover it for use, or _____ it.

10.   _____ memory holds information for a second or two, while _____ holds information for about 30 seconds.

11.   The model of memory that says the human brain does not operate like a computer is called the _____, or connectionist, model.

12. We overcome the limits of short-term memory by grouping small bits of information into larger units, or _____.

13. One way words are organized in long-term memory is by the _____ categories to which they belong.

14. Many models of long-term memory represent its contents as a vast network of interrelated concepts and propositions. These conceptualizations of memory are called _____ models.

15. _____ memories are internal representations of the world, independent of any particular context, whereas _____ memories are internal representations of personally experienced events. Both are types of _____ memories.

16. The fact that recall is best for items at the beginning and end of a list is called the _____ effect.

17. _____ rehearsal will keep information in short-term memory, but to remember things for the long haul, it is better to use _____ rehearsal which involves associating new items of information with material that has already been stored.

18. The hormones released by the adrenal glands during stress and emotional arousal, including _____, enhance memory.

19. The _____ theory of forgetting holds that memory traces fade with time if they are not "accessed" now and then.

20. A type of interference in which new information interferes with the ability to remember old information is called _____ interference. _____ interference is when old information interferes with the ability to remember new information.

21. Often, when we need to remember, we rely on _____ cues, items of information that can help us find the specific information we're looking for. The type of memory failure that occurs when we lack these cues is called _____ forgetting.

22. If your emotional arousal is especially high at the time of an event, you may remember that event best when you are in the same emotional state. This is referred to as _____ memory.

23. Memories from before the age of two are not likely to be real memories because of childhood _____.

PRACTICE TEST 3 - Essay

1.   Identify and describe the three basic processes involved in the capacity to remember.

2.   Imagine that you watched a baseball game yesterday and presently retain many details about the game. According to the "three-box" theory, what kind of sequence have such details followed?

3.   The home team brings in a new pitcher in the fifth inning. In each situation below, suggest the type of memory most likely to be the prime determinant.

        A.   Her warm-up style indicates the fluid and coordinated movements of an experienced athlete.
        B.   After several batters are walked, she tells the umpire that the calls are no better this week than last week.
        C.   As the third batter steps up, the pitcher indicates to the umpire that improper attire is being worn.

4.   Written descriptions of a fight on a school bus have been collected from several students. Explain below how memory processes are likely to influence the various descriptions.

5.   While searching the attic, Henry discovers his senior-year diary, written over 30 years ago and has not seen it since.
        A.   According to decay theory, what will have been forgotten and why?
        B.   The first page contains the title "Happy Times as a Senior." He tries hard to remember but is not successful until he begins reading a description of his homeroom. This triggers a flood of memories. What variable related to forgetting best explains this experience?
        C.   Henry finds another section entitled "Worst Times as a Senior." He is sure there were very few, but begins to change his mind as he reads. This time there is no flood of memories, but many descriptions of unhappy moments. Henry wonders whether he was overly imaginative or whether senior year was that bad. What variables that influence memory best explain this?

6.   For finals week, you have to be prepared for exams in English, math, Spanish, Italian, and history. How should the sequence of study be arranged to minimize the possibility of interference?

CHAPTER ELEVEN

Emotion

LEARNING OBJECTIVES

1.   Define emotion, focusing on its three major components.

2.   Describe the function of emotion.

3.   Describe the role of facial expressions in emotional experience.

4.   Discuss the role of social and cultural context on facial expression.

5.   Review the four reasons that people do not always agree on the meaning of emotional expression.

6.   Using research evidence, discuss the involvement of the 2 cerebral hemispheres, the prefrontal cortex, and the amygdala in the experience and expression of emotion.

7.   Discuss the role of mirror hormones in many aspects of psychology.

8.   Identify the hormones involved in emotions and describe their effects on the body.

9.   Explain why most researchers do not believe the polygraph test is a valid way to ascertain whether a person is lying.

10.   Describe other ways of detecting lying, reviewing their strengths and weaknesses.

11.   Describe the Stoic philosophers' explanation of the human emotional experience.

12.   Define and discuss the Schachter and Singer two-factor theory of emotion.

13.   Explain through the use of examples how cognitive processes can affect emotions.

14.   Discuss how culture can influence the experience and expression of emotion.

15.   Compare and contrast emotional experience and expression in men and women.

16.   Outline five suggestions for constructively managing anger.

BRIEF CHAPTER SUMMARY

Chapter 11 explores the elements of emotions. Emotions have a physical component that involves facial expressions, brain activity, and hormonal activity. There seem to be some basic universal facial expressions. Specific parts of the brain are associated with aspects of emotion. The physiological component does not result directly in the experience of emotion. Events are interpreted, and our perception of events influences our emotional experience. The final element that influences our emotions and their expression is culture. Cultural display rules govern how and when emotions may be expressed. Researchers have searched for primary, or universal, emotions. The search for primary emotions is controversial to those who feel that culture influences even biologically based emotions. The research on gender differences in emotions suggests that men and women experience similar emotions though they differ somewhat in their physiological responses and their perceptions and expectations about emotional experiences.

PREVIEW OUTLINE

Before you read the chapter, review the preview outline for each section of the text. After you have read the chapter, close this book and try to <u>re-create</u> the outlines on a blank piece of paper.

I. **ELEMENTS OF EMOTION 1: THE BODY**
    A. **Primary emotions** are considered to be universal and biologically based, whereas secondary emotions are more culture-specific
    B. **The face of emotion**
        1. Darwin said facial expressions of emotion had survival function
        2. Ekman's found seven universal facial expressions of emotion: anger, happiness, fear, surprise, disgust, sadness, and contempt. New research suggests that pride is a basic human emotion.
        3. Facial feedback - facial expressions can influence feelings
        4. Research on babies shows they use emotions to communicate
        5. Mood contagion - people often mimic the expressions and emotions of those around them
        6. Facial expressions may have different meanings depending on the context and the culture
            a. Cultures differ in the attributions they make about facial expressions (dispositional vs. situational)
            b. Familiarity affects the ability to read facial expressions
            c. Expressions can mean different things at different times
            d. People often use facial expressions to lie about their feelings

C. **The brain and emotion**
 1. **Amygdala** - gives quick appraisal of sensory information, especially important for fear
 2. **Cerebral cortex** - more accurate appraisal of sensory information
 3. **Left prefrontal cortex** - associated with motivation to approach others
 4. **Right prefrontal cortex** - associated with withdrawal from others
 5. **Mirror neurons** – found in various parts of the brain, firing in imitation of actions or emotions of others; involved in empathy
D. **Hormones and emotion** - produce the energy to respond to alarm signals
 1. Epinephrine and norepinephrine produce state of arousal
 2. Emotions differ from one another biochemically

E. **Biology and Deception: Can Lies be detected in the brain and the body?**
 1. The polygraph machine and lie detection - based on idea that lying associated with increased autonomic nervous system activity (increased heart rate, respiration)
 2. Most researchers see polygraph tests as invalid because no physiological response is uniquely associated with lying.
 3. Other physiological approaches to catching liars include the Computer Voice Stress Analyzer and MRI, but these approaches also are questionable

Elements of Emotion 1: The Body

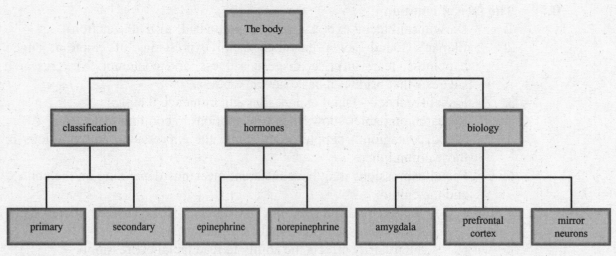

II. ELEMENTS OF EMOTION 2: THE MIND
    A.   **How thoughts create emotions**
           1.   Two-factor theory of emotion - emotion depends on physiological arousal and cognitive interpretation of events
           2.   Attributions and emotion - how perceptions and explanations of events (attributions) affect emotions
                    a.   Appraising events for their personal implications affects emotions
                    b.   Cognitions involved range from immediate perceptions of an event to general philosophy of life
3. Thoughts and emotions operate reciprocally, each influencing the other
    B.   **Cognitions and emotional complexity** - people can learn how their thinking affects their emotions and then they can learn to change their thinking

Elements of Emotion 2: The Mind

III. ELEMENTS OF EMOTION 3: THE CULTURE
    A.   **How culture shapes emotion** - are some emotions specific to culture?
           1.   Language and emotion - words for certain emotional states exist in some languages and not in others (i.e.Schadenfreude)
           2.   Culture affects which emotions are defined as "primary" and what individuals feel emotional about
    B.   **Culture and Emotional Expression**
           1.   Display rules - cultural rules govern how, when emotions are expressed
                    2.   Body language - nonverbal signals; movement, posture, gesture, gaze
           3.   Emotion work - how, when to show an emotion we don't feel

Elements of Emotion 3: The Culture

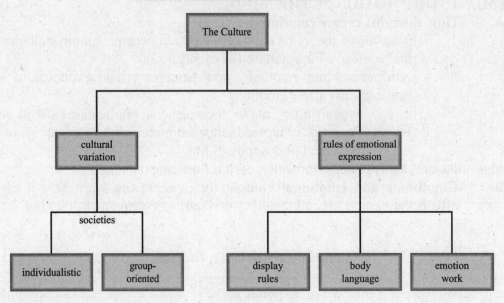

IV. PUTTING THE ELEMENTS TOGETHER: EMOTION AND GENDER
A. Emotional Reactivity
1. Men are more physiologically reactive than women, which might explain their greater discomfort with conflict in marriages
2. May be due to more sensitive and reactive autonomic nervous systems
3. Men are more likely than women to rehearse negative thoughts
C. Cognitions
1. Men and women differ in perceptions and interpretations that create emotions
2. They differ in the kinds of everyday events that provoke their anger

D. **Expressiveness**
1. Women are willing to, and permitted to, express more emotions, while men are expected to control them
2. Women smile more than men do and are more likely to cry
3. Men are more likely to express anger toward strangers
4. Gender differences in expressiveness are affected by gender roles, cultural norms, and the specific situation

E. **Emotion Work**
1. Women tend to try to persuade others they're happy or friendly
2. Men tend to try to persuade others they're unemotional or aggressive

Putting the Elements Together: Emotion and Gender

IDIOMS AND SLANGS

Moved by the beauty (page 415) – arouse a person's emotions, and passions. Creating strong, intense feelings.

Out of tune with the rest of humanity (page 415) – no balance, unable to read the signs and cues from other people's emotions.

Strike you as funny (page 415) – find something to be humorous.

When you are faced with a decision (page 415) – confronted with, have to choose a position

Wired in (page 417) – natural, programmed into the individual.

A snooty maître d' (page 421) – rude, inconsiderate host or headwaiter in a restaurant.

Anger may pale into (page 425) – anger will fade or change into.

Bounced a cheque (page 427) – having insufficient money in your bank account to pay the cheque.

Churning away in high gear (page 429) – quickly changing, excitedly producing new emotions and feelings.

In a clever twist (page 429) – showing ingenuity, different approach to research.

Had a crush for weeks on a fellow student (page 430) – infatuation, liking, and desire to be with a certain person.

Lucky fluke (page 430) – successful by accident, beyond your control.

Hopping mad (page 431) – extremely or excessively mad.

Warm fuzzy feeling (page 432) – not clear, or distinct, an overall feeling of well-being.

Let another person down (page 432) – to disappoint, inconsiderate of another person's expectations and feelings, disrespectful behaviour.

Storm out of the house (page 432) – leave in anger; to exit quickly

He was so remote the previous night (page 432) – distant, distracted, not communicating with his wife.

Sneaky affair (page 434) –hidden relationships of a sexual nature occurring when a person is married.

Loss of face (page 435) – shame, dishonour, inappropriate behaviour resulting in loss of respect in society.

Blips on the radar screen of Western emotion research (page 435) – little or no research as been conducted. Aware of non-Western emotions, but have not been researched by our methods.

Who barely gave poor Ulrich the time of day (page 435) the princess ignored or paid no attention to Ulrich.

Win your heart (page 435) – attracting a person, getting their attention or love through acts of bravery.

Squelched (page 436) – to suppress or silence completely, to stop quickly.

Ruminate (page 439) – think something over, meditate on an idea.

Blows up (page 439) – very angry, acting out, upset.

Mask negative feelings (page 440) – hide or cover up feelings.

Readily sound off at a professor (page 441) – confront, shout and yell, become argumentative with your professor.

Smooth over conflicts (page 441) – make right, correct, restore balance and harmony.

Pop-psych advice (page 442) – suggestions and information from popular trends in psychology.

Out of your system (page 442) – to let go, release emotions that you have held onto.

Their blood pressure shoots up (page 442) – making themselves excited, tense.

Sage old advice (page 442) – advice influenced by wisdom and experience.

Time-out (page 442) – a break from the other person, taking time to relax and calm down.

Benefit of the doubt (page 442) – willing to think the person did it by mistake, not intending to hurt them.

PRACTICE TEST 1 - Multiple Choice

1.   The elements of emotion include
      A.   the face and body.   B.   the mind.
      C.   the culture.   D.   all of the above.

2.   Ekman's studies found that
      A.   there are 15 universal facial expressions of emotion.
      B.   there are really no universal facial expressions of emotion because of the different meaning each culture attaches to the expressions.
      C.   there are seven basic facial expressions of emotion.
      D.   all facial expressions are learned.

3.   The reason that certain emotions are registered on the face is that facial expressions
      A.   help us communicate with others.
      B.   help teach young children which emotions are appropriate.
      C.   can cause problems for those who do not wish their emotions to be known.
      D.   are physiologically uncontrollable.

4.   The ability of our ancestors to tell at a glance the difference between a friendly stranger and a hostile one have survival value and serve a(n) _____ function.
      A.   primary   B.   evolutionary
      C.   biological   D.   cultural

5.   Ekman's cross-cultural studies on facial expressions suggest
      A.   certain facial expressions are universal in their emotional meaning.
      B.   people from different cultures can recognize the emotions in pictures of people who are entirely foreign to them.
      C.   that in the cultures studied most people recognized the emotional expressions portrayed by people in other cultures.
      D.   all of the above.

6.   Dr. Toner is smiling. Based on the research, what can you conclude about what she feels?
      A.   She definitely is feeling happy.
      B.   She is experiencing a primary emotion.
      C.   You cannot be sure what she is feeling since facial expressions can communicate states besides emotions.
      D.   She is experiencing something positive, although you cannot be sure what.

7. "When I clenched my jaw and knitted my brows, I suddenly felt angry." This reflects the
   A. two-factor theory.   B. prototype theory.
   C. facial-feedback hypothesis.   D. neuro-cultural theory.

8. Research with infants demonstrates that facial expressions help us
   A. express internal states.
   B. communicate with others.
   C. evoke a response from others.
   D. to achieve all of the above.

9. A limitation of the role of facial expressions in the experience of emotion includes
   A. the fact that facial expressions can have different meanings depending on the context.
   B. the fact that there is emotion without facial expression and facial expression without emotion.
   C. the fact that there is no way to tell what people are feeling from what they choose to display.
   D. all of the above.

10. The part of the brain that is able to process immediate perceptions of danger or threat is the
    A. left cerebral hemisphere.   B. frontal lobe.
    C. amygdala.   D. cerebellum.

11. With a more accurate appraisal of the situation, the _____ can override the response described in the previous question.
    A. limbic system   B. cortex
    C. temporal lobe   D. corpus callosum

12. Left prefrontal cortex activation is associated with tendencies to _____, while right prefrontal cortex activation is associated with tendencies to _____ .
    A. withdraw; approach   B. approach; withdraw
    C. withdraw; withdraw   D. approach; approach

13. Which of the following is one of the hormones that provide the energy of an emotion?
    A. epinephrine   B. dopamine
    C. insulin   D. serotonin

14. One function of arousal appears to be that it
    A. prepares the body to cope with danger or threat.
    B. exhausts and calms the body.
    C. responds to all emotional states with the same pattern.
    D. makes one feel nauseated and seek protection.

15. Which is (are) involved in the physiological experience of emotion?
    A. amygdala
    B. prefrontal cortex
    C. autonomic nervous system
    D. all of the above

16. The longer Dr. Toner smiles, the more her mood improves. What best accounts for this?
    A. two-factor theory
    B. neuro-cultural theory
    C. theory of primary emotions
    D. facial-feedback hypothesis

17. You feel a tap on your shoulder outside the residence hall at night. What brain structure helps you to evaluate whether this is a dangerous situation?
    A. limbic system
    B. cortex
    C. amygdala
    D. all of the above

18. My heart is beating, I'm hyperventilating, and my pupils are dilated. Which of the following is involved in this response?
    A. epinephrine
    B. adrenal glands
    C. norepinephrine
    D. all of the above

19. The Singer and Schacter two-factor theory suggests that both
    A. facial features and the limbic system are necessary to experience emotion.
    B. physiological arousal and cognitive interpretation are involved in emotion.
    C. primary and secondary emotions are necessary to experience emotion.
    D. display rules and emotion work are involved in emotional experiencing.

20. According to the Singer and Schacter two-factor theory of emotion, if you are physiologically aroused and don't know why,
    A. you will not feel a need to explain the changes in your body.
    B. your interpretations of events will not produce a true emotion.
    C. you will try to label your feeling, using interpretation of events around you.
    D. you will become irritable and angry.

21. In a series of experiments, students reported occasions in which they had succeeded or failed on an exam. Researchers found that the students' emotions were most closely associated with
    A. whether they had passed or failed the exam.
    B. their explanations for their success or failure.
    C. other peoples' perceptions of their performance.
    D. past experiences with success or failure.

22. A study of Olympic athletes found that sometimes the third-place winners were happier than the second-place winners. Their emotional response depended on their
   A. ability to rationalize.   B. desire to win.
   C. interpretations of their award.   D. country of origin.

23. Many researchers argue against the use of polygraphs because
   A. they break often and it is not always easy to get an accurate reading.
   B. no physiological patterns of responses are specific to lying.
   C. they often let the guilty go free.
   D. of the corruption associated with their use.

24. What have studies shown about whether people can learn about the effects of their thinking on their emotions?
   A. People have shown little success at being able to change their thinking.
   B. There is little evidence that changing thinking affects emotions.
   C. People can learn how their thinking affects their emotions and change their thinking accordingly.
   D. People can learn how their thinking affects their emotions, but people's emotions are very irrational and do not respond to reason.

25. Primary emotions
   A. indicate that in all cultures certain behaviours are considered acceptable.
   B. include emotions that are morally superior.
   C. are thought to be experienced universally.
   D. incorporate all of the above.

26. Which of the following represents the position of those who disagree with the search for primary emotions?
   A. There is little agreement in what most people think of as primary.
   B. There is a cultural influence on every aspect of emotional experience.
   C. Some emotions may be "basic" in some cultures and not in others.
   D. All of the above.

27. Primary emotions are _____, whereas secondary emotions are _____.
   A. universal; culture-specific   B. desirable; undesirable
   C. culture specific; subculture-specific   D. agreed upon; controversial

28. Culture can affect
   A. what people feel emotional about.
   B. how particular emotions might be expressed.
   C. the meaning of expressions of emotion.
   D. all of the above.

29. Which of the following statements is true?
    A. Women feel emotions more often and more intensely than men.
    B. Men are more likely than women to reveal negative emotions, such as sadness and fear.
    C. Men and women are fairly similar in how often they experience normal, everyday emotions.
    D. Powerful people are more sensitive to subordinates' nonverbal signals than vice versa.

30. Where are gender differences in emotion found?
    A. There are some physiological differences in response to conflict.
    B. There are differences in the perceptions and expectations that generate certain emotions.
    C. There are different display rules.
    D. All of the above.

31. Which of the following statements about the brain and emotion is FALSE?
    A. Damage to the amygdala can result in exaggerated fear responses.
    B. Parts of the right prefrontal cortex are involved with withdrawal or escape.
    C. Parts of the left prefrontal cortex are involved with approaching others.
    D. Parts of the prefrontal cortex are involved in the regulation of emotion.

PRACTICE TEST 2 - Short Answer

1. The most obvious place to look for emotion is on the _____, where the expression of emotion can be most visible.

2. Ekman's research found seven _____ facial expressions.

3. The _____ hypothesis would predict that the longer you smiled, the happier you would begin to feel.

4. The _____, a small structure in the limbic system, appears to be responsible for evaluating sensory information and quickly determining its emotional importance. The _____ subsequently provides a more accurate appraisal of incoming information.

5. When you are in a situation requiring the body to respond, the _____ nervous system sends out two hormones, _____ and _____, that produce a state of arousal.

6. Each emotion may be associated with somewhat different _____ of autonomic activity that produces differences in the way we experience emotions.

7. Schachter and Singer's two-factor theory of emotion proposed that emotion depends on _____ arousal and the _____ interpretation of such arousal.

8. _____, or how we explain events or behaviours, affect our emotional responses.

9. Cognitive _____ refer to the meanings that people attribute to events, including their thoughts, perceptions, interpretations, and explanations.

10. An understanding of the reciprocal interaction between thoughts and feelings helps us to see that just as _____ affect emotions, so do _____ affect cognitions.

11. Most psychologists believe that it is possible to identify a number of _____ emotions that seem to be universal and _____ emotions that are more culture-specific.

12. Some evidence for the existence of primary emotions comes from the fact that most languages have emotion _____, or agreed upon core examples of the concept emotion.

13. Whatever the emotion, every society has _____ , governing how and when emotions may be expressed.

14. Acting out an emotion we don't really feel is called emotion _____.

15. Emotions are expressed by body language, the countless _____ signals of body movement, posture, gesture, and gaze.

16. Although some basic signals of body language seem to be universal, most aspects of body language are specific to particular languages and _____.

17. If we define being "more emotional" in terms of physiological reactivity to _____, then men are more emotional than women. One possible explanation for this is that the male's autonomic nervous system is, on the average, more _____ than the female's.

18. From a cognitive standpoint, men and women often differ in their _____ of the same event.

19. Sensitivity to other people's emotional states depends on the sex of the sender and receiver, how well the two people know each other, and who has the _____.

20. The one gender difference that undoubtedly contributes most to the stereotype that women are "more emotional" than men is women's greater willingness to _____ their feelings, nonverbally and verbally.

21. The seven universal facial expressions identified by Ekman are _____
_____.

22. People with damage to the _____ often lose their capacity for joy.

23. Someone who is unable to identify fear in other people might have damage to the part of the brain known as the _____.

PRACTICE TEST 3 - Essay

1.   A.   While enacting a role, performers sometimes report being lost in the feelings they are depicting. How might this be explained by the facial-feedback hypothesis?

     B.   Successful negotiators and gamblers are often described as having poker faces. What does such a phenomenon indicate about the outward expression of emotion?

     C.   Emotion work is the acting out of emotions the person does not truly feel. From the standpoint of facial expression and body language, how might this concept be defined?

     D.   Body language is specific to cultures and is not good as a universal indicator of emotions. However, when facial expression is the clue, the ability to identify emotions universally rises dramatically. How might Charles Darwin explain this?

2.   A.   A nurse looks in on a patient shortly before surgery. The patient's heart rate and blood pressure are elevated, breathing is rapid, the pupils are dilated, and the patient appears flushed. The nurse concludes that the patient is fearfully anticipating the surgery. What physiological mechanism produces the pattern observed by the nurse?

     B.   The nurse tries to reassure the patient, but he laughs and denies feeling nervous. In fact, the patient is not very co-operative and the nurse begins to feel irritated but continues to attempt to be comforting and pleasant. Explain the patient's behaviour and the nurse's behaviour in terms of emotion work and display rules.

3.   Larry, Curly, and Moe all got a grade of 75 on a test, yet they each had different reactions to the grade. Larry felt disappointed and depressed. Curly felt relieved that he passed, though he didn't feel particularly happy or sad about the grade. Moe felt extremely happy. Using information about the influence of interpretations on feelings, identify expectations, surrounding events, and interpretations of each student's emotional responses.

4.   Mary was given a surprise party for her 40th birthday. As each gift was being opened, Mary felt the following: shocked, then touched, by the pet caterpillar from her young daughter; delighted at the earrings from her sister; warmly amused at the cane, laxatives, and contributions for a facelift that came from neighbours; insulted and angry over the "girdle for burgeoning hips" from her cousin; and irritated by the insensitivity of her husband's gift of a vacuum cleaner. Regardless of her true feelings, Mary warmly expressed gratitude and appreciation after each gift, and no one except her younger sister sensed Mary's true feelings. When the guests departed, Mary's husband began to assemble the vacuum cleaner. One look at Mary's face made it clear that she was angry. After prodding, Mary angrily revealed that her own husband might have been more thoughtful. To her surprise, another package was produced. It contained 40 beautifully arranged exotic flowers from all over the world. Mary's husband had sent out for the flowers and arranged them himself, but confessed that he was too embarrassed to give

this gift in front of the guests. Mary confessed that she really wanted to punch her cousin. The next day Mary's younger sister called and was virtually perfect in guessing Mary's true feeling about each gift.

A.   Why did Mary find it important to express gratitude for each gift?
B.   What type of performance is illustrated when Mary feigns gratitude for gifts that disturb her?
C.   Mary's husband easily sees anger on her face. Why isn't this surprising?
D.   Mary privately displays aggressive feelings toward her cousin. Her husband privately displays sensitivity and tenderness. What cultural mechanisms contribute to such behaviour?
E.   What advantages does Mary's younger sister have over the other guests when reading Mary's feelings?
F.   Examine Mary's reactions to each gift and think about why she felt as she did. Which reactions tend to result from a process of interpretation that involves culturally determined meanings?

CHAPTER TWELVE

Motivation

LEARNING OBJECTIVES

1. Define motivation and distinguish between drives based on physiological needs and those that are psychological and social in nature.

2. Distinguish between intrinsic and extrinsic motivation.

3. Explain set-point theory and other genetic influences on weight.

4. Summarize the statistics on obesity in the Western world generally and more specifically in Canada.

5. Describe environmental, cultural and gender influences on obesity.

6. Describe the research on eating disorders and distinguish between anorexia nervosa and bulimia.

7. Distinguish between passionate and companionate love.

8. Describe the biological similarities between infant-mother love and adult romantic love.

9. Outline two key predictors of whom we love.

10. Describe the attachment theory of love.

11. Discuss the impact of social and economic influences on gender differences in love.

12. Summarize the findings from biological research on sexual responses and behaviour.

13. List and explain the cognitive, interpersonal, and cultural factors that influence the sexual motives and behaviours of men and women.

14. Discuss the motivational factors involved in rape and coercive sexual behaviour.

15. Describe the various explanations advanced to explain sexual orientation. Discuss the limitations of these hypotheses.

16. Define the need for achievement.

17. Describe the TAT and how it is used to measure achievement motivation.

18. Describe the research on achievement and goal setting.

19. Distinguish between approach goals and avoidance goals.

20. Describe the influence of working conditions on productivity and achievement.

25. List and discuss three types of motivational conflicts.

26. Summarize Maslow's hierarchy of needs and discuss whether motives can be ranked.

27. Describe seven suggestions for goal setting and achievement.

BRIEF CHAPTER SUMMARY

Chapter 12 describes four categories of motives: motives to eat, motives to love, motives for sex, and motives to achieve. Biological and cultural explanations for eating are discussed as are the two types of eating disorders (anorexia nervosa and bulimia). Two approaches to studying love are described: passionate versus companionate love, and attachment theory. Biological, psychological, and cultural influences on the sexual motive are discussed. Kinsey introduces the scientific study of sex, which was continued by Masters and Johnson. Coercive sex, or rape, is considered an act of dominance or aggression rather than an act motivated by sexual desire. Different theories that attempt to explain sexual orientation are reviewed. These theories lead to the conclusion that sexual orientation is a result of the interaction of biology, culture, learning, and circumstances. The motive to achieve is influenced by internal factors, such as one's expectations, values, and needs for achievement, and by external factors, such as working conditions. Three types of motivational conflicts are discussed, and Maslow's hierarchy of needs is described.

PREVIEW OUTLINE

Before you read the chapter, review the preview outline for each section of the text. After you have read the chapter, close this book and try to <u>re-create</u> the outlines on a blank piece of paper.

I. **THE HUNGRY ANIMAL: MOTIVES TO EAT**
   A. **The genetics of weight**
      1. We no longer think that being overweight is related only to emotional problems or overeating; biology plays a role.
      2. Set point - biological mechanism that keeps a body at a genetically influenced set point; genetically programmed basal metabolism rate interacts with fat cells and hormones to keep people at their set point
      3. The protein leptin plays a role in human obesity and the set point, but that role is complicated.
   B. **Culture, gender and weight**
      1. Obesity has increased greatly due to changes in diet and exercise, such as supersized portions and varied food choices.
      2. Cultures' standards for ideal beauty influence eating and activity

C.   The body as battleground:Eating Disorders
1.   Many women in cultures that value thinness become obsessed with weight and continual dieting; some develop eating disorders
    a.   Bulimia involves binge eating and purges
    b.   Anorexia nervosa involves severely reduced eating and distorted body image
    c.   Ten times more common in women, begins in late adolescence
2.   Genes interact with cultural rules, psychological needs, and personal habits to influence weight

The Hungry Animal: Motives to Eat

II. THE SOCIAL ANIMAL: MOTIVES TO LOVE

A.   **The biology of love**

    1.   Passionate (romantic) versus companionate (affectionate) love

    2.   Origins of passionate love start in infancy, with baby's attachment to mother

    3.   Role of endorphins in attachment

B.   **The psychology of love**

    1.   Basic predictors of love include proximity and similarity

    2.   Attachment theory of love (Shaver and Hazan)

        a.   Adult attachment styles originate in infant-parent relationship; people develop "working models" of relationships

        b.   Three styles are secure, avoidant, and anxious

    3.   Ingredients of love: a mixture of passion, intimacy, commitment

C.   **Gender, culture, and love**

    1.   No evidence that one sex is more loving than the other

    2.   Men and women tend to express love differently

The Social Animal: Motives to Love

III. THE EROTIC ANIMAL: MOTIVES FOR SEX
    A.   **The biology of desire**
        1.   The hormone testosterone promotes sexual desire in both sexes, but it doesn't "cause" sexual behaviour in a direct way
        2.   First scientific sex research by Kinsey, furthered by Masters and Johnson, emphasized the similarities in arousal and orgasm by men and women.
        3.   Researchers disagree about whether men and women have different biologically based "sex drives"
    B.   **The psychology of desire**
        1.   Values, expectations, fantasies, and beliefs affect sexual responsiveness
        2.   Motives for sex - enhancement, intimacy, coping, self-affirmation, partner approval, and peer approval
        3.   Consenting to unwanted sex, sexual coercion and rape
            a.Anxiously attached more likely to consent to unwanted sex
            b. Motives for rape vary - primarily an act of aggression

    C.   **The culture of desire**
        1.   Sexual scripts - culture's rules for proper sexual behaviour; they are based on gender roles, which result in different scripts. Scripts can be powerful determinants of behaviour.

D. Gender, culture and sex

        1.   To explain origin of sexual scripts, evolutionary psychologists look to hardwired biological sex differences that resulted from natural selection; cultural psychologists look to gender roles, economic, and social arrangements
    2.Sex ratios influence sexual norms and practices
    E.   **Biology and sexual orientation**
        1.   Biological explanations for sexual orientation are inconclusive; psychological theories have not been supported
        2.   Sexual orientation research can have political goals

The Erotic Animal: Motives for Sex

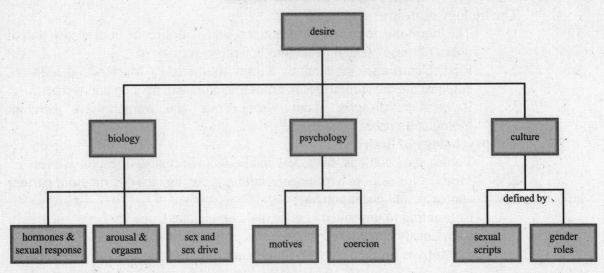

IV.   THE COMPETENT ANIMAL: MOTIVES TO ACHIEVE
A.   The effects of motivation on work
1.   Level of need for achievement can be measured by using Thematic Apperception Test (TAT)
2.   Goals are likely to improve performance when the goal is specific, challenging but achievable, and is defined as getting what you want (approach goals) versus avoiding what you don't want (avoidance goals)
4.

B.   The effects of work on motivation
1.   Working conditions that influence work motivation and satisfaction - meaningfulness, ability to control aspects of work, varied tasks, clear and consistent rules, supportive relationships, useful feedback, opportunities for growth and development
2.   Motivation is not increased by high pay but by how and when money is paid - incentive pay in particular
3.   Motivation lower if lack of opportunity to advance exists

The Competent Animal: Motives to Achieve

V. MOTIVES, VALUES, AND WELL-BEING
A. Kinds of motivational conflicts
1. Approach–approach - equal attraction to two or more goals
2. Avoidance–avoidance - when you dislike two alternatives
3. Approach–avoidance - one activity has a positive and negative aspect
B. Can motives be ranked?
i. Maslow's pyramid
    a. Survival needs at the bottom, self-actualization needs at the top; lower need must be met before higher needs can be addressed
    b. Popular theory but little empirical support
ii. More recent ranking of needs based on study of American and South Korean university students; top needs were autonomy, competence, relatedness, and self-esteem

Motives, Values, and Well-being

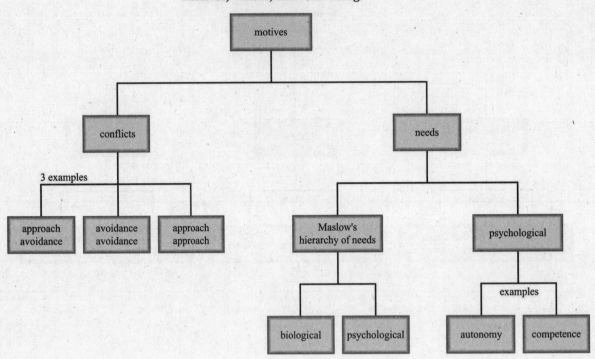

IDIOMS AND SLANGS

Loading up on rich desserts (page 448) – taking more than what you need, excessive amounts of desserts.

Notions (page 453) –standards of your culture.

Pump iron compulsively (page 455) – to lift weights excessively. For example, going to the gym everyday.

Clingy (page 458) – to be emotionally attached, stay near or close to their partner.

Put up with their insecurities (page 459) – endure, willing to accept their insecurities.

Keep in mind (page 459) – remember the information.

Pop up (page 461) – appear, arrive, to appear suddenly.

Relationship was not going anywhere (page 461) – the relationship was not leading to commitment or marriage.

Sweeping away the cobwebs of superstition (page 462) – removing past beliefs or ideas that prevented discovery of new knowledge.

Sex drive (page 464) – a physiological need or desire for sexual activity.

Scoring (page 467) – having casual sex to show their friends that they are masculine.

Gotten through (page 468) – sex done for reproduction or the pleasure of others, not enjoyed by the person.

Give in (page 486) – allows sex to happen after being asked.

Make a move (page 486) – approach someone for casual sex when he or she is really not interested in the person.

Smothering mother (page 462) – over-protective, very involved in her son's life.

Straight (page 471) – people who have sex with people of the opposite sex; heterosexual, male-female couples.

You want to eat your cake and have it, too (page 482) – want to do two things at the same time that are impossible. For example, wanting to fly and stay on the ground at the same time.

PRACTICE TEST 1 - Multiple Choice

1. A process within a person or animal that causes that organism to move toward a goal or away from an unpleasant situation is called
   - A. energy.
   - B. incentive.
   - C. motivation.
   - D. the need for achievement.

2. The desire to do something for its own sake and the pleasure it brings is known as
   - A. a primary goal.
   - B. intrinsic motivation.
   - C. a secondary goal.
   - D. extrinsic motivation.

3. One criticism of the drive theory approach to motivation is that
   - A. biological drives have surprisingly little influence on behaviour.
   - B. they explain social motives better than biological motives.
   - C. they cannot account for the complexity of human motivation.
   - D. they don't explain the motives of sex and hunger very well.

4. Set-point theory suggests that
   - A. a genetically influenced weight range is maintained by a homeostatic mechanism that regulates food intake, fat reserves, and metabolism.
   - B. in almost all cases, being overweight is caused by overeating.
   - C. obesity is an indicator of emotional disturbance.
   - D. weight is not influenced by genes but by learned behaviours.

5. Set point is to _____ as thermostat is to _____.
   - A. basal metabolic rate; furnace
   - B. fat cells; temperature
   - C. weight; furnace
   - D. genes; temperature

6. _____ plays a crucial role in the attachment- caregiving system.
   - A. testosterone
   - B. serotonin
   - C. dopamine
   - D. oxytocin

7. James and Marshall found that non familial child molesters were_____ times more likely to report avoidant relationships than a community sample.
   - A. two
   - B. three
   - C. five
   - D. four

8. Adult love styles originate in a person's first and most important "love relationship," the infant-parent attachment. Which approach to love does this describe?
   - A. affiliation theory
   - B. companionate theory
   - C. attachment theory of love
   - D. narrative theory of love

9. Kinsey made which of the following observations about biological differences in sexual behaviour between men and women?
    A. Males and females are alike in their basic anatomy and physiology.
    B. Males and females differ in frequency of masturbation and orgasm.
    C. Females have a lesser "sexual capacity."
    D. All of the above.

10. Which of the following was a finding of Masters and Johnson?
    A. Male and female arousal and orgasms are remarkably similar.
    B. Orgasms are physiologically the same, regardless of the source of stimulation.
    C. Women's capacity for sexual response infinitely surpasses that of men.
    D. All of the above.

11. Which of the following is true about gender differences in motives for sex?
    A. Motives for sex are generally quite similar.
    B. People rarely have sex when they don't want to.
    C. Women engage in sex when they don't want to but men do not.
    D. None of the above.

12. Which characteristics were found more often in sexually aggressive males?
    A. a history of violence and psychological problems
    B. poor communication and feelings of insecurity
    C. hostile attitudes and sexual promiscuity
    D. a history of being abused and family problems

13. According to the text, motivation for rape includes which of the following?
    A. sexual outlet   B. power and anger at women
    C. crossed signals   D. psychological disturbance

14. In a large-scale sex survey, one-fourth of the women said they had been forced to do something sexually that they did not want to do, but only about 3 percent of the men said that they ever had forced a woman into a sexual act. How might this be explained?
    A. Women are in denial about their sexual behaviour.
    B. What many women experience as coercion is not seen as such by many men.
    C. Women tend to over-exaggerate these experiences.
    D. Women say "no," but they mean "yes."

15. Kissing, sexual arousal, and orgasms are
    A. biologically based behaviours.   B. natural behaviours.
    C. highly influenced by culture and learning. D. normal behaviours.

16. The part of the brain that is involved in the regulation of appetite is the
    A. amygdala.   B. hippocampus.
    C. prefrontal cortex.   D. hypothalamus.

17. Two students from different parts of the world met at university in Ontario. They fell in love and are beginning a sexual relationship. Because of their different cultural backgrounds, they
    A. would agree that kissing is enjoyable.
    B. would both enjoy kissing, but might disagree about whether it is appropriate.
    C. might disagree about whether kissing is erotic or deviant.
    D. would agree that they should not kiss until they have dated for a long time.

18. The fact that boys are motivated to impress other males with their sexual experiences and girls are taught not to indulge in sexual pleasure demonstrates the effects of
    A. hormones.   B. sexual scripts.
    C. game playing.   D. sexual orientation.

19. Which of the following best describes current thinking about the origins of sexual orientation?
    A. Most research supports a genetic basis.
    B. Dominant mothers and absent/passive fathers contribute to male homosexuality.
    C. Brain differences between heterosexuals and homosexuals explain sexual orientation.
    D. Sexual identity and behaviour involve an interaction of biology, culture, and experiences.

20. Which of the following explanations for homosexuality has been supported by research?
    A. bad mothering, absent fathering   B. parental role models
    C. homosexuals have a mental disorder   D. none of the above

21. Which of the following represents an argument against biological explanations of sexual orientation?
    A. The flexible sexual history of most lesbians.
    B. Most gay men and lesbians do not have a close gay relative.
    C. Studies on brain differences have not been reliable or replicated.
    D. All of the above.

22. Which of the following motivations influences people's work habits?
    A. their expectation and values   B. how competent they feel
    C. the type of goals they have   D. all of the above

23. Bonuses that are given upon completion of a goal rather than automatically are known as:
   A.   incentive pay   B.   bonus pay
   C.   mastery pay   D. alternate compensation

24. The person who is more likely to work hard is
   A.   someone who expects to succeed.   B.   someone with a high salary.
   C.   someone who has performance goals.   D.   none of the above.

25. You want to have Chinese food for dinner, but you also have a craving for Italian food.
   This represents a(n)
   A.   approach–approach conflict.   B.   avoidance–avoidance conflict.
   C.   approach–avoidance conflict.   D.   no lose situation.

26. Going to the dentist or having one's teeth fall out is an example of a(n) _____ conflict;
   wanting to go out with Dan while continuing to date Bill is an example of a(n) _____
   conflict; wanting to travel this summer but knowing that you would miss the summer
   with your friends is an example of a(n) _____ conflict.
   A.   avoidance–avoidance; approach–approach; approach–avoidance
   B.   approach–avoidance; approach–approach; avoidance–avoidance
   C.   approach–approach; avoidance–avoidance; approach–avoidance
   D.   approach–avoidance; approach–approach; approach–approach

27. Research on Maslow's hierarchy of needs
   A.   has supported the idea that motives are met in a hierarchy.
   B.   has not supported this theory.
   C.   has found that it is true that lower needs must be met first but that once these
        needs are met, all people do not necessarily go on to meet the higher needs.
   D.   has found that very few people go on to meet the higher needs.

28. The eating disorder of bulimia is characterized by
   A.   episodes of bingeing followed by purging.
   B.   a severely distorted body image.
   C.   restricted eating and emaciation.
   D.   extreme obesity.

29. Extremely obese individuals who lack the protein _____ for genetic reasons
   benefit from injections of it.
   A.   leptin   B.   endorphins
   C.   androgen   D.   melatonin

30. Adult love styles originate in a person's first and most important "love relationship," the infant-parent bond. Which approach to love does this describe?
    A. affiliation theory
    B. companionate theory
    C. attachment theory of love
    D. narrative theory of love

31. Most people agree that the ingredients of love include a mixture of
    A. friendship, passion, and attachment.
    B. passion, intimacy, and commitment.
    C. commitment, sacrifice, and trust.
    D. ambivalence, passion, and game-playing.

32. Risky sexual behaviour, such as not using birth control or having many partners, is associated with
    A. extrinsic motives, such as intimacy or enhancement.
    B. intrinsic motives, such as intimacy or enhancement.
    C. extrinsic motives, such as gaining partner or peer approval.
    D. intrinsic motives, such as gaining partner or peer approval.

PRACTICE TEST 2 - Short Answer

1. Motivation refers to any process that causes a person or animal to move _____ a goal or _____ from an unpleasant situation.

2. _____ refer to states of tension resulting from the deprivation of physical needs, such as those for food and water.

3. One approach to weight holds that a biological mechanism keeps a person's body weight at a genetically influenced _____, which is the weight you stay at when you are not consciously trying to gain or lose.

4. Though there is considerable evidence that genes contribute to size and weight differences, it is also true that environmental influences such as _____and _____also play an important role.

5. In order to improve motivation, it is better to focus on_____ goals.

6. Most agree that love consists of the three ingredients, including intimacy, _____, and _____.

7. Companionate love is affection and _____.

8. _____ theory of love says that the kind of relationships that people have as adults is strongly related to their reports of how their parents treated them.

9. Men and women do differ, on average, in how they _____ love.

10. Gender differences in ways of expressing love and intimacy do not just pop up from nowhere; they reflect social, _____, and cultural forces.

11. The hormone _____ seems to promote sexual desire in both sexes, though it does not "cause" sexual behaviour, or any other behaviour, in a simple, direct way.

12. Kinsey was the first to introduce the idea that men and women are sexually _____, though he did think that women had lesser sexual capacity.

13. A study indicated that there were six factors underlying the many reasons that people give for having sex. The reasons are enhancement, intimacy, coping, self-affirmation, _____ , and _____.

14. Men who coerce women into having sex have _____ that justify their behaviour.

15. The argument that rape is primarily an act of _____ and aggression is supported by the widespread evidence of soldiers who rape captive women during war, and then often kill them.

16. A person following a gender role needs a _____ script that teaches men and women how to behave in sexual matters.

17. The most reasonable conclusion about sexual identity and behaviour is that they involve an interaction of biology, _____, and experience.

18. Those in the field of _____ psychology study work motivation in the laboratory and in organizations, where they study the conditions that influence productivity and satisfaction.

19. The Thematic Apperception Test (TAT) is used to measure the strength of need for _____ .

20. Sometimes minority groups and women lack the _____ to achieve.

21. One criticism of attachment theory is that the individual styles are not a result of how individuals are treated by their mother, but by _____ .

22. Two basic factors that heavily influence who you will fall in love with are _____ and _____ .

23. The three major attachment styles are _____, _____, and _____ .

24. Two types of love proposed are companionate love and _____ .

PRACTICE TEST 3 - Essay

1. Apply the lessons of motivational research to your own life, using the suggestions outlined in "Taking Psychology With You".

2. You are at a party and there is a debate about what "causes" homosexuality. David says it is a choice that people freely make. Amy says that it is clearly biological. Describe the information that supports and refutes each of their positions. Also discuss the political implications of each point of view.

3. Identify the type of conflict associated with each example below.
   A. Hank promised the counsellor that his third switch between chemistry and physics would be the last. He dreaded both courses but had to take one to fulfill requirements.
   B. When the networks put her favourite shows on at the same time, Lucy bought a VCR so she could watch one program and record the other for later viewing.
   C. Jason, an avid fisherman, just met new neighbours who made his day. The neighbours agreed to clean his fish and split the catch. Jason loved catching the fish, but couldn't do the cleaning because it made him nauseous.

4. What are some criticisms of Maslow's hierarchy of needs?

CHAPTER THIRTEEN

Theories of Personality

LEARNING OBJECTIVES

1. Define personality.

2. Summarize the competing theories that have been considered over the 20th century that have attempted to explain personality. Outline the position offered by the text.

3. Explain the basic principles of Freud's psychoanalytic approach to the study of personality and list the emphases shared by modern psychodynamic theories.

4. Describe the structure of the personality, according to Freud.

5. Describe Freudian defence mechanisms.

6. Describe the five psychosexual stages of personality development identified by Freud.

7. Discuss the challenges to psychoanalytic theory made by Horney, Jung, and the object-relations school.

8. Review the strengths and weaknesses of Freudian theory specifically and psychodynamic theories in general.

9. Describe characteristics of popular personality tests and compare them to standardized personality inventories.

10. Define traits. Distinguish between central and secondary traits.

11. Summarize the Big Five theory of personality, including cross-cultural research findings.

12. Review the research evidence on animals and personality.

13. Discuss the issue of heritability of personality, temperament, and traits including cautionary considerations.

14. Describe the social-cognitive concept of reciprocal determinism.

15. Review the evidence regarding parental and peer influence on personality development.

16. Discuss how culture influences how we define our selves, noting the limitations of cultural explanations.

17. Distinguish between individualistic and collectivist cultures.

18. Discuss how culture influences aggression and altruism.

19. Define culture of honour.

20. Summarize the principles of humanistic psychology proposed by Maslow, Rogers, and May.

21. How do the stories we tell define who we are?

22. Review the strengths and weaknesses of humanistic psychology.

23. Define the Barnum effect and preventative measures to avoid it.

BRIEF CHAPTER SUMMARY

Chapter 13 defines personality and reviews the major theoretical approaches that have been advanced to explain its development. The psychodynamic approach focuses on the role of unconscious processes and the development of the id, ego, and superego. Freud originally developed this approach, and then other theorists modified his work. The biological approach focuses on the heritability of traits and the idea that there is a genetic basis for certain temperaments. The social-cognitive approach emphasizes the reciprocal interactions between specific situations and a person's cognitions and behaviours. Cognitions and behaviour are also influenced by culture. The humanist and existential approaches reject the negative and deterministic views of the psychoanalytic and behavioural approaches. Instead, they focus on the positive aspects of humanity and the idea that humans have free will to shape their own destinies.

PREVIEW OUTLINE

Before you read the chapter, review the preview outline for each section of the text. After you have read the chapter, close this book and try to <u>re-create</u> the outlines on a blank piece of paper.

  Personality is a distinctive pattern of behaviour, thoughts, motives, and emotions that characterizes an individual over time

I. PSYCHODYNAMIC INFLUENCES ON PERSONALITY

    A.   **Psychodynamic theories** emphasize unconscious, intrapsychic dynamics, and the importance of early childhood experiences

    B.   **Freud and psychoanalysis**

        1.   The structure of personality - id (source of sexual energy and aggressive instinct), ego (source of reason), superego (source of conscience)

        2.   Defence mechanisms - reduce anxiety from conflict between id and society

        3.   The development of personality occurs in five psychosexual stages; if demands of a stage are too great, a child may get fixated or stuck at a stage:

            a.   The oral stage - babies take the world in through their mouths

            b.   The anal stage - may become over-controlled (anal retentive) or under-controlled (anal expulsive)

c. The Oedipal stage - desire for opposite-sex parent, then identification with the same-sex parent

d. The latency stage - supposedly nonsexual stage

e. The genital stage - beginning of mature adult sexuality

4. Psychologists disagree about the value of Freud's theory

C. **Other Psychodynamic Approaches**

1. Karen Horney - challenged the notion of penis envy and female inferiority

2. Jungian theory - biggest difference was the nature of the unconscious

a. Collective unconscious contains the universal memory and history

b. Concerned with archetypes - themes that appear in myths

3. The object-relations school - emphasizes need for human relationships

a. Emphasis on children's need for mother, which in early years is only a representation of her

b. Males and females both identify first with mother, then boys must separate which can result in more rigid boundaries with others

D. **Evaluating psychodynamic theories**

1. Principle of falsifiability violated - can't confirm or disprove ideas

2. Theories based on the patients' fallible memories and retrospective accounts, which creates an illusion of causality between events

3. In response to criticisms, some are using empirical methods and research

II. THE MODERN STUDY OF PERSONALITY

A. **Personality tests**

1. Extremely popular but not useful from an empirical point of view

2. Objective tests or inventories - standardized questionnaires

B. **Identifying central traits**

1. Allport's trait theory - not all traits are equally important

a. Central traits - characteristic ways of behaving

b. Secondary traits - the more changeable aspects of personality

2. Cattell - studied traits using factor analysis; found 16 factors and developed the 16 Personality Factors (PF) Questionnaire

3. The "Big Five" traits - introversion versus extroversion, neuroticism, agreeableness, conscientiousness, openness to experience

a. Big Five have been replicated in many countries, but there are some cultural differences

b. Stable over a lifetime though some maturational changes exist

c. Four of the Big Five even apply to dogs

Modern Study of Personality

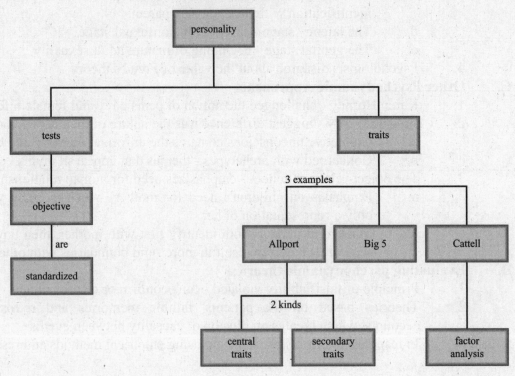

III. GENETIC INFLUENCES ON PERSONALITY
A. Heredity and temperament
1. Temperaments are physiological dispositions to respond to the environment in relatively stable ways that may later form the basis of personality traits
2. Kagan's study on reactivity - highly reactive infants are excitable and nervous, whereas nonreactive infants lie there, don't cry, and are happy

B. Heredity and traits
1. Heritability estimates based on studies of adopted children and identical twins reared together and apart; for many traits, heritability is around .50
2. Genetic predisposition does not imply genetic inevitability

Genetic Influence on Personality

IV. ENVIRONMENTAL INFLUENCES ON PERSONALITY
    A.   **Situations and circumstances**
         1.   How reinforcement history and cognitions influence both responses and situations and vice versa - reciprocal determinism
         2.   Helps explains why a person may behave differently in different situations
         3.
    B.   **The power of parents is weak**
         1.   The shared environment of the home has little influence on personality
         2.   Few parents use a consistent child-rearing style
         4.   Even with consistency, parental behaviour may not influence children
         5.   Parents can modify extreme traits and things other than personality
    C.   **The power of peers**
         1.   Once children are in school, peer influence becomes stronger than parental influence
         2.   Peer acceptance is often more important than parental approval

Environmental Influences on Personality

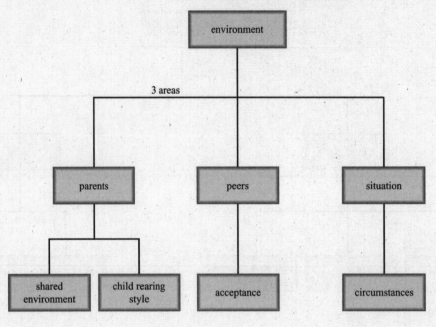

IV. CULTURAL INFLUENCES ON PERSONALITY
A. **Culture** - program of shared rules that govern the behaviour of people in a community or society
B. **Culture, values, and traits**
   1. Individualistic vs. collectivist cultures
   2. Influence of culture on perception of time and altruism
   3. Culture of honour can increase male aggression
C. **Evaluating Cultural Approaches**
   1. Difficult to describe cultural influences without stereotyping or exaggerating
   2. Key aspects of personality include the valued traits, sense of self versus community, and notions of the right way to behave.

Cultural Influences on Personality

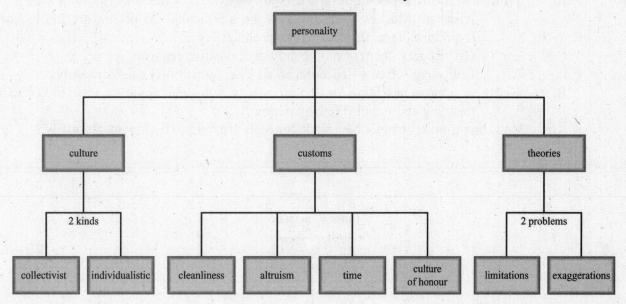

Psychodynamic Influences on Personality

VI. THE INNER EXPERIENCE
A. **Humanist approaches** focus on a person's own view of the world and free will
1. Abraham Maslow - the traits of the self-actualized person are the most important - meaning, challenge, productivity
2. Carl Rogers - benefit of unconditional positive regard
3. Rollo May - free will accompanied by responsibility causes anxiety

B. Narrative approaches focus on the story a person develops over time to create meaning about their life experience.

C. Many assumptions cannot be tested; concepts are hard to define operationally

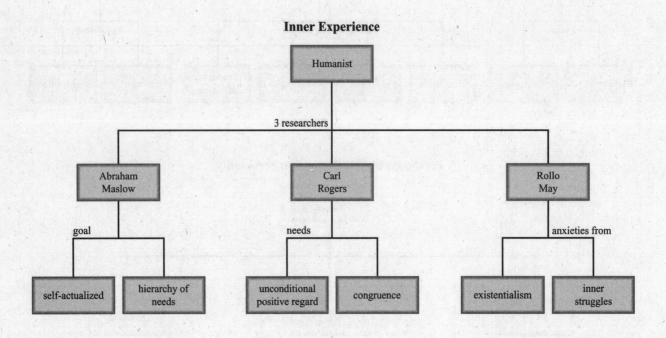

IDIOMS AND SLANGS

Robust factors (page 500) – these were the five most reliable factors of personality research.

Eager to be in the limelight versus inclined to stay in the shadows (page 500) – this is one way to differentiate extr0verted people (likes fame and being important) versus introverted (not being in the public).

Ready to see the sour side of life and none of its sweetness (page 500) – people who are neurotic usually worry, even when there is nothing to worry about. They fail to see the good things in life.

They came out of the womb that way (page 503) – this is another way of saying inborn or innate.

More set with time (page 506) – as we get older, we find it hard to get used to change. We usually like things done a certain way.

Growing into a tidal wave that threatens to engulf (page 507) – the idea that personality is inherited or has genetic influences is becoming very popular and widespread.

Began to crumble under the weight (page 509) – the idea that personality is a major factor of parenting style is being argued because of some important evidence.

Clash (page 511) – refers to situations where the two people or sides do not agree on an idea.

Moulding facets of our personalities (page 512) – the textbook is talking about the strong influences of our peers. We tend to change our personalities with peer pressures.

Pay off (page 508) – this means that there will be some reward or a positive outcome for this behaviour.

Appalling slob (page 514) – this is a negative name for someone who is dirty or does not clean themselves.

I was stunned (page 518) – this is said when someone can't believe a situation is occurring.

Break away from his mother (page 496) – for boys to develop into a masculine boy, he must leave home and not be too close with his mother. She may influence him negatively.

House rules (page 520) – these are rules that are set out by your parents that you may have to follow while you are living in their house.

PRACTICE TEST 1 - Multiple Choice

1. A distinctive and stable pattern of behaviour, thoughts, motives, and emotions that characterizes an individual over time is the definition of
    A. traits.
    B. temperament.
    C. personality.
    D. locus of control.

2. Allport's trait theory suggests there are
    A. central and secondary traits.
    B. surface and source traits.
    C. 16 factors.
    D. the "Big Five" traits.

3. The "Big Five" refers to
    A. the five main trait theories.
    B. five types of traits, including cardinal, central, secondary, surface, and source.
    C. robust factors that are thought to be able to describe personality.
    D. five stages of personality development.

4. William is a complainer and a defeatist. He always sees the negative side of life. This demonstrates which of the following of the "Big Five" traits?
    A. introversion
    B. depressiveness
    C. neuroticism
    D. disagreeableness

5. As a child, Pam was anxious and negative. She complained frequently about health problems even though she was not sick. As an adult, Pam will probably
    A. outgrow these characteristics.
    B. be equally likely to keep these characteristics or to change.
    C. continue to have the same characteristics.
    D. become even more negative and disturbed.

6. A study investigating personality in dogs found that dog owners, their friends, and neutral observers agreed strongly on the dogs' personalities for all of the following traits EXCEPT
    A. neuroticism.
    B. agreeableness.
    C. extroversion.
    D. conscientiousness.

7. Studies of twins have found that heritability for most traits is around .50. This means that
    A. if one twin has a trait, there is a 50-percent chance the other twin will have the same trait.
    B. most people have a 50-percent chance of having a given trait.
    C. within a group about 50 percent of the variance in a trait is attributable to genes.
    D. the differences between two groups of people can be explained.

8. Based on studies of twins, which of the following environmental factors would be expected to have the greatest influence on the personality of two siblings?
   A. having the same parents
   B. going to the same schools
   C. having different extracurricular activities
   D. having the same religious training

9. A study of Finnish twins, ages 18 to 59, found that the heritability of extroversion decreased from the late teens to the late twenties. What does this suggest?
   A. Heritability of traits diminishes over time.
   B. The influence of the environment increases over time.
   C. For some traits, experiences at certain periods in life become more important.
   D. All of the above.

10. Which of the following suggests caution about the heritability of personality?
    A. Not all traits are equally heritable or unaffected by shared environment.
    B. Even highly heritable traits are not rigidly fixed.
    C. The relative influence of genes versus environment can change over time.
    D. All of the above.

11. The social-cognitive theory can explain how a person can be friendly at work and hostile at home. The explanation is
    A. based on whether the person has internal or external locus of control.
    B. the difference between a person's public and private personalities.
    C. that personality traits can change depending on the situation and on how people perceive and interpret those situations.
    D. an interaction of the id, ego, and superego.

12. Which of the following is NOT one of the shared elements among psychodynamic theories?
    A. an emphasis on environmental influences
    B. the assumption that adult behaviour is determined primarily by childhood experiences
    C. the emphasis on the unconscious mind
    D. the belief that psychological development occurs in fixed stages

13. Which part of the personality would be likely to want to go for a pizza rather than study for a test?
    A. id   B. superego
    C. ego   D. ego ideal

14. The function of defence mechanisms is
    A.   to make us look good in the eyes of other people.
    B.   to protect ourselves from negative environmental consequences.
    C.   to protect us from the conflict and stress of reality.
    D.   all of the above.

15. When the Aherns brought home baby John, four-year-old Andy began acting like a baby himself by crawling around and wanting to drink out of a bottle. This is an example of
    A.   regression.   B.   identification.
    C.   reaction formation.   D.   projection.

16. The psychosexual stages of personality development identified by Freud are (in order)
    A.   oral, anal, latency, phallic, genital.
    B.   oral, phallic, anal, genital, latency.
    C.   oral, anal, phallic, latency, genital.
    D.   anal, phallic, genital, oral, latency.

17. According to Freud, the resolution of the _____ marks the emergence of the superego.
    A.   anal stage   B.   unconscious conflict
    C.   Oedipus complex   D.   latency stage

18. Priscilla is having relationship problems. Which of the following approaches to her difficulties represents one of the shared elements of psychodynamic theories?
    A.   The problems are a result of her interpretation of what is going on.
    B.   The problems are a result of her previous relationship history.
    C.   The problems result from the lack of unconditional positive regard.
    D.   The problems are determined by experiences in her early childhood.

19. "I don't want to study; let's go get pizza." "If you go get pizza, you'll fail the test." "You owe it to your parents to get good grades." Which parts of the personality would make each of these statements, according to Freudian theory?
    A.   id; ego; superego   B.   id; superego; ego
    C.   ego; id; superego   D.   superego; id; ego

20. Johnny was aggressive as a child. He now plays professional football. This is an example of
    A.   regression.   B.   sublimation.
    C.   reaction formation.   D.   projection.

21. Max has just had his sixth birthday. Freud would expect that
    A.   he has resolved the Oedipal complex.
    B.   his personality pattern is basically formed.
    C.   his superego has emerged.
    D.   all of the above have occurred.

22. The fact that several basic archetypes appear in virtually every society supports which Jungian idea?
    A.   penis envy   B.   the strength of the ego
    C.   psychosocial stages   D.   the collective unconscious

23. Julia disagrees with Dr. Sigmund's interpretation that she is very angry at her mother. Dr. Sigmund says that Julia's disagreement is denial and, therefore, confirms that she is angry at her mother. This is an example of which criticism of psychodynamic theories?
    A.   They draw universal principles from a few atypical patients.
    B.   They base theories of development on retrospective accounts of patients.
    C.   They violate the principle of falsifiability.
    D.   They are based on the illusion of causality.

24. Horney disagreed with Freud about
    A.   the nature of the unconscious.
    B.   the notion of the inferiority complex.
    C.   the notion that personality development continues into adult life.
    D.   penis envy and female inferiority.

25. The idea that the human psyche contains the universal memories and history of mankind was contributed by
    A.   Freud.   B.   Jung.
    C.   Erikson.   D.   Horney.

26. Which of the following is NOT one of the criticisms of psychodynamic theories?
    A.   It violates the principle of falsifiability.
    B.   It is based on retrospective memories.
    C.   It is overly comprehensive; it tries to explain too much.
    D.   It draws universal principles from studying selected patients.

27. Dr. West is studying depression. He has interviewed 50 participants about their early lives and childhoods, and he has identified common threads that fit an overall theory. This example represents which of the criticisms of psychodynamic theories?
    A.   It violates the principle of falsifiability.
    B.   It is a prospective study.
    C.   It is based on the retrospective memories of participants.
    D.   People are seen as too malleable, like jellyfish.

28. The object-relations school predicts that adult males will have problems permitting close attachments because
    A. their identities are based on <u>not</u> being like women, so they develop more rigid ego boundaries.
    B. their superegos are too strong.
    C. they have great difficulty resolving the anal stage.
    D. all of the above.

29. Congruence and unconditional positive regard are part of
    A. Roger's theory.
    B. Maslow's theory.
    C. May's theory.
    D. existential philosophy.

30. Humanism focuses on
    A. full human potential.
    B. measurable traits.
    C. environmental influences.
    D. unconscious dynamics.

31. The defence mechanism that occurs when people direct their emotions (such as anger) toward safer targets than the source of those emotions is known as
    A. repression.
    B. sublimation.
    C. reaction formation.
    D. displacement.

32. A man who has some homosexual feelings, but who transforms those feelings into negative actions against homosexuals is most likely exhibiting the defence mechanism of
    A. reaction formation.
    B. sublimation.
    C. projection.
    D. displacement.

PRACTICE TEST 2 - Short Answer

1.   Personality refers to a distinctive pattern of _____, _____, motives, and emotions that characterize an individual over time.

2.   The personality assessment industry is growing. _____ tests are standardized questionnaires that require written responses. These tests are also known as _____.

3.   _____ has identified two types of traits; _____ traits that reflect a characteristic way of behaviour and reacting, while secondary traits are more _____ aspects of personality, such as music preferences.

4.   The Big Five personality traits include introversion versus extroversion, neuroticism, _____, _____, and openness to experience.

5.   The fact that Joey was excitable, nervous, and overreacted to every little thing suggests that he falls into Kagan's category of a _____ temperamental style.

6.   In behavioural genetics, the _____ of an enormous range of personality traits is typically between .50.

7.   In numerous behavioural genetic studies, the only environmental contribution to personality differences comes from having unique experiences that are _____ with other family members.

8.   The process of _____ can account for why a person may be cheerful and friendly at work but hostile and obnoxious at home.

9.   Over time, people learn that some acts will be rewarded and others punished, and thus they develop generalized _____ about which situations and acts will be rewarding. This is known as the theory of _____.

10. In _____ cultures, group harmony takes precedence over the wishes of the individual.

11. In _____ cultures, the needs of friends and family supersede appointments, and time is organized along parallel lines.

12. _____ theories, which are based on the work of Freud, emphasize the movement of psychological energy within the person, in the form of attachments, conflicts, and motivations.

13. According to Freud, the _____ contains two competing basic instincts, the ego bows to the _____ of life, whereas the _____ represents morality.

14. In psychodynamic theory, the ego has tools, called _____, that deny or distort reality and operate unconsciously. These tools protect us from conflict and the stresses of reality.

15. Johnny was always aggressive as a child. Now that he is in high school, he has become the top football player. From the psychodynamic perspective, Johnny's athletic success might be attributable to the defence mechanism of _____.

16. _____ challenged some of Freud's theories about women, suggesting that when women feel inferior to men, the explanation may be related to disadvantages that women live with and their second-class status.

17. Jung introduced the idea of the _____ unconscious, which contains _____, universal memories, symbols, and images that are the legacy of human history.

18. Object-relations theory states that a child creates a(n) _____ of the mother and this unconsciously affects personality throughout life.

19. One of the criticisms of psychodynamic theories is that they violate the principle of _____.

20. Abraham Maslow said that people who strive for a life that is meaningful, challenging, and productive are _____. Carl Rogers believed that to become a fully functioning person, you must receive _____ regard.

21. According to Jung, the _____ represents the feminine archetype in men, whereas the _____ represents the masculine archetype in women.

22. If Jung were alive today, he might point to Darth Vader, Lord Voldemort, and Sauron as examples of the evil _____ archetype.

PRACTICE TEST 3 - Essay

1. Lynne is having aggressive fantasies about her husband. Over a long period, he has gotten drunk on a regular basis. Lynne remembers her alcoholic father, who was never there when she needed him. She also remembers her mother, who suffered silently for years. Lynne swears this will not happen to her, but she can't seem to make anything change. She is hostile toward her children and her neighbours. Her husband is always repentant the next day, but his sorrow never lasts more than a week. Yet, Lynne doesn't take the final step of leaving.

   Identify which approach to personality each of the following set of comments represents:

   A. The perseverance of Lynne's mother is the significant determinant in this case. Her mother's behaviour taught Lynne that marriage was for better or for worse, but also that silence produces suffering. Lynne's pattern was acquired from an important role model.

   B. Aggressiveness is Lynne's outstanding characteristic and it dominates her actions and relationships with most people.

   C. Lynne's marriage to and anger with an alcoholic suggests many unresolved feelings toward her father. Her marriage to an alcoholic demonstrates her ongoing attachment to her father and the effort to resolve her issues with him. Her anger most likely is unresolved anger at her father. Her reluctance to leave reflects her desire to stay united with her father.

   D. Lynne is struggling with her choices. While marriage is important to her, she realizes that her husband's alcoholism is a source of despair. She is struggling with her values, principles, desires for growth and fulfillment, and how they should influence her choices.

2. Bernard had studied for his psychology test, but before he was finished studying, he agreed to go partying with his friends and stayed out late. The test was very difficult, and he found he did not know many of the answers. The class was crowded, and a good student was sitting very close to him. It would have been very easy to look over at her paper. He was worried because this test grade would make a big difference on his final grade. He struggled with whether or not he should cheat. He decided not to cheat because he felt that he would have let his parents down if he did. Instead, he decided that this grade really didn't matter so much. He felt guilty about not having studied enough and about having considered cheating.

   Indicate whether the id, ego, or superego is involved in each of the following examples and explain the basis for your answer:

   A. Bernard's studying for his test
   B. Going out partying with his friends rather than studying
   C. Wanting a good grade under any circumstance

D.   Evaluating whether or not to cheat
E.   Deciding not to cheat
F.   Deciding that the grade did not matter so much
G.   Feeling guilty about his behaviour

3.   Identify which defence mechanism each example represents:

A.   A mother shows exaggerated concern and love for her children, even though she unconsciously feels trapped and frustrated by motherhood.
B.   Bob often feels that other people don't like him and are talking behind his back.
C.   Jack is unconsciously attracted to his sister-in-law and, though he seems to have no awareness of it, his sister-in-law senses these feelings.
D.   Even after finding his lighter in the jacket worn the other day, Tony swears he never misplaces anything and someone must be playing a trick on him.
E.   Whenever he is frustrated, Jack has a tantrum and destroys anything he can get his hands on.
F.   The football coach loves to insult John and make him angry. Whenever he does this, the opposing team really suffers because then John begins to hit extra hard.

4.   Identify the most likely stage of fixation demonstrated in the following descriptions:

A.   A husband has had long-term marital problems due to a continuing lack of interest in sex.
B.   A chain smoker begins to eat whenever he becomes the least bit upset.
C.   A man is attracted to much older women because of their protective, caring ways.
D.   A woman has all her CDs and the food in her cabinets organized alphabetically, and the clothes in her closets are organized by colour. The pencils on her desk all must be sharpened and her desk cleared off before she can work.

5.   Below are criticisms of Freudian psychoanalysis. Identify which theorist would have been most likely to make each comment.

A.   Freud saw the importance of the individual's past but failed to see the contribution of humanity's past. People have universal memories owing to the ancestry they share.
B.   Freud misunderstood women. He believed they were motivated by envy for men when the true determining forces were social injustice and second-class treatment.
C.   Freud emphasized a child's fear of the powerful father, but ignored the child's need for a powerful mother, especially during the baby's early years. He emphasized the dynamics of inner drives and impulses, but paid little attention to the child's relationship with others.

6.   Based on the three humanistic theorists, indicate how each thinker might account for a person's failure to reach his or her full potential.

7.   Using the "Big Five" trait approach, indicate which set of traits would be most useful for describing each of the individuals described below.

   A.   Bob is stable, happy to meet people, and well liked. He has many friends and few worries.
   B.   Mary is neat, timely, and dependable. She has relatively few interests or hobbies, but she is a good listener and is liked by her co-workers.
   C.   John complains constantly and worries about his health and his life in general. He reads a lot and loves going to movies and to museums, but he always goes alone.

CHAPTER
FOURTEEN

Development over the Lifespan

LEARNING OBJECTIVES

1. Describe the field of study of developmental psychologists.

2. Distinguish between cross-sectional and longitudinal studies.

3. List and summarize the stages of prenatal development.

4. Describe some possible harmful influences to the embryo or fetus.

5. Describe the physical and perceptual abilities of infants that are present at birth. What is the effect of culture on infant development?

6. Describe the importance of contact comfort in early life.

7. Define separation anxiety and describe how it is measured.

8. Distinguish between secure and insecure attachment.

9. Describe those factors that influence the development of the healthy attachment relationship.

10. Describe the stages of language development.

11. Describe Piaget's theory of cognitive development. Distinguish between assimilation and accommodation.

12. Outline Piaget's four stages of cognitive development.

13. Describe Vygotsky's theory of sociocultural influence.

14. Describe the strengths and weaknesses of Piaget's theory.

15. Describe Kohlberg's theory of moral development.

16. Distinguish between power assertion and induction as parenting styles.

17. Distinguish between gender typing and gender identity and describe the explanations that have been given for gender development. Explain how gender typing changes over the lifespan.

18. Describe the events that signal the onset of puberty in males and females, and the relationship between age of onset of puberty and later adjustment.

19. Summarize the evidence on the relationship between adolescence and emotional turmoil.

20. List and discuss the stages of Erikson's theory of psychosocial development.

21. Summarize the biological and emotional changes associated with midlife.

22. Describe the changing role of women in Canadian society.

23. Discuss the effects of aging on intelligence and memory.

24. Distinguish between fluid and crystallized intelligence.

25. Discuss the impact of childhood experience on adulthood. Describe the variables that are associated with resilience in children and adolescents.

26. Outline the basic guidelines that child development research suggests for raising children.

BRIEF CHAPTER SUMMARY

Chapter 14 describes the stages of prenatal development, which include the germinal stage, the embryonic stage, and the fetal stage. The newborn is capable of processing information, though there are many limitations to the newborn's abilities. According to Piaget's theory of cognitive development, thinking develops in four stages: the sensorimotor stage, the preoperational stage, the concrete operations stage, and the formal operations stage. While parts of Piaget's theory have been refuted, other parts of it have been confirmed. Language, another aspect of cognitive development, is an evolutionary adaptation of the human species. Children are responsive to aspects of language in the first months of life, and by about two years of age, they are using two- to three-word combinations. Moral reasoning is another aspect of cognitive development. Kohlberg's theory of moral reasoning is described. Development of gender identity is discussed. Language, thinking, gender identity, and moral reasoning are all areas of development that influence one another. Myths and realities of adolescent development are discussed. The physiology of puberty is described, along with the psychological issues of this period of development. Aspects of adulthood are examined, including midlife and aging. Erickson's theory identifies eight stages of psychological development that occur across the lifespan.

PREVIEW OUTLINE

Before you read the chapter, review the preview outline for each section of the text. After you have read the chapter, close this book and try to re-create the outlines on a blank piece of paper.

I. FROM CONCEPTION THROUGH THE FIRST YEAR
   A. **Developmental psychologists** study universal aspects of life-span development as well as cultural and individual variations; many study socialization
   Socialization – the process by which children learn rules and behaviour expected of them by society
   B. **Prenatal development** - maturation is the sequential unfolding of genetically influenced behaviour and physical characteristics
   1. Three stages - germinal stage (fertilized egg divides and attaches to the uterine wall); embryonic stage (embryo develops); fetal stage (organs and systems develop)

2.   Harmful influences, like German measles, X-rays, sexually transmitted diseases, cigarette smoking, alcohol, drugs can cross the placental barrier

C.   **The infant's world**
1.   Physical abilities - newborns have a series of reflexes, perceptual abilities, sensations that are not fully developed
2.   Culture and maturation - infants all go through the same maturational sequence, but many aspects of development depend on culture

D.   **Attachment**
1. **Contact comfort** - Harlow studies show need for being touched and held
2. **Separation and security -** separation anxiety develops between six and eight months and lasts until middle of second year; experienced by all children
3. Ainsworth - studied attachment using the "Strange Situation" method
   a.   secure - cry when mom leaves, happy upon return
   b.   avoidant - don't care what mom does
   c.   anxious/ambivalent - cry when mom leaves, resists upon return

E. Causes of insecure attachment
Factors that may cause insecure attachment include
1. abandonment and separation in the first two years of life
2. abusive, neglectful or erratic parenting style
3. the child's genetic disposition
4. stressful family circumstances

F. How critical are the early years?
There are critical periods for perceptual development; unclear whether critical period for intellectual development

From Conception Through the First Year

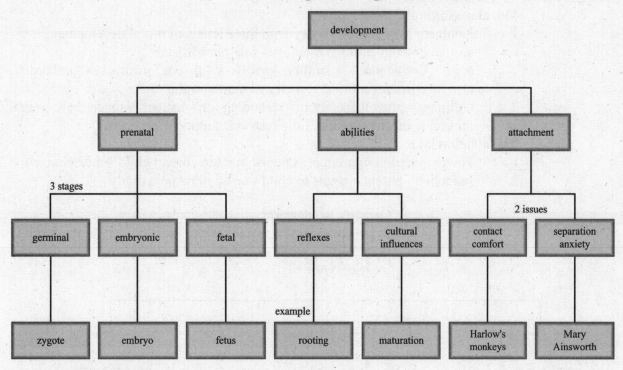

II. COGNITIVE DEVELOPMENT

    A.   **Language** - an evolutionary adaptation of the human species

        1.   In first months, responsive to pitch, intensity, and sound of language

        2.   By 4 to 6 months, learn many basic sounds of own language

        3.   Between 6 months to 1 year, become more familiar with own language

        4.   At 1 year, babies develop symbolic gestures

        5.   Between 18 months and 2 years, use telegraphic communication

    B.   **Thinking**

        1.   Piaget's theory - children make two mental adaptations to new experiences

             a.   Assimilation - fitting new information into existing schemas

             b.   Accommodation - changing schemas because of new information

        2.   Piaget proposed children go through four stages of cognitive development

             a.   Sensorimotor stage - birth to 2 years old, object permanence

             b.   Preoperational stage - ages 2 to 7, able to pretend

             c.   Concrete operations stage - ages 7 to 12, conservation,identity, math

             d.   Formal operations stage - ages 12 to adulthood, abstract reasoning

        3.   Piaget underestimated children's abilities, overestimated adults' abilities

        4.   Vygotsky's theory - development depends on social/cultural context

        5.   Research has challenged many of Piaget's ideas (e.g., cognitive abilities develop more continuously, he underestimated children but overestimated many adults)

III. LEARNING TO BE GOOD
A. Moral reasoning
1. Kohlberg developed a theory with three levels of moral development
   a. Preconventional morality - fear punishment
   b. Conventional morality, ages 10 or 11 - conformity, law, and order
   c. Postconventional - universal human rights
2. Gilligan - men base moral reasoning on justice, women base moral reasoning on compassion; little research support

B. Moral behaviour
1. Power assertion - parent uses punishment to correct child's misbehaviour
2. Induction - parent appeals to child's sense of responsibility

Cognitive Development

IV. GENDER DEVELOPMENT
A. Terms
1. Gender identity - sense of being male or female independent of behaviour
2. Gender typing - process of learning what culture considers "appropriate"
3. Transgender – don't fit comfortably into male/female categories
4. Gender schema – a mental network of beliefs and expectations about what it means to be male or female

B.   **Influences on gender development**
  1.   Biological influences - toy and play preferences may be inborn
  2.   Cognitive influences - children, especially boys, develop gender schemas
  3.   Learning influences - gender socialization, adults' treatment of children
C.   **Gender over the lifespan** - gender differences are greatest in childhood

Gender Development

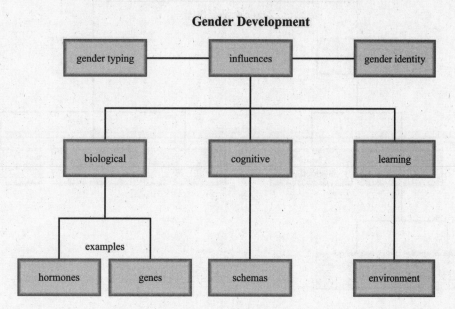

V. ADOLESCENCE
  A.   **Adolescence** - period of development between puberty, the age at which a person becomes capable of sexual reproduction, and adulthood
  B.   **The physiology of adolescence** - puberty and the onset of reproductive capacity
  1.   Become capable of reproduction, emergence of secondary sex characteristics (e.g., deepened voice for boys)
  2.   Timing of puberty depends on genes and environment; is occurring earlier
  3.   Different adjustment issues related to early and late maturation
  4.   Brain development – changes in prefrontal cortex and limbic system
  C.   **The psychology of adolescence**
  1.   Teenagers have greater conflict with parents, mood swings, and risky behaviour
  2.   Conflict with parents can reflect teens' desire for more autonomy

Adolescence

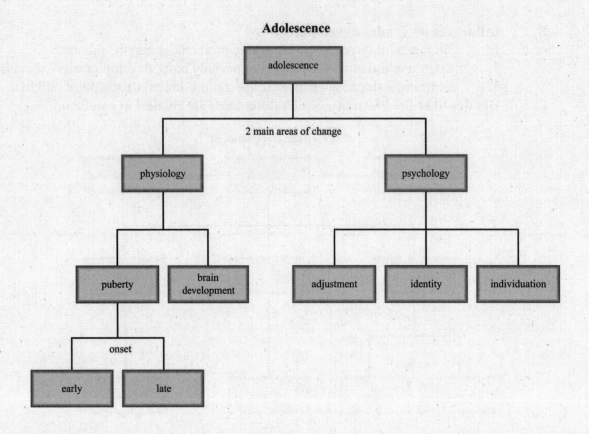

VI. ADULTHOOD

  A. **Stages and ages** - Erikson identifies eight stages from childhood to old age

    1. Trust versus mistrust - first year

    2. Autonomy versus shame and doubt - toddler

    3. Initiative versus guilt - preschooler

    4. Competence versus inferiority - school-age children

    5. Identity versus role confusion - adolescence

    6. Intimacy versus isolation - young adulthood

    7. Generativity versus stagnation - middle years

    8. Ego integrity versus despair - old age

  B. **The transitions of life** – the social clock tells us the "right" time for transitions

    1. Emerging adulthood - stage of life before career, marriage

    2. The middle years - for most people, the prime of life

  C. **Old age** - gerontologists have challenged stereotypes

    1. Crystallized intelligence (knowledge and skills built over a lifetime) remains stable over the lifespan, but fluid intelligence (independent of education and experience) declines

    2. Aging associated with improved well being and increased happiness

Adulthood

VII. THE WELLSPRING OF RESILIENCE
A. Events of childhood do not necessarily have permanent effects
B. Evidence comes from studies of children who recovered from wars, from abusive or alcoholic parents, and sexual abuse; resilience is rather ordinary

STAGES OF COGNITIVE DEVELOPMENT ACCORDING TO PIAGET

Complete the following chart by describing the characteristics, limitations, and achievements of each stage of Piaget's theory of cognitive development.

STAGE OF DEVELOPMENT	CHARACTERISTICS	LIMITATIONS	ACHIEVEMENTS
SENSORIMOTOR STAGE			
PREOPERATIONAL STAGE			
CONCRETE OPERATIONS STAGE			
FORMAL OPERATIONS STAGE			

IDIOMS AND SLANGS

Screens out some (page 530) – refers to the role of the umbilical cord to try and keep the harmful substances away from the baby.

Are not as clear (page 571) – the scientific results of the effects of drinking some alcohol are not obvious.

Developmental milestones (page 534) – these are important stages of behavioural change in a child's development.

Right kind of mothering (page 536) – as shown in the research, babies need contact and love from a mother, not just food.

For a few hours at a stretch (page 536) – this is referring to babies being left alone for a while so they can become independent.

Out of sight, out of mind (page 541) – when children are young, they believe things do not exist if they cannot see them.

Peekaboo (page 542) – this is a game parents play with babies where they hide their faces from them and then suddenly appear. Babies like to play this game.

Train of thought (page 542) – this is referring to a mental ability that can be performed forwards and backwards.

Experienced first-hand (page 543) – these are experiences that children have themselves. After age 12, they can think of situations that they haven't experienced. This shows higher cognitive thought.

Children are not passive vessels into which education and experience are poured (page 546) – this refers to the idea that children are active learners and thinkers.

Still behave like scoundrels (page 547) – when talking about moral behaviours, we may think about doing the right thing, but in reality, we may do the wrong thing or a mean thing.

Sexual overtures (page 555) – these are comments or behaviours that are sexual in nature.

Gender crossover (page 555) – later in life, people are not so worried about being masculine or feminine, so they explore different behaviours they may not have done in the past.

Sink into confusion (page 560) – according to Erikson, if one doesn't develop one's personal identity, he or she may end up being confused and not knowing who they really are.

Parallels other biological capacities (page 567) – fluid intelligence is related to biological development, slow at the beginning, then it gets stronger, but then it slows down as we get older.

Sedentary lifestyle (page 567) – this refers to people who do not exercise.

Dwindle with age (page 566) – some intellectual abilities decline or get weaker with age.

Use it or lose it (page 568) – refers to the idea that people have to use their cognitive and physical abilities or else these abilities will get weaker and then you will not have them anymore.

Fewer signposts and road maps to guide us (page 569) – as the world changes, growing older will be unpredictable. We can learn to do our best in any situation or we can let our past experiences hurt us.

PRACTICE TEST 1 - Multiple Choice

1. The order of the three stages of prenatal development is
   A. embryonic, germinal, fetal.
   B. germinal, fetal, embryonic.
   C. germinal, embryonic, fetal.
   D. fetal, germinal, embryonic.

2. Which of the following could be a problem during pregnancy?
   A. coffee
   B. alcohol
   C. cigarettes
   D. all of the above

3. Embryos that are genetically male will begin to secrete _____ during the
   _____ stage of prenatal development.
   A. adrenalin; embryonic
   B. testosterone; embryonic
   C. hormones; fetal
   D. estrogen; germinal

4. Jane has smoked heavily during her pregnancy. What are the risks?
   A. increased chance of miscarriage
   B. premature birth
   C. her child may be hyperactive
   D. all of the above

5. An infant touched on the cheek or corner of the mouth will turn in the direction from
   which he or she was touched and search for something to suck on. This is called the
   A. sucking reflex.
   B. rooting reflex.
   C. sneeze reflex.
   D. grasping reflex.

6. "Hermaphroditism" is now usually referred to as:
   A. intersex conditions.
   B. emerging adulthood.
   C. identity crisis.
   D. gender schema activation.

7. The deep emotional tie that babies and children develop for their primary caregivers, and
   their distress at being separated from them, is called
   A. attachment.
   B. affiliation.
   C. contact comfort.
   D. security.

8. Harry and Margaret Harlow's studies, in which infant rhesus monkeys ran to soft, terry-
   cloth "mothers" when they were frightened or startled, demonstrated the need for
   A. affiliation.
   B. food.
   C. contact comfort.
   D. love.

9. Lucia's mom is not very comfortable with physical affection. Although she loves Lucia and takes good care of her, she does not hold or cuddle her. In contrast, Lucia's dad likes to hug and cuddle. Based on Harlow's experiments, to which parent would Lucia be most likely to go to when she is upset?
   A. her mom
   B. her dad
   C. either
   D. impossible to say

10. Baby Huey cries for his mother to pick him up, yet when she does, he wants to be put back down. According to Ainsworth's studies, Huey exhibits a(n)
    A. avoidant attachment style.
    B. ambivalent attachment style.
    C. secure attachment style.
    D. psychological problem.

11. Ainsworth identified mother's treatment of their babies as the primary determinant of attachment styles. What are other influences on attachment?
    A. infant temperament
    B. stressful events
    C. family circumstances
    D. all of the above

12. The order of Piaget's stages of cognitive development is
    A. preoperational, sensorimotor, concrete operations, formal operations.
    B. concrete operations, preoperational, sensorimotor, formal operations.
    C. sensorimotor, preoperational, formal operations, concrete operations.
    D. sensorimotor, preoperational, concrete operations, formal operations.

13. Fitting new information into your present system of knowledge and beliefs is called
    A. assimilation.
    B. organization.
    C. accommodation.
    D. sensorimotor development.

14. According to Piaget, during the concrete operations stage the child
    A. thinks egocentrically.
    B. develops object permanence.
    C. grasps conservation.
    D. can reason abstractly.

15. While on a walk with his father, Billy points to a cardinal and his father says, "Birdie." A little bit later, Billy sees a blue jay and says, "Birdie." This is an example of
    A. assimilation.
    B. conservation.
    C. accommodation.
    D. an operation.

16. During the first months, babies are highly responsive to
    A. emotions and rhythms in voices.
    B. the basic sounds of their native language.
    C. the pitch and intensity of language.
    D. all of the above.

17. Based on the stages of language development, which of the following would a four- to six-month-old baby be able to do?
    A. have a repertoire of symbolic gestures
    B. use telegraphic speech
    C. recognize "mommy" and "daddy"
    D. all of the above

18. In the first few months of life, a baby is most likely to respond to
    A. his or her name.
    B. the words "mommy" and "daddy."
    C. the basic sounds of his or her native language.
    D. speech in which the pitch is higher and more varied and spoken with exaggerated intonation.

19. "Mama here," "go 'way bug," and "my toy" are examples of
    A. baby talk.   B. telegraphic speech.
    C. babbling.   D. parentese.

20. A child's fundamental sense of maleness or femaleness that exists regardless of what one wears or does is called
    A. gender schema.   B. gender socialization.
    C. gender identity.   D. sex-typing.

21. According to gender schema theory,
    A. gender-typed behaviour increases once a gender schema is developed.
    B. gender schemas do not develop until a child is about four years old.
    C. gender schemas are formed early and basically do not change throughout life.
    D. gender schemas disappear during adolescence.

22. Both Fran and Dan know that girls play with dolls and become nurses and that boys play with trucks and become doctors. This demonstrates
    A. gender typing.   B. fixations in the oral stage.
    C. gender identity.   D. all of the above.

23. The belief by children that bears, fire, anger, dogs, and the colour black are "masculine" and butterflies, hearts, the colour pink, and flowers are feminine indicates that
    A. children have accurate gender identity.
    B. children have been reinforced for these types of distinctions.
    C. children are learning gender schemas.
    D. there is a biological basis for these distinctions.

24. Kohlberg's theory describes
    A. moral emotions.
    B. moral behaviour.
    C. moral reasoning.
    D. moral actions.

25. Which of the following statements is FALSE regarding recent research on cognitive development?
    A. Preschoolers are more egocentric than Piaget thought.
    B. Cognitive development is greatly affected by a child's culture.
    C. Piaget underestimated the understanding of children.
    D. Cognitive development is more continuous than in discrete or stage form.

26. Early-maturing boys
    A. generally have a negative body image compared to late-developing boys.
    B. are more likely to smoke, drink, use drugs, and break the law than later-maturing boys.
    C. feel worse about themselves than do late-developing boys at first, but they end up the healthiest group.
    D. have more self-control and emotional stability than late-developing boys.

27. Michelle is going through menopause. If she is like most women, she will
    A. experience depression and other emotional reactions.
    B. will not experience unusually severe symptoms.
    C. will regret reaching menopause.
    D. will experience severe physical discomfort.

28. The findings of gerontologists have changed our understanding of old age by
    A. reevaluating when "old age" begins.
    B. separating aging from illness.
    C. recognizing some of the benefits of aging.
    D. doing all of the above.

29. Fluid intelligence
    A. tends to remain stable or even improve over the lifespan.
    B. is influenced by an inherited predisposition, and it parallels other biological capacities in its growth and, in later years, decline.
    C. is the knowledge and skills that are built up over a lifetime.
    D. gives us the ability to solve math problems, define words, or summarize a prime minister's policy.

30. According to Erikson, Heather, who is 16 years old, will
    A. experience an identity crisis.
    B. fight against stagnation.
    C. learn to share herself with another person and make a commitment.
    D. deal with her feelings of competence versus inferiority.

PRACTICE TEST 2 - Short Answer

1. The psychological and social processes by which children learn the rules and behaviour expected of them by their society is called _____.

2. Prenatal development is divided into three stages: the _____ begins at conception, the _____ begins once the implantation of the _____ into the wall of the uterus is completed.

3. The _____, connected to the embryo by the umbilical cord, serves to screen out some, but not all, harmful substances. Some harmful influences, such as _____ and _____ can cross the barrier.

4. Substances that interfere with normal embryonic development are known as _____.

5. In the Harlow experiments, the baby monkeys ran to the _____ "mother" when they were frightened or startled. This reaction demonstrated the need for _____.

6. A mother brings her baby into an unfamiliar room containing lots of toys. After a while a stranger comes in and attempts to play with the child. The mother leaves the baby with the stranger. She returns, plays with the child, and then the stranger leaves. Finally, the mother leaves the baby alone for three minutes and returns. This describes the research method used by _____ and it is called the _____.

7. In the research situation described in question 5, babies who did not care if their mothers left the room and made little effort to seek contact with the mothers when they returned demonstrated one of the insecure types of attachment, called _____ attachment style.

8. Ainsworth believed that attachment styles were based on the way _____ treated their babies in the first year. Subsequent research has found that other factors contribute to insecure attachment. These other factors include family circumstances, later stressful events in childhood and the child's _____.

9. Jennifer is about _____ months old, and she has started to smack her lips when she is hungry, to blow on something to show that it is hot, and to shrug her shoulders to indicate that she doesn't know an answer to a question. Jennifer is demonstrating her developing repertoire of _____ gestures.

10. The Swiss psychologist, _____, proposed a theory of cognitive development.

11. When Leah learns a _____ for birdies, she is able to identify robins, cardinals, and pet parakeets, as birdies. This demonstrates Piaget's concept of _____, or fitting new information into existing categories.

253

12. Jean-Paul is 12 months old. When his mother puts his favourite toy out of sight at meal time, he still cries for it. Jean-Paul has developed _____.

13. Hillary's dad asks her advice about a birthday present for her mom. Five-year-old Hillary suggests that they buy mom one of Hillary's favourite toys. Piaget's theory proposes that Hillary is demonstrating _____. Hillary is in Piaget's _____ stage of cognitive development.

14. Jack understands the principles of conservation and cause and effect, yet he cannot think in abstractions or use logical deductions. He is in the _____ stage of cognitive development.

15. Bill will not cross the road unless he is at a crosswalk, even when he is on a small road and there is no traffic in sight. He says, "It is the law, and it is important that we obey the laws we have chosen because society is based on them." Based on this reasoning, Bill would be about _____ years old according to Kohlberg.

16. Learning theorists point to the role of _____, or the reinforcers and societal messages children get about what "girls" and "boys" do.

17. The onset of menstruation is called _____. The cessation (end of) of menstruation is called _____.

18. When teenagers have conflicts with their parents over autonomy, they are usually trying to _____, to develop their own opinions, values, and style of dress and look.

19. Intersexed individuals often refer to themselves as _____.

20. Erik Erikson wrote that all individuals go through _____ stages in their lives, resolving an inevitable _____ at each one.

21. _____ intelligence is relatively independent of education and experience and in later years it _____. _____ intelligence depends heavily on culture, education, and experience, and it tends to remain _____ over the lifespan.

22. An approach to disciplining a child that emphasizes the child's own abilities, empathy, and sense of responsibility is known as _____.

PRACTICE TEST 3 - Essay

1. Prenatal development is associated with several dangers. Identify the dangers associated with

   A. X-rays B. cigarettes
   C. alcohol D. drugs

2. A. You are part of a pediatric medical team and you are conducting an evaluation of a newborn infant. Discuss all the behaviours and sensory abilities that a normal newborn should have.

   B. Many people think newborn attachment is instinctive. Discuss behaviours that contribute to attachment between the newborn and the caregiver.

3. A. A four-year-old girl insists small people must live in the TV because they are right there behind the glass. Identify her stage of cognitive development and the phenomenon being displayed by this child.

   B. A child who is good at roller-skating goes ice skating for the first time. She keeps trying to stand and move just as she would on roller skates but she falls again and again. According to Piaget, what is necessary for mastery of this new skill?

   C. A child threatened to tell his parents when his older brother gave him only one of the three candy bars they were supposed to share. The older child then broke his brother's bar in half and gave him two pieces. This satisfied both children because they each had two pieces. Identify the cognitive stages of these children and the disadvantage that allows the younger child to be cheated.

   D. Previously, whenever Johnny banged with a spoon, his mother would put it in a drawer and Johnny would quickly move on to something else. Now that he's eight months old, this isn't working. The child continues to demand the spoon even though he can't see it. Identify the cognitive stage of this child and the change that has taken place.

4. Harold has been babysitting Jennie since she was an infant. She is now 23 months old. Harold has always tried to get Jennie to speak. He is now trying to get her to say, "The apple is on the table." Describe what Jennie's response might have been at 4 months old, 10 months old, 14 months old, and 23 months old.

5. Describe "resilience". And some of the variables associated with it.

CHAPTER FIFTEEN

Health, Stress, and Coping

LEARNING OBJECTIVES

1. Describe the Social Readjustment Rating Scale noting its advantages and disadvantages.
2. Distinguish between hassles and stressors.
3. List five chronic or uncontrollable stressors.
4. Describe the relationship between poverty and health and stress.
5. Describe the relationship between immigration and stress.
6. Describe Selye's stages of stress response and compare his theory to current theories.
7. Describe the role of the hypothalamus when under stress.
8. Describe the functioning of the immune system and its response to stress.
9. Summarize the aims of the interdisciplinary field of psychoneuroimmunology.
10. Discuss the relationship between emotions and illness.
11. Describe the relationship between personality and hostlity and heart disease.
12. Describe the link between depression and disease.
13. Describe the influence of positive emotions on health.
14. Describe emotional inhibition and describe its effects.
15. Describe the nature of loneliness and its effects.
16. Outline the benefits of confession.
17. Compare optimistic and pessimistic explanatory styles and describe their relationship to illness and coping with stress.
18. Define locus of control and explain its relationship with health and well-being.
19. Distinguish between primary and secondary control and explain how culture influences their use.
20. List and explain the major methods of coping with stress.
21. Distinguish between emotion-focused and problem-focused coping.
22. Describe four conditions under which men find it easier to ask for help.
23. Discuss the relationship between social networks, health, and well-being.
24. Describe how health psychology can help Canadians become healthier.

25. To what degree we have control over our health? Review the factors that increase the risk of illness.

26. List and describe six practical guidelines for maintaining good health.

BRIEF CHAPTER SUMMARY

Chapter 15 examines the effects of stress on our lives. Hans Selye began the modern era of stress research and identified a stress response cycle. This cycle includes an alarm phase, a resistance phase, and an exhaustion phase. Health psychologists study the relationship between psychological factors and health. Stress is no longer considered a purely biological condition that leads directly to illness, but rather an interaction between aspects of the individual and aspects of the environment. The area of psychoneuroimmunology examines the relationship among psychological processes, the nervous and endocrine systems, and the immune system. The current view of the relationship between stress and illness considers aspects of the external stressor, characteristics of the individual, emotional style of the individual and perceived coping abilities. Several coping methods are reviewed, including reducing bodily arousal, solving the problem, thinking about the problem differently, and drawing on social support. Optimistic and pessimistic explanatory styles, and internal versus external locus of control have been researched extensively and play a significant role in physical and psychological health. Finally, the chapter examines the extent to which we can control our health.

PREVIEW OUTLINE

Before you read the chapter, review the preview outline for each section of the text. After you have read the chapter, close this book and try to <u>re-create</u> the outlines on a blank piece of paper.

I. **WHAT IS STRESS?**
   A. **Definitions**
      1. Stress – refers to recurring conflicts, traumatic experience, continuing pressures that seem uncontrollable, and small irritations
      2. Stressors – environmental factors that throw the body out of balance
      3. Health psychology studies the sources of wellness and illness to learn why some people succumb to stress and disease and others do not

II. **THE STRESS-ILLNESS MYSTERY -** The following may threaten health:
   A. **Noise**
   B. **Bereavement and loss** (e.g., through divorce or death)
   C. **Work-related problems**
   D. **Poverty, powerlessness and low status -** related to health care, diet, continuous environmental stressors (crime, discrimination, housing)
   E. **Recent Immigration**

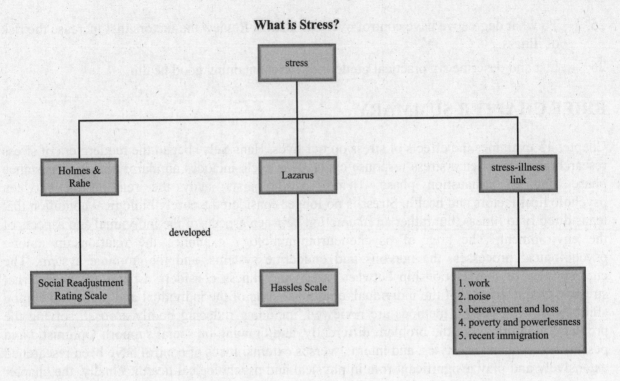

What is Stress?

stress

Holmes & Rahe

Lazarus

stress-illness link

developed

Social Readjustment Rating Scale

Hassles Scale

1. work
2. noise
3. bereavement and loss
4. poverty and powerlessness
5. recent immigration

III. THE PHYSIOLOGY OF STRESS

A. **Hans Selye's General Adaptation Syndrome**
1. Alarm phase - the body mobilizes to meet threat
2. Resistance phase - resists or copes with a stressor which makes the body more susceptible to *other* stressors
3. Exhaustion phase - occurs if the stressor persists; body's resources are depleted and vulnerability to illness increases
4. Some stress is positive; but it is important to minimize its negative effects
5. Current approaches - "fight or flight" response initiates activity along the HPA axis for increased energy; long-term activation can be harmful

B. **The mind–body link**
1. Researchers study mechanisms that link mind and body; interdisciplinary specialty is called psychoneuroimmunology (PNI)
2. PNI researchers study psychological factors that influence the immune system (e.g., feeling crowded) as well as the white blood cells of the immune system (which recognize foreign substances and destroy or deactivate them).Some evidence exists that stress causes specific cell damage.

The Physiology of Stress

- stress
  - general adaptation syndrome
    - 3 stages
      - alarm
      - resistance
      - exhaustion
  - psychoneuroimmunology
    - interact
      - mind
      - body

IV. THE PSYCHOLOGY OF STRESS

A. Emotions and illness

1. Evidence that negative emotions affect the course of illness once a person has a medical condition; less clear whether negative emotions <u>cause</u> illness
2. Hostility and heart disease
   - a. Early research on the Type A pattern as risk factor for heart disease
   - b. Cynical or antagonistic hostility found to be related to heart disease
3. Depression may be a risk factor for heart disease and other diseases, but the evidence is somewhat contradictory
4. Experiencing positive emotions correlated with longevity (study on nuns)

B. Managing negative emotions

1. Emotional inhibition
   - a. Trying to avoid bothersome thoughts has the opposite effect
   - b. Those who suppress feelings of anxiety, anger, or fear are at greater risk of becoming ill than those who acknowledge their fears. New research suggests that loneliness may contribute to poor management of negative emotions.
   - c. "Confessing" worries and fears can reduce chance of illness if it produces insight and understanding

C. Optimism and pessimism

1. Pessimistic style associated lower achievement, illness, slower recovery from trauma, and self-destructive behaviour
2. Optimistic style associated with "positive illusions" (not denial), active problem solving, persistence, and better health habits
3. Optimism can be learned, such as counting one's blessings.

D.   The sense of control

      1.   Locus of control - your expectation of whether you can control the things that happen to you

           a.   Internal locus of control - those who believe they are responsible for what happens to them

           b.   External locus of control - those who believe they are victims of circumstances

      2.   The benefits of control

           a.   Difficult events more tolerable if more predictable or controllable

           b.   Feeling in control reduces chronic pain, improves adjustment to surgery and illness, speeds up recovery from diseases

      3.   The limits of control

           a.   Trying to control the uncontrollable or blaming control are problems

           b.   Ideas about control are influenced by culture: primary control (modify situation) versus secondary control (modify desires)

           c.   Goal is to avoid guilt and self-blame while retaining self-efficacy

The Psychology of Stress

V. COPING WITH STRESS

    A.   **Coping** - what people do to control, tolerate, or reduce the effects of stressors

    B.   **Cooling off** - techniques that reduce bodily arousal have a variety of benefits, such as relaxation, massage and "contact comfort," and exercise

    C.   **Solving the problem**

        1.   Emotion-focused coping - giving in to emotions right after tragedy

        2.   Problem-focused coping - learning information about how to cope

D.   Rethinking the problem
    1.   Reappraising the situation - thinking about a problem differently which changes a person's emotional response
    2.   Learning from experience - finding benefit from a bad experience
    3.   Making social comparisons - comparing self to others less fortunate

E.   Drawing on social support
    1.   Studies show positive effects of friends on health and longevity
    2.   Men ask for help less often, but they are more likely to ask for help when they think the problem is prevalent, the problem isn't central to the self, other men support help-seeking, and they feel they can reciprocate
    3.   Friends can be source of stress when there is arguing and hostility

F.   Healing through helping – strength derived from focusing on and helping others

Coping With Stress

V.   HOW MUCH CONTROL DO WE HAVE OVER OUR HEALTH?
  A.   Relationship between stress and illness – is not direct
    1.   Many factors influence outcome, such as personality traits, biological vulnerabilities, emotional inhibition, explanatory styles, coping strategies
    2.   Behaviour (smoking, diet, exercise) has a strong influence on health
  B.   Avoid oversimplification or emotional reasoning about health

IDIOMS AND SLANGS

Fall ill (page 576) – to get sick.

Lower rungs of the socioeconomic ladder (page 577) – this expression refers to poorer people.

Under the skin (page 579) – Hans Selye was the first researcher to look at the biological and physiological effects of stress.

Personal space (page 582) – this is the area around each person that is related to how close another person can come. A large personal space means that an individual is not comfortable with people being too close to him or her.

Banish an unwelcome thought (page 585) – when one tries to stop thinking about bad things.

Trivial topics (page 587) – these are minor or unimportant ideas.

Betrays your confidence (page 587) – When someone tells others about your secrets when you have asked them not to.

Bitter and brooding (page 585) – these are two negative emotions that are opposite emotions of someone who expresses positive emotions and has lots of friends.

Taking care of herself (page 592) – refers to the idea that some women play an active role in their health.

Wallowing around in negative emotions (page 593) – this can happen when we feel that bad emotions or feelings are taking over and we don't feel that we are in charge of ourselves.

Keep their heads above water (page 593) – a saying that means that people are able to handle their problems although not very well.

Cool off when you are upset (page 594) – after getting very angry, one has to be able to stop being upset because anger is stressful.

Out of the blue (page 604) – when something happens suddenly or without warning.

Brain, not brawn (page 595) – the example in the book came from people who lost physical movement to their bodies (brawn), but they could still think (brains).

Awful bout with cancer (page 596) – this is a battle or an episode of an illness, like cancer.

Healing through helping (page 600) – refers to social support or friends being important when you are having problems.

Mind over matter (page 603) – in terms of health, positive thoughts and a good attitude are very important to keeping healthy.

PRACTICE TEST 1 - Multiple Choice

1. According to Selye, the body mobilizes to meet a threat during which stage?
   A. alarm
   B. resistance
   C. activation
   D. exhaustion

2. Ellen is in the middle of final exams, and she has been getting very little sleep. She is managing to prepare for her tests, but she is more irritable than usual and feels like she might be getting the flu. This would be compatible with the _____ of Selye's model.
   A. alarm stage
   B. exhaustion stage
   C. resistance stage
   D. activation stage

3. You have the flu. The _____ are designed to recognize this foreign substance and _____ it.
   A. white blood cells; destroy
   B. brain chemicals; transform
   C. antigens; heal
   D. red blood cells; stimulate

4. White blood cells of the immune system are designed to recognize
   A. foreign substances.
   B. flu viruses and bacteria.
   C. antigens.
   D. all of the above.

5. Jerry has been under stress for a long period of time. He is lonely at university, under pressure to do well, and in the middle of finals. Which of the following is true?
   A. He is at higher risk for getting sick.
   B. Persistent stress depletes the body of energy.
   C. How he responds will depend on his coping skills.
   D. All of the above are true.

6. Dr. Weller is conducting research on the health behaviours of people who become ill and those who do not. What field of study does this represent?
   A. health psychology
   B. psychoneuroimmunology
   C. psychosomatic medicine
   D. any of the above

7. Hank is stuck in traffic and he is already late for his important appointment. This type of stressor
   A. does not pose much threat to health.
   B. increases the risk of illness.
   C. is related to heart disease.
   D. decreases the risk of illness.

8. Crowding is most stressful
   A. in a small room.
   B. on a hot day.
   C. in a crowd of strangers.
   D. when you feel crowded.

9. Which of the following would most stress researchers believe to be the most serious threat to health?
   A. being chronically unemployed
   B. crowding
   C. traffic jams
   D. the demands of a deadline

10. Scientists interested in exploring the links between psychological processes and the immune system created an interdisciplinary field called
   A. health psychology.
   B. psychosomatic medicine.
   C. psychoneuroimmunology.
   D. behavioural medicine.

11. Negative emotions
   A. are influential in affecting the course of the illness, once a person is already ill.
   B. are influential in causing an illness.
   C. have an impact on a person's psychological, not physical, well-being.
   D. are directly related to heart disease and cancer.

12. The stressfulness of noise depends on _____.
   A. whether the noise is your choice of noise.
   B. whether it is unpleasant.
   C. the type of noise it is.
   D. how loud it is.

13. The part of the Type A personality pattern that seems to be hazardous to health is
   A. a fast work pace.
   B. intensity.
   C. an achievement orientation.
   D. hostility.

14. Who among the following men has a higher risk for coronary heart disease?
   A. John is intense, ambitious, hard-working, and successful.
   B. Bill is complaining and irritable.
   C. Don is aggressive, confrontational, rude, cynical, and unco-operative.
   D. Jack is easy-going and calm.

15. Which of the following is NOT one of the hypothesized relationships between emotion and illness?
   A. Emotions may contribute to illness, but illness also influences emotions.
   B. Specific emotions are known to cause certain diseases.
   C. Researchers disagree about the strength of the link between emotion and illness.
   D. The mind and body interact.

16. A person _____ is at greater risk of becoming ill.
   A. who expresses his or her emotions
   B. with a problem-focused coping style
   C. who is emotionally inhibited
   D. who has an optimistic explanatory style

17. Optimists
    A. are the best judges of reality.   B. have positive illusions.
    C. deny that problems exist.   D. don't take care of themselves.

18. Which of the following is likely to have been said by someone with a pessimistic explanatory style?
    A. "This problem is all my fault and it's going to ruin my life."
    B. "I couldn't do anything about this."
    C. "I have had terrible luck today."
    D. "Everything will be fine."

19. "To lose is to win" and "The true tolerance is to tolerate the intolerable" are statements that reflect
    A. primary control.   B. secondary control.
    C. locus of control.   D. external locus of control.

20. Scheduled exams should be less stressful than pop quizzes because
    A. students can vent their emotions.   B. students are more optimistic.
    C. students have more control.   D. students can get more rest.

21. Compared to Western cultures, Eastern cultures, such as Japan's, emphasize
    A. primary control.   B. internal control.
    C. secondary control.   D. external control.

22. Which of the following demonstrates a problem that can result from the belief that an event is controllable?
    A. People could be unrealistically confident and try to control the uncontrollable.
    B. People could blame themselves for a problem they could not control.
    C. For some people, the realities of their lives are less controllable than for others.
    D. All of the above.

23. Identifying a problem and learning as much as possible about it is part of
    A. emotion-focused coping.   B. rethinking the problem.
    C. problem-focused coping.   D. cooling off.

24. _____ tends to increase self-efficacy, reduce anger, anxiety, and psychological stress.
    A. problem-focused coping.   B. avoidance.
    C. external locus of control.   D. looking outward.

25. When is it best to use emotion-focused coping and when should one use problem-focused coping?
    A. Problem-focused coping should be used at all times; it is never desirable to use emotion-focused coping.
    B. Emotion-focused coping is useful following a trauma, but a shift should be made to problem-focused coping.
    C. Emotion-focused coping is called for when stressors are continuous or can be prepared for; problem-focused coping should be used when the stressor is sudden.
    D. Emotion-focused coping should be used by people with Type A personalities, and problem-focused coping is appropriate for those with emotional inhibition.

26. Amanda has experienced high levels of stress lately. She is coping by meditating regularly and exercising daily. Which category of coping techniques is she using?
    A. solving the problem
    B. reappraising of the problem
    C. reducing bodily arousal
    D. making social comparisons

27. The positive effects of social supports may be a result of
    A. providing attachment.
    B. improved immune function.
    C. help evaluating problems.
    D. all of the above.

28. Social support
    A. helps heart rate return to normal more quickly after a stressful episode.
    B. can extend the survival time of people with serious illnesses, in some cases.
    C. can contribute to longer life.
    D. all of the above.

29. Social support can actually be harmful if
    A. the two parties frequently argue.
    B. friends resist positive changes.
    C. friends try to stem grief prematurely.
    D. all of the above conditions exist.

30. Anne has quit drinking. Her friend, Carl, continually asks her to join their group for drinks after work. This is an example of
    A. a situation in which a friend might contribute to stress.
    B. a way that friends can help reduce the effects of stress.
    C. an example of healing through helping.
    D. external locus of control.

31. Which of the following is a psychological factor that is thought to be important to good health?
    A. social support
    B. ability to relax
    C. feelings of control
    D. all of the above

32. Students who were asked to write about a personal traumatic experience 20 minutes a day for four days
    A. had fewer visits to the student health center than a control group.
    B. wrote about fairly mild experiences.
    C. had more physical symptoms of disease than a control group.
    D. had subsequent higher levels of anger and fear than a control group.

33. Although men on average are less likely to ask for help, all of the following conditions will make them more likely to ask for help EXCEPT
    A. when the man is able to reciprocate the help.
    B. when the problem is peripheral to the man's self-concept.
    C. when other men support the decision to seek help.
    D. when the problem is seen as "normal" rather than unique to him.

PRACTICE TEST 2 - Short Answer

1. _____ psychology is concerned with the psychological factors that influence how people stay healthy, why they become ill, and how they respond when they do get ill.

2. _____ introduced the modern era of stress research. He concluded that "stress" consists of a series of physiological reactions that occur in three phases: the _____ phase, the _____ phase, and the _____ phase.

3. In the two years following bereavement, _____ are more vulnerable to illness.

4. People who live in poverty or have little power in their lives have _____ health and _____ mortality rates for almost every disease and medical condition than do those at the higher end of the socioeconomic scale.

5. When an _____ invades the body, the _____ system deploys white blood cells that produce chemicals that go to the brain.

6. The interdisciplinary specialty that investigates the exact mechanisms that link mind and body, and studies how stress causes problems is called _____.

7. Negative emotions, like loneliness and worry, can suppress the _____ system.

8. The factor that can be dangerous for health in the behaviour of some Type A personalities is _____.

9. People who tend to deny feelings of anxiety, anger, or fear and pretend that everything is fine exhibit a personality trait called _____.

10. People with an _____ explanatory style tend to live longer and may engage in unrealistic, but healthy, positive _____.

11. People can tolerate all kinds of stressors if they feel able to _____ them. For example, the crowd you choose to join for a hockey game is not as stressful as being trapped in a crowd on a busy street.

12. If you do not like a situation, you are supposed to change it or fight it. This represents _____ control, whereas if you try to accommodate to reality by changing your own desires, you are demonstrating _____ control.

13. All the things people do to control, tolerate, or reduce the effects of life's stressors is called _____.

14. _____ coping in which a person focuses on the anger, anxiety, or grief the problem has caused is normal after a tragedy or trauma. However, over time _____ coping strategies are associated with better adjustment.

15. _____ the situation can help a person to think about the problem differently.

16. In a difficult situation, people who cope successfully often _____ themselves to others who are less fortunate.

17. Friends and social supports can both _____ and _____ stress.

18. Debate continues to rage over the extent to which _____ factors are involved in the onset or course of some illnesses.

19. Health professionals worry about the _____ industry that oversimplifies findings from health research.

20. It is important to avoid _____ thinking when a person is deciding about treatments for health problems.

21. _____ does not mean that the offended person denies or excuses the offence but that he or she is able to "let go" of the hurt and the desire for revenge.

PRACTICE TEST 3 - Essay

1. Indicate which member of each pair is likely to experience greater stress. Explain why.

    A. Air traffic controllers versus fishermen
    B. Type A personalities versus Type B personalities
    C. Subjects with an external locus of control versus subjects with an internal locus of control
    D. Subjects with a large social network versus single subjects
    E. Subjects with an optimistic versus pessimistic explanatory style

2. Apply Hans Selye's phases of stress response to people being held hostage. Describe what they would experience in the alarm, resistance, and exhaustion phases.

3. Over a period of years, David has been under treatment for a variety of disorders, including depression and ulcers. Visits to the doctor and prescriptions have been fairly regular because symptoms recur or new ones break out whenever medication is stopped. The doctor is now beginning to suggest that the origin of the problems must be related to stress or his depression.

    A. How could stress make recurring symptoms possible?
    B. What are some possible relationships that might exist between David's depression and his illnesses?
    C. What must David examine about himself and his life?

4. Assume that a group of hostages has been held by terrorists for several years. For each description, indicate whether stress has been reduced through attempts to solve, reappraise or live with the problem, and identify the specific coping strategy being used.

    A. Margaret has decided her captors have no bad intentions and are just trying to make an important philosophical point.
    B. Frank believes escape would be difficult but not impossible. He keeps formulating escape plans and explaining them to others.
    C. Joe believes this disaster has a bright side. Had another terrorist group taken them, there might have been torture as well as captivity.
    D. Like Frank, Tony believes escape is possible, but only if the terrorists unexpectedly make a mistake. His goal is to remain as calm as possible and look for an opportunity. He refuses to waste energy and lose hope by developing or considering unrealistic escape plans.
    E. Joan believes the group will remain in captivity virtually forever. Her goal is to eat as regularly as possible and combat inactivity through exercise.

CHAPTER
SIXTEEN

Psychological Disorders

LEARNING OBJECTIVES

1. Define mental disorder.

2. Describe three criteria commonly used to distinguish mental disorder from abnormal behaviour.

3. Distinguish mental disorder from the legal definition of insanity.

4. Describe the structure and aim of the *Diagnostic and Statistical Manual of Mental Disorders* (DSM). Describe the five axes of the DSM on which clinicians can evaluate a person.

5. Summarize the positions supporting and criticizing the DSM.

6. Distinguish between objective and projective psychological tests.

7. List and describe the general characteristics of the anxiety disorders.

8. Distinguish between generalized anxiety disorder and post-traumatic stress disorder.

9. Distinguish between panic disorder and phobias.

10. Describe obsessive-compulsive disorder, distinguishing between obsessions and compulsions.

11. Describe the symptoms of major depression.

12. Describe the symptoms of bipolar disorder.

13. Explain the various theories that attempt to account for major depression.

14. List the general features of personality disorders and three specific personality disorders.

15. Describe the features of antisocial personality disorder and the theories explaining its causes.

16. List the signs of substance abuse.

17. Distinguish between the biological and the learning models of addiction.

18. List the components that interact to influence addiction and abuse.

19. List and discuss the characteristics of dissociative identity disorder.

20. Describe the current controversy about the validity and nature of dissociative identity disorder.

21. Describe the symptoms of schizophrenia.

22.   Discuss the five theories that researchers are investigating to understand schizophrenia.

23.   Summarize the debate concerning mental disorder and personal responsibility.

24.   Describe rates of suicide and differences between men and women.

25.   Outline four strategies to consider when someone you know is threatening suicide.

BRIEF CHAPTER SUMMARY

Chapter 16 defines mental disorders and distinguishes abnormal behaviour from mental disorders. The issues and difficulties involved in developing a reliable and valid diagnostic system are also discussed. The *Diagnostic and Statistical Manual of Mental Disorders* (DSM), which is the manual that contains descriptions of all diagnostic categories of mental disorders, is reviewed. Some of the advantages and problems with this diagnostic system are described. There are numerous tools used to diagnose an individual, including projective tests (e.g. Rorschach Test) and objective tests (e.g. MMPI). Six general categories of disorders are reviewed. They consist of anxiety disorders (e.g., PTSD, phobias, panic disorder), mood disorders (e.g., depression, bipolar disorder), personality disorders (e.g., narcissistic personality disorder, antisocial personality disorder), addictions, dissociative identity disorder, and schizophrenia. The text describes symptoms, predisposing factors, and theories of causation for specific mental disorders under each broad disorder category.

PREVIEW OUTLINE

Before you read the chapter, review the preview outline for each section of the text.   After you have read the chapter, close this book and try to <u>re-create</u> the outlines on a blank piece of paper.

I. DEFINING AND DIAGNOSING DISORDER
    A.   **Defining mental disorders** - abnormal behaviour is not the same as mental disorder
        1.   Legal definition of insanity - awareness of the consequences of one's actions
        2.   Violation of cultural standards - depends on the culture and time
        3.   Behaviour that is self destructive or harmful to others
        4.   Emotional distress
    B.   **Text's definition** - any behaviour or emotional state that causes an individual to suffer, is self-destructive, seriously impairs the person's ability to work or get along with other, or endangers others or the community
    C.   **Dilemmas of diagnosis**
        1.   *The Diagnostic and Statistical Manual of Mental Disorders* (DSM) - standard reference used to diagnose disorders; primary aim is descriptive
            a.   Lists symptoms and associated information for each disorder
            b.   Classifies each disorder according to five axes or dimensions:

		(1)	Primary clinical problem

(1)	Primary clinical problem
(2)	Ingrained aspects of the individual's personality
(3)	Medical conditions relevant to the disorder
(4)	Social and environmental problems
(5)	Global assessment of the patient's overall functioning

2. Problems with the DSM - danger of over-diagnosis, power of diagnostic labels, confusion of serious mental disorders with normal problems, the illusion of objectivity and universality– beliefs about what is "normal" can change

3. Benefits of the DSM - new studies are improving empirical support for its categories, improves accuracy of diagnosis, biases in certain diagnosis can be corrected with awareness and better research

D. Dilemmas of measurement

1. Projective tests are used to infer a person's motives and conflicts based on interpretation of ambiguous stimuli (e.g., Rorschach Inkblot Test), but these tests have low reliability and validity

2. Objective tests - standardized questionnaires requiring written responses (e.g., MMPI-2); are generally more reliable and valid but weaknesses include cultural and socioeconomic differences not taken into account

Defining and Diagnosing Disorders

II. ANXIETY DISORDERS

A. **Anxiety and panic**
  1. Generalized anxiety disorder
     a. Characteristics - continuous and uncontrollable anxiety, feelings of dread, restlessness, difficulty concentrating, sleep disturbance
     b. May occur without specific anxiety-producing event, but may be related to physiological tendency to experience anxiety
  2. Post-traumatic stress disorder (PTSD) - anxiety results from uncontrollable and unpredictable dangers such as rape, war, torture, or natural disasters
     a. Symptoms include reliving the trauma, "psychic numbing," increased arousal, inability to feel happy, and detachment from others
     b. Associated with damage to hippocampus
  3. Panic disorder - recurring attacks of intense fear or panic
     a. Symptoms include trembling, dizziness, heart palpitations, feelings of unreality, fear of dying, going crazy, or losing control
     b. Usually occurs in the aftermath of stress or frightening experiences
     c. Interpretation of bodily reactions is part of the cause

B. **Fears and phobias -** exaggerated fear of a specific situation, activity, etc.
  1. Some may have an evolutionary basis
  2. Social phobia - fear of being observed by others
  3. Agoraphobia - fear of being alone in a public place from which escape might be difficult or help unavailable

C. **Obsessions and compulsions (OCD)**
  1. Obsessions - recurrent, persistent, unwished-for thoughts that are frightening or repugnant
  2. Compulsions - repetitive, ritualized behaviours over which people feel a lack of control (e.g., hand washing, counting, checking)
  3. Most sufferers know the behaviour is senseless and they don't enjoy it
  4. PET scans find parts of the brain are hyperactive in people with OCD

Anxiety Disorders

III. MOOD DISORDERS
- A. **Major depression** - emotional, behavioural, cognitive, physical changes; more common in females than males
- B. **Bipolar disorder** - depression alternates with mania, an abnormally high state of exhilaration, where person is full of energy, ambition, self-esteem and often gets into trouble with risky behaviour
- C. **Theories of depression**
    1. Biological explanations emphasize genetics, brain chemistry (deficiencies in serotonin) and shrinkage of some brain structures
    2. Life experiences explanations emphasize stressful circumstances of people's lives such as violence, poverty, loss of status and discrimination; may explain gender differences in depression rates
    3. Problems with close relationships (e.g., separations and losses, insecure attachments)
    4. Cognitive explanations emphasize habits of thinking (e.g. rumination) and interpretion of events - depressed people have a pessimistic explanatory style
    5. "Vulnerability–stress" explanations draw on all four previous explanations as an interaction between individual vulnerability and environmental stress

Mood Disorders

IV. PERSONALITY DISORDERS

    A.   **Definition** - rigid, maladaptive traits that cause great distress or inability to get along with others

    B.   **Problem personalities**
        1.   Narcissistic personality disorder - exaggerated sense of self-importance
        2.   Paranoid personality disorder - pervasive, unfounded suspiciousness
        3.   Borderline personality disorder - intense but unstable relationships, fear of abandonment, unrealistic self-image, emotional volatility

    C.   **Antisocial personality disorder (APD)**
        1.   Individuals who lack a connection to anyone so they can cheat, con, and kill without any problem; used to be called psychopaths or sociopaths
        2.   Symptoms include - repeated law breaking, deception, acting impulsively, fighting, disregarding safety, and lacking remorse
        3.   Often begin with problem behaviours in childhood; more common in males
        4.   Causes of APD
            a.   CNS abnormalities - inability to feel emotional arousal
            b.   Genetically influenced problems with impulse control
            c.   Brain damage from physical abuse or neglect (prefrontal cortex)

Personality Disorders

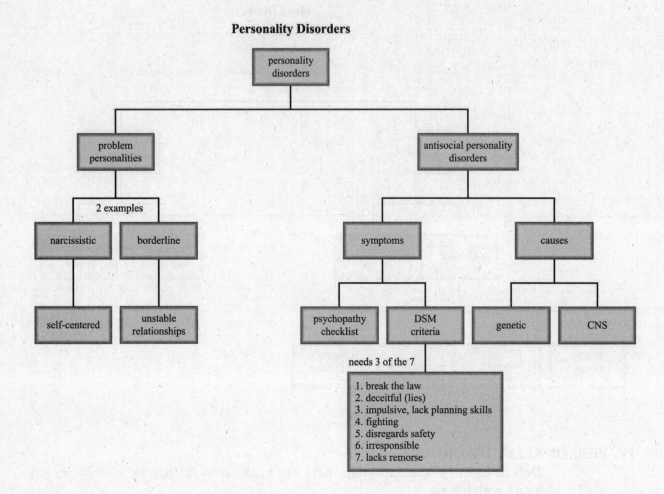

V. DRUG ABUSE AND ADDICTION

    A.   **DSM definition of substance abuse** - maladaptive pattern of substance use leading to clinically significant impairment or distress

    B.   **Biology and addiction** - addiction is a biochemical process influenced by genes

        1.   Biological model - addiction due to biochemistry, metabolism, and genetics

        2.   Genetic factors may affect impulsivity, protection against alcoholism

        3.   Causal relationship also works the other way: heavy drinking reduces endorphins, shrinks cortex, damages liver

    C.   **Learning, culture, and addiction** - challenges the biological model

        1.   Addiction patterns vary with cultural practices and social environment

        2.   Policies of total abstinence tend to increase rates of addiction

        3.   Not all addicts go through withdrawal symptoms when they stop the drug

        4.   Addiction depends on the drug AND the reason the person is taking it

D. **Debating the causes of addiction**
1. Biological and learning models contribute to our understanding
2. Theoretical differences have treatment implications
3. Most heated disagreement is about controlled drinking; research finds that many people can switch to moderate drinking under certain conditions

Drug Abuse and Addiction

VI. DISSOCIATIVE IDENTITY DISORDER

A. **Definition** - the appearance of two or more distinct identities within one person
B. **The MPD controversy -** two views among mental health professionals
1. A real disorder, common but often underdiagnosed; usually develops in childhood as a response to repeated trauma
2. A creation of mental health clinicians who believe in it - pressure and suggestion by clinicians elicit additional personalities
C. **The sociocognitive explanation -** an extreme form of a normal ability to present different aspects of our personalities to others

Dissociative Identity Disorder

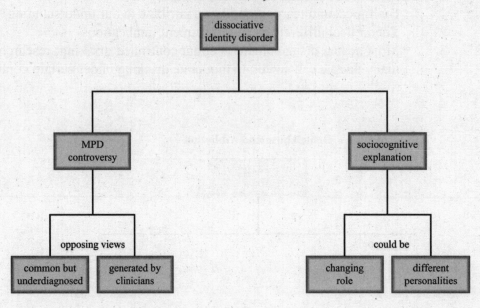

VII. **SCHIZOPHRENIA**
   A.   **Schizophrenia** - a psychosis or condition involving distorted perceptions of reality and an inability to function in most aspects of life
   B.   **Symptoms of schizophrenia**
      a.   Bizarre delusions - false beliefs
      b.   Hallucinations - usually auditory - seem intensely real
      c.   Disorganized, incoherent speech - illogical jumble of ideas
      d.   Grossly disorganized and inappropriate behaviour
      e.   Impaired cognitive abilities
      f.   Loss of motivation - inability to pursue goals
      g.   Poverty of speech - empty replies reflecting diminished thought
      h.   Emotional flatness - general unresponsiveness
      i.   Catatonic stupor

C. **Origins of schizophrenia** - many variations and symptoms
1. Genetic predispositions exist though no specific genes identified (new research looking at one specific gene DISCI)
2. Structural brain abnormalities (enlarged ventricles, smaller hippocampus, and thalamus)
3. Neurotransmitter abnormalities (e.g., serotonin, dopamine and glutamate)
4. Prenatal problems possibly related to malnutrition or a virus; Birth complications
5. Adolescent abnormalities in brain development - over-pruning synapses

Schizophrenia

PSYCHOLOGICAL DISORDERS

Complete the following chart indicating the major symptoms, predisposing factors, and explanatory theories for each of the disorders described in the left-hand column.

TYPE OF DISORDER	MAJOR SYMPTOMS	PREDISPOSING FACTORS	EXPLANATORY THEORIES
ANXIETY DISORDERS **Generalized Anxiety Disorder**			
Social Phobia			
Agoraphobia			
Panic Attack			
Obsessive– Compulsive Disorder			
MOOD DISORDERS **Major Depression**			
Bipolar Disorder			
PERSONALITY DISORDERS **Borderline**			
Narcissistic			
Antisocial			
Dissociative Identity Disorder			
SUBSTANCE ABUSE			
SCHIZOPHRENIA			

IDIOMS AND SLANGS

May not be wholly relevant to legal judgments (page 612) – referring to the idea that the DSM of psychological disorders is not a legal term and should not be used in a court of law.

Rambunctious (page 613) – having a lot of energy, especially little boys.

Veneer of science on an inherently subjective process (page 614) – one complaint of the DSM is that is a subjective interpretation of a mental disorder, but it is accepted as scientific proof.

Fuzzy and often difficult to determine (page 614) – this refers to the difficulty of distinguishing between abnormal and normal behaviours.

False positives (page 617) – when someone tests positive for something, but in reality, they should not have tested positive. Sometimes people are diagnosed positively with a disorder when they do not have it.

Racing heart (page 619) – this refers to a symptom where the heart is beating very quickly.

A far cry from the clinical disorders (page 624) – extreme sadness is normal when a tragedy happens, so this is not a case of a psychological disorder.

Women think and men drink (page 624) – this expression means that women usually solve their problems by talking about them, while men may drink alcohol to forget them.

Puts a premium on youth and beauty (page 628) – referring to a culture where youth and beauty are valuable things and people are encouraged to look young and be beautiful.

Abstainers are not sneered at (page 633) – when talking about alcohol use, abstainers, i.e., people who don't drink, are not laughed at.

Binge drinking (page 636) – referring to people who go out and drink for long periods of time and try to get drunk.

Word salads (page 642) – another phrase that means a number of words put together although they may not make any sense at all.

Hoard scraps of food (page 642) – this is an inappropriate behaviour related to schizophrenia, where someone may keep or hide pieces of food from others.

Track down the genes (page 644) – when referring to the biological cause of schizophrenia, scientists are trying to find the specific genes that cause it.

The traffic control center (page 644) – this refers to the part of the brain called the thalamus, which is responsible for sending sensations to the right part of the brain for processing.

The riddle of schizophrenia (page 645) – Scientists are trying to find the causes of schizophrenia, but they are not able to solve this complex problem.

PRACTICE TEST 1 - Multiple Choice

1. According to the _____ definition of mental disorder, a person living in Canada who hears voices and sees images of deceased loved ones exhibits:
    A. harmful behaviour
    B   violation of cultural standards
    C. emotional distress
    D. impaired judgment

2. Which of the following is <u>NOT</u> one of the definitions of mental disorder?
    A. statistical deviation
    B. self-destructive
    C. violation of cultural standards
    D. emotional distress

3. Whether a person is aware of the consequences of his or her actions and can control his or her behaviour is at the heart of the legal term,
    A. mental disorder.
    B. insanity.
    C. neurotic.
    D. psychotic.

4. The primary aim of the *Diagnostic and Statistical Manual of Mental Disorders* (DSM) is
    A. to provide clear criteria of diagnostic categories.
    B. to describe the causes of particular disorders.
    C. to describe the best course of treatment for a particular disorder.
    D. all of the above.

5. Clinicians are encouraged to evaluate each client according to five axes, or dimensions, in the DSM. The third dimension is
    A. the primary clinical problem.
    B. ingrained aspects of the client's personality.
    C. medical conditions that are relevant to the disorder.
    D. social and environmental problems that can make the disorder worse.

6. Which of the following is <u>NOT</u> one of the principle criticisms of the DSM discussed in the test?
    A. It confounds serious "mental disorders" with normal problems in living.
    B. Its heavy emphasis on theory may alienate clinicians from different perspectives.
    C. It gives the illusion of objectivity.
    D. It may foster over-diagnosis and self-fulfilling prophecies.

7. The diagnoses of disorder of written expression and caffeine-induced sleep disorder represent which criticism of the DSM?
    A. the idea that diagnosis can be made objectively scientific
    B. misusing diagnoses for social and political purposes
    C. confounding serious "mental disorders" with normal problems in living
    D. the fostering of over-diagnosis and self-fulfilling prophecies

8.   Generalized anxiety disorder is marked by
     A.   unrealistic fears of specific things or situations.
     B.   continuous, uncontrollable anxiety or worry.
     C.   the sudden onset of intense fear or terror.
     D.   unwished-for thoughts and repetitive behaviours.

9.   The most disabling fear disorder that accounts for more than half of the phobia cases for
     which people seek treatment is called
     A.   panic disorder.   B.   social phobia.
     C.   claustrophobia.   D.   agoraphobia.

10. Checking the furnace repeatedly before one can sleep and washing one's hands many
     times in one hour are examples of
     A.   obsessions.   B.   phobias.
     C.   compulsions.   D.   superstitions.

11. Unlike normal sadness or grief, major depression involves
     A.   panic attacks.   B.   low self-esteem.
     C.   a lack of interest in outside activities. D.   a negative mood.

12. Recently John has been over-eating, having difficulty sleeping through the night,
     experiencing a lack of energy and interest, and having trouble concentrating. These
     physical changes can be signs of
     A.   a phobia.   B.   mania.
     C.   depression.   D.   panic disorder.

13. Mania is an abnormally
     A.   chronic state of depression.   B.   apathetic state.
     C.   intense feeling of despair.   D.   high state of exhilaration.

14. Most manic episodes alternate with
     A.   episodes of depression.   B.   panic attacks.
     C.   obsessive–compulsive episodes.   D.   periods of elation.

15. More women receive a diagnosis of depression than men. Which of the following is a
     possible explanation for this gender difference in depression?
     A.   Women are more likely to have a history of sexual abuse.
     B.   Women are more likely to lack fulfilling jobs.
     C.   Mothers are vulnerable to depression.
     D.   All of the above.

16. Social theories of depression suggest that women are more likely to be depressed than men because they are more likely to lack
   A. endorphins and key neurotransmitters.   B. positive self-images.
   C. fulfilling work and family relations.   D. a stable network of friends.

17. In Canada, mental disorders are the_____ cause of disability in people aged_____ .
   A. leading; 16-25 years   B. secondary; 16-25 years
   C. leading; 15 – 44 years   D. secondary; 15-44 years

18. Individuals suffering from antisocial personality disorder are often charming and can be highly successful
   A. psychotherapists.   B. con men.
   C. actors.   D. business executives.

19. Hypothesized causes of antisocial personality disorder include
   A. problems in behavioural inhibition. B. neurological impairments.
   C. social deprivation.   D. all of the above.

20. Having a genetic disposition toward impulsivity, addiction, hyperactivity; being neglected or rejected by parents; having a history of physical abuse or birth complications are all
   A. contributors to mood disorders.
   B. risk factors for antisocial personality disorder.
   C. foundations for any mental disorder.
   D. paths to dissociative disorders.

21. According to the DSM-IV, the key feature of substance abuse is
   A. the length of time a person has been using the drug.
   B. the inability to stop using the drug or to cut down on use.
   C. a maladaptive pattern of use leading to significant impairment or distress.
   D. all of the above.

22. The disease model of addiction
   A. requires abstinence.
   B. maintains that people have an inherited predisposition for alcoholism.
   C. holds that addiction is related to biochemistry, metabolism, and genetics.
   D. incorporates all of the above.

23. At the heart of the debate between the disease and learning models of addiction is the question of whether
    A. moderate drinking is possible for former alcoholics.
    B. alcoholics should be blamed for their alcoholism.
    C. there is an alcoholic personality.
    D. alcoholics are "bad" or "sick."

24. Luis is emotionally unstable, quite impulsive, and has serious fears of being abandoned by his girlfriend. He is most likely suffering from which personality disorder?
    A. narcissistic   B. paranoid
    C. antisocial   D. borderline

25. The controversy among mental health professionals about dissociative identity disorder has to do with
    A. whether it is a common and underdiagnosed disorder or whether it is concocted by mental health professionals and suggestible patients.
    B. whether it should be treated with traditional techniques or whether special treatments should be utilized.
    C. whether it is a biologically based disorder or whether it results from psychosocial factors.
    D. whether the alternate personalities should be "seen" in treatment or whether they should be ignored by the therapist.

26. Elizabeth thinks she is the Queen of England. When she speaks, she often does not make any sense at all, and at times she appears to be talking to herself. She is experiencing
    A. symptoms of schizophrenia.
    B. symptoms of bipolar disorder
    C. catatonic symptoms
    D. emotional flatness.

27. Bizarre delusions, hallucinations, incoherent speech, and disorganized and inappropriate behaviour are symptoms of _____.
    A. Schizophrenia   B. Bipolar Disorder
    C. MPD   D. PTSD

28. Symptoms of schizophrenia
    A. may begin during adolescence.
    B. include loss of motivation.
    C. include diminished thought and emotional flatness.
    D. include all of the above.

29. Support for the idea of an infectious virus during prenatal development as a cause of schizophrenia comes from the fact that
   A. there is a significant association between a mother's exposure to a virus during prenatal development.
   B. most schizophrenics have very low immune functioning.
   C. most schizophrenics show abnormalities on chromosome 5.
   D. most schizophrenics have extra dopamine receptors.

30. Which of the following has been advanced as one of the biological explanations of schizophrenia?
   A. brain abnormalities
   B. dopamine abnormalities
   C. genes
   D. all of the above

31. The idea that genetic or brain abnormalities combine with family or other pressures to trigger schizophrenia reflects the
   A. interactionist model
   B. learning theory model
   C. vulnerability–stress model
   D. biology–pressure model

32. Brain abnormalities that have been found to be associated with schizophrenia include
   A. decreased brain weight.
   B. reduced numbers of neurons in specific layers of the prefrontal cortex.
   C. enlarged ventricles.
   D. all of the above.

33. Mike is suspicious of most people in his life, does not open up to people because he mistrusts them, and consequently has few friends. He is most likely suffering from which personality disorder?
   A. narcissistic
   B. paranoid
   C. antisocial
   D. borderline

34. An "alter" is
   A. an emerging personality in dissociative identity disorder.
   B. someone with bipolar disorder.
   C. someone co-dependent with an individual with borderline personality disorder.
   D. a principal symptom of post-traumatic stress disorder.

35. Neurotransmitter abnormalities associated with schizophrenia include which of the following neurotransmitters?
   A. endorphins
   B. GABA
   C. norepinephrine
   D. dopamine

36. A recent approach to understanding the causes of schizophrenia has focused on adolescence, when
   A. a shortage of intimate friends may predispose someone to schizophrenia.
   B. an over-pruning of synapses may occur.
   C. punitive parental treatment may predispose someone to schizophrenia.
   D. viruses may damage the hippocampus.

37. Schizophrenia typically becomes apparent during
   A. childhood.   B. middle adulthood.
   C. adolescence or early adulthood.   D. infancy.

PRACTICE TEST 2 - Short Answer

1.   One perspective defines mental disorders as a violation of _____ standards.

2.   The official manual describing the major categories of mental disorder is the _____.

3.   The fact that attention deficit/hyperactivity disorder is the fastest-growing disorder in America (where it is diagnosed at least ten times as often as it is in Europe) supports the criticism of the DSM that it fosters _____.

4.   _____ anxiety disorder is continuous, uncontrollable anxiety, or worry.

5.   Typical anxiety symptoms of _____ include reliving the trauma in recurrent, intrusive thoughts or dreams.

6.   The essential difference between people who develop panic disorder and those who do not lies in how they _____ their bodily reactions.

7.   John will not take a class if a class presentation is one of the requirements. He is terrified of speaking in class because he worries that he will do or say something humiliating or embarrassing. The most likely diagnosis for John is _____.

8.   The most disabling fear disorder which accounts for more than half of the phobia cases for which people seek treatment is _____.

9.   _____ are recurrent, persistent, unwished-for thoughts or images, whereas _____ are repetitive, ritualized, stereotyped behaviours that the person feels must be carried out to avoid disaster. If the person does not carry out the behaviours, he or she will experience high levels of _____.

10. People who suffer from major depression experience emotional, _____, and _____ changes severe enough to disrupt their ordinary functioning.

11. _____ occurs two or three times as often among women as among men, all over the world.

12. _____ explanations of depression emphasize problems with close relationships.

13. The DSM-IV describes _____ disorders as "an enduring pattern of inner experience and behaviour that deviates markedly from the expectations of the individual's culture [and] is pervasive and inflexible."

14. People with antisocial personality disorder may have problems in behavioural _____, the ability to control responses to frustration and provocation.

15. The _____ model of APD says that disorder is more likely to develop when biological predispositions are combined with physical abuse, parental neglect, lack of love, or other environmental _____.

16. _____, or the tendency to brood about all that is wrong with your life, is associated with depression.

17. On one side of the MPD controversy, there are those who think MPD is _____, but often misdiagnosed. On the other side are those who believe that most cases of MPD are generated by _____, either knowingly or unknowingly.

18. The _____ explanation of MPD holds that it is simply an extreme form of the ability we all have to present different aspects of our personalities to others.

19. The biological model holds that addiction, whether to alcohol or any other drug, is due primarily to a person's _____, metabolism, and genetic predisposition.

20. The fact that within a particular country, addiction rates can rise or fall rapidly in response to cultural changes supports the _____ model of addiction.

21. Schizophrenia is an example of a _____, a mental condition that involves distorted perceptions of reality and an inability to function in most aspects of life.

22. Two active symptoms of schizophrenia include bizarre _____ or false beliefs, and auditory _____.

23. There is good evidence for the existence of a _____ contribution to schizophrenia. In addition, _____ abnormalities are associated with schizophrenia.

24. An infectious _____ during prenatal development may affect the likelihood of schizophrenia developing.

25. The Rorschach Inkblot Test and similar _____ tests typically have low _____ and _____.

26. Because depressed people have given up on the future, "learned helplessness" theory of depression might be more accurate if it were renamed the "learned _____" theory.

27. Damage to the part of the brain known as the _____ has been linked to both schizophrenia and antisocial personality disorder.

PRACTICE TEST 3 - Essay

1. Jason spends all day at the shopping mall. Every day he stops people who look in his direction and literally begs for their forgiveness. Jason's boldly coloured sweatshirts make Jason quite noticeable. These are worn every day, over his coat when it's cold, and each one has exactly the same inscription or saying: "Jason is not a thief." Discuss the aspect of Jason's behaviour that conforms to each of the following definitions of mental disorder.

    A.   Violation of cultural standards
    B.   Self – destructive or harmful behaviour
    C.   Emotional distress

2. In the formulation of Jason's diagnosis according to the DSM-IV, indicate whether the types of information identified below would be included. Explain your answers.

    A.   A diagnostic label for Jason's condition
    B.   The suspected cause(s) for Jason's symptoms
    C.   An estimate of potential treatment effects
    D.   How well Jason is functioning
    E.   Any medical condition that Jason might have

3. For each description below, indicate whether the anxiety that is present is normal or abnormal. When it is abnormal, suggest the most likely diagnostic category.

    A.   Carl loves the racetrack but he will not go there again. The last time he was there he suddenly felt his heart racing, he was gasping for breath, his hands began to tremble and he broke out into a cold sweat.
    B.   Sandy is very clean! She feels contaminated unless she bathes and changes her clothes at least four times a day, and she is meticulous about the house as well. Every room is scrubbed at least twice a week and the bathroom is cleaned daily.
    C.   A university student becomes anxious whenever assigned a project that requires speaking in front of class. The anxiety motivates meticulous preparation and the student rehearses material again and again.
    D.   Marsha was stranded in a building for over two hours. The stairway was blocked by men moving large cartons, and the only way down was the elevators. Elevators cause Marsha to sweat, tremble and suffer from images of being crushed. She decided to wait rather than take the elevator.
    E.   Harry has had problems since returning from Afghanistan. He is listless and quarrelsome, and has fitful sleeps, reliving his past in nightmarish dreams.

294

4. Decide whether each of the statements below is correct or incorrect. When it is incorrect, rewrite it in a more factual form.

    A. Mood disorders consist primarily of emotional symptoms and have little impact on behavioural, cognitive, or physical functioning.
    B. In bipolar disorder, periods of sluggishness alternate with active attempts to commit suicide.
    C. Antidepressant drugs work by altering the activity level of the limbic system.
    D. Lack of fulfilling work and family relationships are a good predictor of depression.
    E. Negatively distorted thinking is the result, not the cause, of depression.
    F. Repeated failure is an unlikely source of major depressive episodes.

5. Josephine is highly mistrustful of airline personnel. She believes that airplanes dirty the streets and sidewalks by dripping oil and that pilots have a power called "telectic penetration." On hearing a plane, Josephine becomes introspective and claims she is being used as radar. She feels the pilots are tuning in to her latitude and longitude and asking her questions about her location. She is unable to speak until they are through.

    A. Does Josephine have delusions? If so, what?
    B. Is Josephine hallucinating? If so, describe her hallucinations.
    C. Is Josephine having any disorganized or incoherent speech? If so, describe.
    D. Is Josephine demonstrating any disorganized or inappropriate behaviour? If so, what?
    E. Is Josephine demonstrating emotional flatness? If so, describe.

6. Imagine that you suspect that a friend might be suicidal. What are some of the danger signs, and what should you do to help your friend?

CHAPTER
SEVENTEEN

Approaches to Treatment and Therapy

LEARNING OBJECTIVES

1. Distinguish between a licensed psychologist and a psychotherapist.

2. Discuss the use of antipsychotic drugs, reviewing their strengths and limitations.

3. Describe the different antidepressants, noting their side effects.

4. Discuss the use of tranquilizers and lithium carbonate in treating mental disorders.

5. Summarize the problems inherent in treating psychological disorders with drugs.

6. Discuss the problem of overprescription of drugs commonly used to treat mental disorders.

7. Describe the procedures used in attempts to alter brain function directly.

8. List and explain the goals and principles of psychodynamic therapy.

9. List and explain the goals and principles of behaviour therapy.

10. List and explain the goals of cognitive therapy.

11. List and explain the goals of humanist and existential therapy.

12. List and explain the goals of family and couples therapy.

13. Describe what is meant by the integrative approach.

14. Define the therapeutic alliance and describe those factors that are most likely to lead to successful therapy.

15. Explain the scientist–practitioner gap and why it has developed.

16. Describe the problems of assessing therapy and current evaluation methods.

17. Discuss which therapies work best for specific problems.

18. Discuss the circumstances under which therapy can be harmful.

19. Distinguish between Western and Eastern approaches to change and the value of psychotherapy.

20. Review the three considerations the text suggests consumers should think about when contemplating psychotherapy.

21. Describe the self-help movement and cautions for its use.

BRIEF CHAPTER SUMMARY

Chapter 17 describes various approaches to the treatment of mental disorders. Three general types of approaches are reviewed. Medical approaches include drug treatments, psychosurgery, and electroconvulsive therapy. Drug treatments include medications that treat psychoses (neuroleptics like Haldol and Clozaril), depression (antidepressants like MAOIs and Prozac), anxiety (tranquilizers like Valium and Xanax), and bipolar disorder (lithium carbonate). Although drugs have contributed to significant advances in the treatment of mental disorders, they require great caution in their use. Psychosurgery, which was used more commonly in the 1950s, is rarely used any longer because of its serious and irreversible side effects. Electroconvulsive therapy is still used for serious cases of depression that do not respond to other treatments. Types of psychotherapy exist based on each of the major perspectives (e.g., psychodynamic, humanistic). The general principles and techniques of each of these approaches are reviewed along with research on their effectiveness. Although there are certain commonalities among all the different types of psychotherapy, research indicates that some approaches are more effective for particular problems. Cognitive and behavioural approaches, for example, are successful in treating depression, phobias, and other anxiety disorders, as well as childhood behaviour problems.

PREVIEW OUTLINE

Before you read the chapter, review the preview outline for each section of the text. After you have read the chapter, close this book and try to <u>re-create</u> the outlines on a blank piece of paper.

I. **BIOLOGICAL TREATMENTS FOR MENTAL DISORDERS**
   A.   **The question of drugs**
       1.   Biological treatments are enjoying a resurgence because of evidence that some disorders have a biological component
       2.   Drugs commonly prescribed for mental disorders
           a.   Antipsychotic drugs (neuroleptics) for schizophrenia and other psychoses; may shorten length of schizophrenic episodes
           b.   Antidepressant drugs - include (MAO) inhibitors, tricyclics, and SSRIs - nonaddictive, but can have unpleasant side effects
           c.   Tranquilizers - increase activity of GABA
           d.   Lithium carbonate - prescribed for bipolar disorder; must be administered in the correct dose or can be dangerous
       3.   Cautions about drugs include overprescription, relapse, and dropout rates, dosage problems, unknown long term risks and placebo effect (to what extent is the effectiveness of a drug due simply to belief in the drug's effectiveness?)

B. Direct brain intervention
    1.   Psychosurgery - surgery to destroy selected areas of the brain (e.g., prefrontal lobotomy, cingulotomy)
    2.   Electrically stimulating the brain - Electroconvulsive therapy or ECT (works for severely depressed people, though it is unclear why it works) and transcranial magnetic stimulation or TMS (involves magnetic coil)

Biological Treatments for Mental Disorders

II. KINDS OF PSYCHOTHERAPY
    A.   **Commonalities among psychotherapies** - help clients think about their lives in new ways and find solutions to their problems
    B.   **Psychodynamic therapy**
        1.   Probes the past and the unconscious with techniques such as free association and transference
        2.   Traditional psychoanalysis evolved into psychodynamic therapies
        3.   They do not aim to solve an individual's immediate problem - symptoms are seen as the tip of the iceberg
    C.   **Behavioural and cognitive therapy** - focus is behaviour change, not insight
        1.   Behavioural techniques - derived from classical and operant conditioning

        a.   Systematic desensitization – step-by-step process of "desensitizing" a client to a feared object or experience; uses counterconditioning

        b.   Graduated exposure treatment (or flooding) - therapist accompanies client into the feared situation

        c.   Behavioural self monitoring

        d.   Skills training - practice in behaviours necessary for achieving goals

2.   Cognitive techniques

        a.   Aim is to identify thoughts, beliefs, and expectations that might be prolonging a person's problems

        b.   Albert Ellis and rational emotive behaviour therapy - therapist challenges unrealistic beliefs directly with rational arguments

        c.   Beck's approach uses other, less direct techniques

D.   **Humanistic and existential therapy**

1.   Humanistic therapies - assume that people seek self-actualization

2.   Do not delve into the past; help people to develop will and confidence to change and achieve goals

3.   Client-centered or nondirective therapy by Carl Rogers - unconditional positive regard and empathy by therapist

4.   Existential therapy - helps client explore meaning of existence, choose a destiny and accept self-responsibility

E.   **Family and couples therapy**

1.   Family therapy - believes that the problem developed and is maintained in the social context, and that is where change must occur

2.   The family as a changing pattern in which all parts affect each other and efforts to treat a single member are doomed to fail; observing the family together reveals family tensions and imbalances

3.   Couples therapy involves both parties; integrative approach popular

F.   **Psychotherapy in practice** - integrative approach

Kinds of Psychotherapy

III. EVALUATING PSYCHOTHERAPY

A. **The scientist–practitioner gap**

1. Conflict between scientists and practitioners about the relevance of research findings to clinical practice

2. Breach between scientists and therapists has widened, partly due to professional schools that are unconnected to academic departments

B. **The therapeutic alliance**

1. Some participants will do better than others in therapy (e.g., those motivated to improve or who have family support)

2. Understanding role of the client's culture is also important

C. **When therapy helps**

1. Randomized controlled trials reveal empirically validated treatments

2. Which therapy for which problem?

   a. Behaviour and cognitive therapies are the method of choice for depression, anxiety disorders, anger and impulsive violence, health problems, sleeps disorders, and childhood behaviour problems

   b. Family intervention therapies help schizophrenics by teaching their families skills for dealing with the schizophrenic children

   c. No single type of therapy can help everyone

D.   When therapy harms
1.   Sexual intimacies or other unethical behaviour
2.   Prejudice or cultural ignorance on the part of a therapist
3.   Inappropriate or coercive influence
4.   Use of empirically unsupported, potentially dangerous techniques

Evaluating Psychotherapy

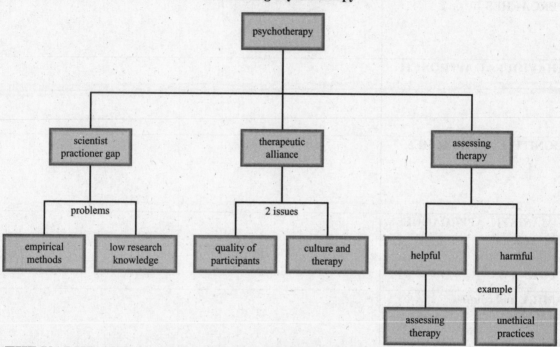

IV. THE VALUE AND VALUES OF PSYCHOTHERAPY
A.   Does psychotherapy promise too much or foster a preoccupation with the self?
B.   Make wise decisions when choosing a therapist, choosing a therapy, and deciding when to leave

APPROACHES TO PSYCHOTHERAPY

Complete the following chart by listing specific techniques and general goals of therapy for each of the approaches in the left-hand column.

THERAPEUTIC APPROACH	SPECIFIC TECHNIQUES	GENERAL GOALS OF THERAPY
PSYCHODYNAMIC APPROACHES		
BEHAVIOURAL APPROACH		
COGNITIVE APPROACHES		
HUMANISTIC APPROACHES		
FAMILY and couples THERAPY		

302

IDIOMS AND SLANGS

Hundreds of offshoots and specialties (page 653) – this refers to the hundreds of different types of psychotherapy besides the major types.

Physicians and pharmaceutical companies are promoting biomedical solutions (page 654) – meaning that there is an increase in biological therapies because of economics (money making).

Jumbled thoughts (page 654) – when people are thinking about a number of different things, but there doesn't seem to be any sense or order to them. This is a symptom with schizophrenia.

Before Prozac, she loathed company (page 655) – this cartoon is commenting on the use of drugs, like Prozac, to make people (and animals) happy.

Repeated TMS seems to give it a boost (page 660) – TMS, or transcranial magnetic stimulation, is used to stimulate the left prefrontal cortex, making it more active.

Problems that plague them (page 661) – some people feel that their problems will not go away, like the disease, the plague.

Tip of the mental iceberg (page 661) – Freud compared the consciousness to an iceberg. The part that you can see, or the tip, is only a surface problem. Usually the therapist is more interested in the problems that a person is hiding.

Make small talk with others (page 663) – this is the kind of conversation that we have with strangers. Usually this includes conversations of the weather, news events, or other common events.

No-nonsense, get-on-with-it attitude (page 665) – this type of therapy gets at the problem directly.

They contain the seeds of wisdom and redemption (page 668) – according to existential therapy, one must find knowledge in experiences. One example was Victor Frankl who was in a Nazi concentration camp but used his experiences to further himself.

Tomorrow man (page 668) – this is a nickname given to the fictional character, Murray, because he puts things off until tomorrow and they never seem to get done.

Interconnected as that of two dancers (page 669) – the textbook is trying to show that the family plays a large role in the member's behaviours.

Anything more than pseudoscientific window dressing (page 675) – they are referring to a questionable technique, EMDR (Eye Movement Desensitization and Reprocessing) that is being supported by psychologists without scientific proof.

Toxic families (page 683) – some therapists believe the family does more harm to a person, so they refer to them as toxic.

Eradicate these psychological weeds from their life (page 684) – this is referring to the Japanese therapy, where people live with their troubling emotions. The weeds are compared to these bad emotions that they learn to live with and not get rid of.

PRACTICE TEST 1 - Multiple Choice

1.   The most widespread biological treatment is
      A.   medication.   B.   psychosurgery.
      C.   ECT.   D.   psychotherapy.

2.   Antipsychotic drugs do <u>NOT</u>
      A.   restore normal thought patterns.   B.   lessen hallucinations.
      C.   reduce dramatic symptoms.   D.   have side effects.

3.   Randolf is taking antipsychotic medication. Which of the following should concern him?
      A.   the possibility of tardive dyskinesia
      B.   the fact that while the more dramatic symptoms may be helped, normal thinking
            may not
      C.   though he may be well enough to be released from a hospital, he may not be able
            to care for himself
      D.   All of the above are concerns.

4.   Lithium carbonate is often effective in treating people who
      A.   have schizophrenia.   B.   have tardive dyskinesia.
      C.   complain of unhappiness or anxiety.   D.   have bipolar disorder.

5.   Jay is taking a medication that elevates the levels of norepinephrine and serotonin in his
      brain. What is his most probable diagnosis?
      A.   depression   B.   an anxiety disorder
      C.   bipolar disorder   D.   a psychosis

6.   Felicia has been prescribed an antidepressant. Based on the cautions about drug
      treatment, Felicia should probably have concerns about
      A.   whether the drug is more effective than a placebo.
      B.   whether the drug has been tested for long-term use.
      C.   whether the right dosage has been identified.
      D.   all of the above.

7.   A problem with using drugs in treating psychological disorders is that
      A.   there are high dropout rates.
      B.   tests of drug effects in long-term usage are often missing.
      C.   there is a strong placebo effect in evaluating their effectiveness.
      D.   all of the above are potential problems.

8. The original intention of prefrontal lobotomy was to
   A. reduce the patient's emotional discomfort without impairing intellectual capacity.
   B. get rid of evil impulses or mental pressures.
   C. remove an abnormal organic condition, such as a tumour.
   D. replace drugs and electroconvulsive therapy, which were considered dangerous.

9. Among the following patients, who would be a likely candidate for electroconvulsive therapy (ECT)?
   A. Fran is suicidally depressed.
   B. Dan is anxious.
   C. Stan is moderately depressed.
   D. ECT should not be used on any of them, since it is outdated and barbaric.

10. Critics of ECT say that it
    A. only helps people with minor psychological problems.
    B. is too often used improperly, and it can damage the brain.
    C. requires high voltages that could be fatal.
    D. causes epileptic seizures.

11. In psychodynamic therapies, the patient's displacement of emotional elements in his or her inner life onto the therapist is called
    A. free association.   B. transference.
    C. insight.   D. dynamic focus.

12. A type of therapy that takes the individual right into the most feared situation is called
    A. systematic desensitization.   B. aversive conditioning.
    C. flooding or exposure treatment. D. brief psychodynamic therapy.

13. Systematic desensitization, aversive conditioning, flooding, and skills training are all
    A. techniques used in cognitive therapies.   B. psychodynamic techniques.
    C. methods employed by humanists.   D. behavioural techniques.

14. To help Bob with his fear of flying, Dr. Rose teaches Bob to relax while they proceed through a series of steps that go from reading a story about an airplane, to visiting an airport, to boarding a plane, to taking a short flight. This _____ technique is called _____.
    A. cognitive; rational emotive therapy   B. humanistic; flooding
    C. behavioural; systematic desensitization   D. behavioural; flooding

15. Cognitive therapies focus on changing _____, whereas humanistic therapies focus on _____.
    A. beliefs; self-acceptance   B. behaviours; changing families
    C. behaviours; insight into the past D. thoughts; skills

16. Which two therapies often borrow each other's methods, so that a combination of the two is more common than either method alone?
    A. psychoanalysis; behaviour therapy
    B. family therapy; group therapy
    C. cognitive therapy; behaviour therapy
    D. support groups; group therapy

17. In which approach does the therapist challenge the client's illogical beliefs?
    A. cognitive therapy
    B. humanistic therapy
    C. psychodynamic therapy
    D. existential therapy

18. What type of therapist would try to provide unconditional positive regard?
    A. cognitive
    B. humanistic
    C. psychodynamic
    D. existential

19. Which type of therapist might make use of insight, transference, and free association?
    A. a humanistic therapist
    B. a behaviourist therapist
    C. a psychodynamic therapist
    D. a cognitive therapist

20. Professionals who help those who are physically disabled to work and live independently are called
    A. behavioural psychologists.
    B. family therapists.
    C. rehabilitation psychologists.
    D. group therapists.

21. Based on controlled clinical trials, which of the following is true about the effectiveness of therapy?
    A. Psychotherapy is better than doing nothing at all.
    B. People who do best in psychotherapy are those who have less serious problems and are motivated to improve.
    C. For the common emotional problems of life, short-term treatment is usually sufficient.
    D. All of the above

22. Good therapeutic candidates are those who
    A. are introspective and want to talk about their childhoods.
    B. want a chance to talk about their feelings without any limits.
    C. recognize the expertise of the therapist.
    D. are unhappy and motivated enough to want to work on their problems.

23. A therapeutic alliance is
    A. an organization of therapists who advocate for the benefits of therapy.
    B. a group of consumers who were harmed because of a therapist's incompetence or unethical methods.
    C. a bond between the client and therapist that depends on their ability to understand each other.
    D. a support group in which people share common problems.

24. Depth therapies work best for
    A. anxiety disorders.
    B. people who are introspective and want to explore their pasts and examine their current lives.
    C. people with sex problems.
    D. people who are drug abusers.

25. Research suggests that cognitive and behavioural approaches are very successful with many types of problems; however, they are NOT thought to work well for
    A. personality disorders and psychoses.
    B. phobias and panic disorder.
    C. moderate depression.
    D. agoraphobia and anxiety disorders.

26. In which of the following cases is Melissa most likely to find the therapeutic experience harmful?
    A. Her therapist firmly believes that Melissa was sexually abused in childhood, though she has no memories of this and does not believe it is so.
    B. Her therapist disagrees with her about several issues.
    C. Her therapist does not always give her an immediate appointment when she calls.
    D. All of the above may be harmful.

27. Which factors can cause psychotherapy to be harmful?
    A. coercion   B. bias
    C. therapist-induced disorders   D. all of the above

28. A realistic expectation for the outcome of psychotherapy is
    A. to learn that any change is possible.
    B. to help make decisions and clarify values and goals.
    C. to be happy all, or almost all, of the time.
    D. to help eliminate the problems from one's life.

29. One type of modern psychosurgery for intractable OCD or depression involves burning holes in the frontal lobes. It is called
    A. lobotomy.   B. thalamectomy.
    C. lobectomy.   D. cingulotomy.

30. Which category of antidepressant drug is least prescribed nowadays due to the risky side effects?
    A. SSRIs   B. tricyclics
    C. MAOIs   D. neuroleptics

PRACTICE TEST 2 - Short Answer

1. Neuroleptics, or antipsychotic drugs, are used in the treatment of _____ and other _____.

2. One of the side effects of the antipsychotic drugs is a neurological disorder called _____, which is characterized by hand tremors and other involuntary muscle movements.

3. Monoamine oxidase inhibitors, tricyclics, and selective serotonin reuptake inhibitors are all examples of _____ drugs.

4. _____ is a special category of drug which often helps people who suffer from bipolar disorder.

5. People who take antidepressant drugs without also learning how to cope with their problems are more likely to _____ in the future.

6. A form of psychosurgery that was supposed to reduce the patient's emotional symptoms without impairing intellectual ability, called a _____, left many patients apathetic, withdrawn, and unable to care for themselves.

7. _____ is used as a treatment for severe depression, for patients who are at risk of committing suicide and who cannot wait for antidepressants or psychotherapy to take effect.

8. To bring unconscious conflicts to awareness, _____ therapists often ask the client to say whatever comes to mind. This technique is called _____.

9. Bob has been seeing Dr. Sigmund. Bob has always felt that his mother rejected him and now he finds that he is furious at Dr. Sigmund for planning a vacation. This element of psychodynamic therapy is called _____.

10. _____ is one of the _____ techniques that involves a step-by-step process of desensitizing a client to a feared object or experience.

11. The technique of _____ involves having clients who are suffering from specific anxieties confront the feared situation or memory directly.

12. Cognitive therapists require clients to examine the _____ for their beliefs and to consider other _____ of events that might result in less disturbing emotions.

13.   One of the best known schools of cognitive therapy was developed by Albert Ellis and is now called rational _____ behaviour therapy.

14.   _____ therapy, developed by Carl Rogers, the therapist listens to the client in an accepting, nonjudgmental way and offers _____ positive regard.

15.   _____ therapists maintain that problems develop in a social context, and that any changes a person makes in therapy will affect that context.

16.   The scientist–practitioner gap refers to the breach between scientists and therapists about the importance of _____ methods and findings on the practice of psychotherapy.

17.   In some cases, psychotherapy has been found to be harmful because the therapist may be _____, inducing the client to produce the symptoms the therapist is looking for.

18.   The personality of the therapist is also critical to the success of any therapy, particularly the qualities that Carl Rogers praised: _____, expressiveness, warmth, and _____.

19.   A task force from the American Psychological Association found that _____treatment is particularly effective for depression and _____ disorders.

20.   The APA task force also found that young adults with schizophrenia are greatly helped by family therapies that teach parents _____ skills in dealing with their troubled children.

21.   _____ to accept the therapist's advice, sexual intimacies, or other unethical behaviour can result in harm to the client.

22.   Therapist influence is a likely reason for the growing number of people diagnosed with _____ disorder in the 1980s and 1990s.

23.   _____ psychologists set up programs to help people who are mentally ill in their own communities rather than in hospitals. _____ psychologists are concerned with the assessment and treatment of people who are physically disabled.

24.   One alternative to transcranial magnetic stimulation involves implanting an electrode into the brain and connecting it to a pacemaker. This method is known as _____.

25.   The lack of communication between those who research therapy and those who conduct it is called the _____.

PRACTICE TEST 3 - Essay

1. Identify the three major categories of approaches to psychological problems and briefly describe the help they offer. Indicate under what circumstances each would be desirable.

2. Identify the drugs typically prescribed for each of the disorders listed below and then briefly explain why drugs alone may not be sufficient treatment.

    A. Anxiety disorders
    B. Mood disorders
    C. Psychotic disorders

3. Summarize the major features of each of the five major approaches to psychotherapy. Specify the goals and common techniques of each.

4. Identify the features of the client, the therapist, and their relationship that are associated with therapeutic success.

5. Identify and briefly describe the factors that contribute to therapeutic harm.

A P P E N D I X

Statistical Methods

LEARNING OBJECTIVES

1. Describe the function of statistics.

2. Distinguish between descriptive statistics and inferential statistics.

3. Describe a frequency distribution and explain how one is constructed.

4. Describe the different types of graphs and explain how graphs can mask or exaggerate differences.

5. Describe the three measures of central tendency and how each is calculated.

6. Describe what is meant by a measure of variability. Define the range.

7. Define standard deviation and describe how it is calculated.

8. Compare and contrast percentile scores and z-scores.

9. Describe a normal distribution and the two types of skewed distributions.

10. Describe the characteristics of a normal curve.

11. Distinguish between the null hypothesis and the alternative hypothesis.

12. Explain what is meant by statistical significance, and discuss the relationship between statistical significance and psychological importance.

13. Define sampling distribution.

PREVIEW OUTLINE

Before you read the appendix, review the preview outline for each section. After you have read the appendix, close this book and try to <u>re-create</u> the outlines on a blank piece of paper.

I. ORGANIZING DATA

    A.   **Constructing a frequency distribution** - often the first step in organizing data

        1.   Shows how often each possible score actually occurred

        2.   Grouped frequency distributions (groups adjacent scores into equal-sized classes or intervals) are sometimes used with many possible scores

    B.   **Graphing the data**

        1.   A graph is a picture that depicts numerical relationships

        2.   Types of graphs

            a.   Histogram or bar graph - draw rectangles or bars above each score indicating the number of times it occurred from the bar's height

            b.   Frequency polygon, or line graph - each score is indicated by a dot placed directly over the score on the horizontal axis

        3.   Caution about graphs - they can mask or exaggerate differences

II. DESCRIBING DATA

    A.   **Measuring central tendency** - single representative number for a set of data

        1.   The mean or "average"

            a.   Add up a set of scores and divide by the total number of scores

            b.   Means can be misleading because very high or very low scores can dramatically raise or lower the mean

        2.   The median

            a.   The median is the midpoint in a set of scores ordered

            b.   A more representative measure when extreme scores occur

        3.   The mode

            a.   The score that occurs most often

            b.   Used less often than other measures of central tendency

    B.   **Measuring variability** - tells whether the scores are clustered closely around the mean or widely scattered

        1.   The mode - simplest measure of variability - found by subtracting the lowest score from the highest one

        2.   The standard deviation - tells how much, on average, scores in a distribution differ from the mean

            a.   To compute the standard deviation - Subtract the mean from each score, yielding deviation scores. Square deviation scores, average the squared deviation scores, then take the square root of the result

            b.   Large standard deviations signify that scores are widely scattered and the mean is probably not very representative

C. **Transforming scores** - used when researchers don't want to work directly with raw scores
    1.   Percentile scores - percentage of people scoring at or below a given raw score
    2.   Z-scores or standard scores
        a.   Tell how far a given raw score is above or below the mean, using the standard deviation as the unit of measurement
        b.   They preserve the relative spacing of the original raw scores
        c.   Z-scores comparisons must be done with caution

D. **Curves** - or the pattern of the distribution
    1.   A normal distribution has a symmetrical, bell-shaped form when plotted in a frequency polygon - called a normal curve
    2.   Characteristics of a normal curve - symmetrical, all measures of central tendency (mean, median, mode) have the same value
    3.   Not all types of observations are distributed normally; some are lopsided or skewed
        a.   When the tail goes to the left, it is a negative skew
        b.   When the tail goes to the right, it is a positive skew

III. DRAWING INFERENCES with inferential statistics
A. **The null versus the alternative hypothesis**
    1.   The null hypothesis states the possibility that the experimental manipulations will have no effect on the participants' behaviour
    2.   The alternative hypothesis states that the average experimental-group score will differ from the average control-group score
    3.   The goal is to reject the null hypothesis

B. **Testing hypotheses**
    1.   Goal - to be reasonably certain the difference did not occur by chance
    2.   Sampling distribution is used - the theoretical distribution of differences between means
    3.   When the null hypothesis is true, there is no difference between groups
    4.   If there is a difference, how likely is it to occur by chance?
    5.   If it is highly improbable that a result occurs by chance, it is said to be statistically significant
    6.   Characteristics of statistical significance
        a.   Finding accepted as statistically significant if the likelihood of its occurring by chance is five percent or less ($p < .05$)
        b.   Statistically significant results are not always psychologically interesting or important
        c.   Statistical significance is related to sample size - results from a large sample are likely to be found statistically significant

PRACTICE TEST 1 - Multiple Choice

1. The first step in organizing raw data is to
   A. get a measure of the central tendency.
   B. establish the range.
   C. construct a frequency distribution.
   D. identify standard deviation.

2. Dr. Starr gives 10-question quizzes in her psychology class. When she returns quizzes, she puts on the board how many people scored a 10, 9, 8, 7, 6, 5, 4, 3, 2, and 1. This is called a
   A. normal curve.
   B. frequency distribution.
   C. frequency polygon.
   D. histogram.

3. A "histogram" is the technical term that describes a
   A. bar graph.
   B. polygon.
   C. mean.
   D. line graph.

4. A histogram is to a polygon as
   A. a line is to a bar.
   B. null is to alternative.
   C. a bar is to a line.
   D. normal is to skewed.

5. The most frequently occurring score in a distribution is called the
   A. mean.
   B. median.
   C. standard deviation.
   D. mode.

6. The mean, median, and mode are
   A. measures of central tendency.
   B. measures of variability.
   C. characteristics of a normal distribution, but not a skewed distribution.
   D. characteristics of a skewed distribution, but not a normal distribution.

7. A measure of variability that indicates the average difference between scores in a distribution and their mean is called the
   A. range.
   B. standard deviation.
   C. mode.
   D. z-score.

8. A score that indicates how far a given score is from the mean is called a
   A. range.
   B. mode.
   C. standard deviation.
   D. z-score.

9. Students in Dr. Gauthier's class got the following scores on their first test: 75, 77, 87, 63, 93, 77, 72, 80, 57, 68, 76. What is the mode?
   A. 77
   B. 75
   C. 36
   D. 76

10. What is the median in the distribution of scores in question 9?
    A. 77
    B. 75
    C. 36
    D. 76

11. What is the range in the distribution of scores in question 9?
    A. 77
    B. 36
    C. 30
    D. 76

12. If the mean is 10, and the standard deviation is 2, a person with a raw score of 8 has a z-score of
    A. 8.
    B. -1.
    C. 1.
    D. 2.

13. A lopsided distribution in which scores cluster at the high or low end of the distribution is referred to as
    A. normal.
    B. bimodal.
    C. skewed.
    D. standard.

14. What asserts that experimental manipulations have no effect?
    A. null hypothesis
    B. sampling distribution
    C. alternative hypothesis
    D. statistical significance

15. If the null hypothesis is true, differences between experimental and control groups are due to
    A. standard deviations.
    B. skew.
    C. chance fluctuations.
    D. true differences.

16. Results that are not attributable to chance are referred to as
    A. nonchance fluctuations.
    B. skewed.
    C. statistically significant.
    D. all of the above.

17. The theoretical distribution of the results of the entire population is called the
    A. null hypothesis.
    B. sampling distribution.
    C. statistical significance.
    D. random error.

18. Statistical significance
    A. suggests that a result would be highly improbable by chance alone.
    B. does not necessarily have anything to do with psychological importance.
    C. is a likely outcome with a large sample.
    D. incorporates all of the above.

PRACTICE TEST 2 - Short Answer

1. A _____ distribution shows how often each possible score occurs.

2. In a frequency _____, each score is indicated by a dot placed on a horizontal axis at the appropriate height on the vertical axis.

3. The _____ is calculated by adding up a set of scores and dividing by the number of scores in the set. The _____ is the score that occurs most often.

4. The above terms are ways of characterizing an entire set of data in terms of a representative number. They are measures of _____ tendency.

5. The _____ is the simplest measure of variability, whereas the standard _____ tells how much, on average, scores in a distribution differ from the _____.

6. When researchers don't want to work directly with raw scores, they can convert the scores to either _____ or to _____.

7. A _____ distribution has a symmetrical, bell-shaped form when plotted on a frequency polygon.

8. When a distribution of scores is lopsided and the longer tail goes to the left, it is characterized as _____ skewed.

9. The _____ hypothesis states the possibility that the experimental manipulations will have no effect on the behaviour of the participants.

10. If it is highly improbable that a result occurs by chance, it is said to be _____ significant.

PRACTICE TEST 3 - Essay

1. Researchers organize and describe data in a variety of ways. Below, different statistical devices have been grouped together. Examine each grouping and describe the common purpose of the statistics within each.

    A. Mean, median, mode
    B. Range and standard deviation
    C. Frequency distributions, bar graphs (histograms), and line graphs (frequency polygons)
    D. Percentile scores and z-scores

2. Assume that the height of the male population is normally distributed with a mean of 178 centimetres and a standard deviation of 8 centimetres. Given such information, examine each of the statements below and decide whether it is justified or unjustified. Explain the basis for your answer.

    A. The most frequently occurring male height is 178 centimetres.
    B. The percentage of men above 178 centimetres inches is much higher than the percentage below this height.
    C. If the height requirement for entering the police academy were set at 185 centimetres, less than half the male population would qualify.
    D. A curve depicting the height of players in professional basketball would also be normally distributed.

3. Below are two inaccurate statements about hypothesis testing and statistical significance. Revise each statement so that it is accurate.

    A. The null hypothesis is accepted whenever results are statistically significant.
    B. Statistical significance is a measure of the relative strengths of experimental and control treatments.

ANSWER KEY

ANSWER KEYS FOR CHAPTER ONE

ANSWER KEY - PRACTICE TEST 1 - MULTIPLE CHOICE

1. B	2. B	3. B	4. A
5. D	6. D	7. A	8. C
9. D	10. D	11. A	12. A
13. C	14. A	15. D	16. A
17. C	18. B	19. D	20. D
21. B	22. A	23. A	24. C
25. C	26. D	27. A	28. B
29. C	30. D	31. A	32. A

ANSWER KEY - PRACTICE TEST 2 - SHORT ANSWER

1. behaviour and mental processes
2. empirical
3. critical thinking
4. any two of the following: ask questions, define your terms, examine the evidence, analyze assumptions and biases, avoid emotional reasoning, don't oversimplify, consider other interpretations, tolerate uncertainty
5. predict, modify
6. trained introspection
7. structuralism
8. conflicts and traumas from early childhood
9. psychodynamic
10. biological, learning, cognitive, sociocultural, psychodynamic
11. learning
12. free will
13. cognitive
14. social and cultural forces
15. social rules and roles, groups, authority and how we are affected by other people; cultural
16. feminist
17. basic; applied
18. industrial/occupational; educational
19. nonclinical
20. clinical psychology, counselling psychology, school psychology
21. developmental
22. province; doctoral; master's
23. psychotherapist, psychoanalyst, psychiatrist
24. psychiatrists; psychotherapists

25. social workers, school counsellors, marriage, family and child counselors
26. evolutionary
27. humanist

ANSWER KEY - PRACTICE TEST 3 - ESSAY

1 A. This activity is an area of basic psychology because this research is not applying the measurement of intelligence for a particular use. This falls in the area of psychometrics, which is a nonclinical specialty.

   B. The study of vision falls in the area of basic research, since the findings are not concerned with the practical uses of its findings. This research is conducted by experimental psychologists because they conduct laboratory studies of sensation as well as other areas. Experimental psychology is a nonclinical specialty.

   C. Piaget's work is an example of basic psychology because the theory does not address practical uses of the knowledge. This activity falls in the area of developmental psychology because Piaget studied how people change and grow over time. It is a nonclinical area.

   D. Studying work motivations falls in the basic psychology area because this project does not involve direct use or application of the findings. This type of research falls into the specialty area of industrial or organizational psychology, which studies behaviour in the workplace. It is a nonclinical specialty.

   E. Milgram's study represents basic psychology because there is no direct application of the findings. It falls under the nonclinical specialty area, social psychology. The study examines how the social context influences individuals.

   F. Strupp's study is basic research because direct application for these findings is not part of the purpose of the study. It falls under the specialty of clinical psychology, which is interested in treating mental or emotional problems and is a clinical specialty area.

   G. The study of children's self-esteem is applied research, since it was used to make changes in the school systems. This type of research falls under the specialty area of developmental psychology, since it deals with how people change and grow over time. Developmental psychology is a nonclinical specialty.

   H. Using findings from career development research to assist students is an example of applied psychology. This activity falls into the specialty of counselling psychology, a clinical area, because it is dealing with problems of everyday life rather than with mental disorders.

2. Learning theory or behaviourism would explore how Harold learned his behaviour and how his environmental conditions encouraged his drug abuse. Specifically, behaviourists would be interested in the payoffs or rewards that result from the drug use. Social learning theorists might wonder if Harold had learned this behaviour from observing or imitating others, such as peers or parents.

Psychologists from a psychodynamic perspective would understand Harold's drug abuse as a result of unconscious conflicts that remain unresolved from his early childhood. Harold is unaware of his true motivations because they are unconscious.

The biological perspective understands Harold's drug abuse as a direct result of addictive processes by which the body comes to crave and depend on drugs. If Harold were to attempt to discontinue his drug use, he would experience unpleasant bodily sensations related to withdrawal. Therefore, to avoid bodily withdrawal symptoms, his drug use is continued. Biological predispositions may be operating that may have made Harold more sensitive to drug exposure.

Cognitive psychologists would be interested in Harold's perception and reasoning about drug use. Are his ideas about drugs irrational or unreasonable? What does he tell himself about drug use or nonuse? For example, does he believe that he must use drugs to be accepted by his peers? Cognitive psychologists would be interested in whether Harold believes he has control of himself or whether he sees his drug use as a problem. Sociocultural psychologists would look to the attitude in the culture toward alcohol use. They would understand the role alcohol plays for people and how it is expected to be used. For example, attitudes and expectations for alcohol use are different in other countries where alcohol is used as a beverage at meals and is consumed at meal times by adolescents and sometimes children.

According to humanists, Harold's drug abuse represents a choice. He is freely choosing to use drugs and is equally free to choose not to do so. Humanists may inquire whether he believes it assists him in dealing with questions about reaching his full potential.

Feminist psychologists would be interested in gender differences in drug abuse. They would see Harold's drug use as a way of dealing with emotions that are compatible with the male gender role in this society. Since the expression of certain emotions is not considered masculine, they might speculate that drug use would be a way of dealing with "unmasculine" emotions.

3. A psychologist would use psychotherapy based on psychological theories to treat Juanita's depression. The psychologist would have formal training and would hold either a Ph.D., an Ed.D., or a Psy.D. A psychiatrist would be likely to prescribe medication for Juanita's depression. A psychiatrist is a medical doctor (M.D.) with a residency in psychiatry. A psychoanalyst would use psychoanalysis, which is a type of psychotherapy based on the work of Sigmund Freud. To practise psychoanalysis, specialized training at a recognized psychoanalytic institute is required. A psychotherapist would use psychotherapy. A psychotherapist may or may not have formal education in psychology or a related field.

4. Zainab's experience is obviously a very emotional one, but she should not let her emotions dominate her thinking. She should examine the evidence more closely, and she should define her terms: what does she mean by "psychic" anyway? Has she had experiences like this before? Even better, how could she gather additional evidence to investigate her supposed powers? She could write down her dreams for two weeks and see how many come true and how many do not. In addition, Zainab should not rely only on her personal experience but other sources of evidence. One important source is

whether or not psychologists have found evidence in controlled research for psychic phenomena.

Zainab should try not to oversimplify, and she should consider other explanations. For example, is it possible that the dream coming true was a coincidence? One coincidence by itself is (by definition) very rare, but coincidences in general always happen sooner or later! Is it possible that Zainab dreamed about her hero because he was planning to come to her campus soon? In other words, we might dream about events that are likely to come true anyway (how many people dream about tests?). Is it possible that her dreaming about this issue actually influenced her behaviour (going to listen to a speech by her hero), such that she had a role in the dream being fulfilled that does not involve any supernatural process? Zainab should analyze any assumptions or biases she might have, even including a tendency to provide supernatural explanations for events.

ANSWER KEYS FOR CHAPTER TWO

ANSWER KEY - PRACTICE TEST 1 - MULTIPLE CHOICE

1. B	2. A	3. C	4. D
5. A	6. C	7. A	8. B
9. D	10. D	11. C	12. A
13. B	14. B	15. C	16. D
17. C	18. B	19. B	20. C
21. C	22. B	23. A	24. D
25. B	26. C	27. D	28. A
29. D	30. A	31. A	32. B
33. D	34. A	35. D	36. C

ANSWER KEY - PRACTICE TEST 2 - SHORT ANSWER

1.   unfounded belief
2.   hypothesis
3.   operational
4.   principle of falsifiability
5.   replicated
6.   descriptive
7.   case study
8.   naturalistic observational studies
9.   objective; projective
10.   norms
11.   reliability
12.   validity
13.   criterion validity
14.   representative
15.   volunteer
16.   correlation; variables
17.   positively; a causal relationship
18.   experimental method
19.   independent; dependent
20.   experimental; control
21.   placebo; expectations
22.   single
23.   descriptive
24.   significant
25.   cross-sectional; longitudinal
26.   experimenter effects
27.   innumeracy

ANSWER KEY - PRACTICE TEST 3 - ESSAY

1.   A.   Survey. Adolescents constitute a large population, and the information sought should be accessible through questionnaires or interviews. Care is needed to construct a sample that is representative of the population under consideration.

     B.   Psychological tests. The goal is to measure psychological qualities within an individual. Other methods (e.g., case history, naturalistic observation) might be employed, but they are more time-consuming and do not offer the degree of standardization, reliability, and validity found in a well-constructed test.

     C.   Experiment. Cause-and-effect information is being sought. In science this information is obtained through experiments in which the proposed causal variable is manipulated under controlled conditions.

     D.   Correlation. This technique is used to determine if and how strongly two variables are related. Establishing that a correlation exists, however, does not address the problem of why two things are related.

     E.   Naturalistic observation. A description of behaviour as it occurs in a real-life situation is being sought. Making the observations without arousing suspicion in subjects could be problematic.

     F.   Case study. Making this determination requires in-depth information about the way a variety of psychological factors - expectation, values, motives, past experiences, and so forth - blend together within the person. This kind of information is unique to the person under consideration and could not be assessed through standardized tests.

     G.   Laboratory observation. The goal is to identify what the parents are doing that may be contributing to the child's problems and help them to parent differently. To ascertain what is currently going on in the family, observing them interact in the laboratory would be the best way to actually see what is occurring. Information could be collected with an interview or questionnaire, but parents may not be aware of what they are doing.

2.   A.   Hypothesis: Caffeine improves studying
          Independent variable and its operational definition: caffeine; ounces
          Dependent variable and its operational definition: studying; test score
          Experimental condition: group receiving caffeine
          Control group: group receiving decaffeinated beverage

B.   Hypothesis: Heavy metal music increases aggression
      Independent variable and its operational definition: music; jazz, classical, heavy metal
      Dependent variable and its operational definition: aggression; amount of time spent punching bag
      Experimental condition: groups exposed to jazz, classical, and heavy metal music
      Control group: group exposed to white-noise machine

C.   Hypothesis: Exercise increases relaxation
      Independent variable and its operational definition: exercise; aerobics, number of sit-ups and push-ups
      Dependent variable and its operational definition: relaxation; heart rate, muscle tension, respiration, blood pressure
      Experimental condition: groups engaging in aerobics, sit-ups, and push-ups
      Control group: group having supervised study session

3.   A.   Positive   B.   Negative
     C.   Negative   D.   Positive
     E.   Zero   F.   Negative
     G.   Negative   H.   Positive
     I.   Negative   J.   Zero

4.   A.   Unethical. Requiring research participation for a course, without providing an alternative way of satisfying the course requirement, violates the principle of voluntary consent.
     B.   Unethical. Not only should participants be free to withdraw at any time, but they should also be informed of this right before they begin to participate.
     C.   Ethical. Although it is controversial, outright deception has not been ruled out by the Tri-Council policy guidelines.
     D.   Ethical. Under the Tri-Council policy guidelines, the use of animals is acceptable in research that reduces human suffering and promotes human welfare.
     E.   Ethical. The investigator is obligated to protect participants from physical and mental discomfort by using both voluntary and informed consent.

5.   Independent variables are those variables manipulated by the experimenter. For example, in an experiment designed to evaluate the effectiveness of weight loss programs on long-term weight loss, the independent variable is the actual program (i.e., Jenny Craig, Weight Watchers). The dependent variables are those variables affected by manipulations of the independent variable. In this case, actual weight loss over a specified period would be an example of a dependent variable.

6.   Subjects in experimental groups are actually exposed to the treatment or manipulation of the independent variable. In the above example, subjects would participate in weight loss programs. Subjects in control groups are treated exactly the same as experimental subjects, except they are not exposed to the treatment. In this example, to control for the placebo effect, control subjects may participate in a discussion group.

7. In single-blind studies, subjects do not know which condition they are in. That is, they don't know which level of the IV (e.g., experimental group versus control group) they are experiencing. In double-blind studies, both the subjects and those who are running the experiment are unaware of which condition subjects are in. These methods improve the quality of the experiments because they can rule out potential expectancy effects as causing the change in the dependent variables. For example, if the people running the experiment don't know which condition subjects are in, it is impossible for them to (consciously or unconsciously) influence the behaviour of subjects in a biasing manner.

8. Experiments allow conclusions about cause and effect, and allow the researcher the greatest amount of control; however, the experimental situation is often artificial, limiting the generalization of results. As well, it is somehow difficult to avoid experimenter effects.

9. The key elements of an experiment are the manipulation of an independent variable and random assignment to groups. There must be at least two levels of the independent variable. Your experiment should label the variable you manipulated as the independent variable, and the variable affected by the IV as the dependent variable. Subjects must be randomly assigned to the different levels of the IV.

ANSWER KEYS FOR CHAPTER THREE

ANSWER KEY - PRACTICE TEST 1 - MULTIPLE CHOICE

1. C	2. B	3. C	4. D
5. A	6. C	7. C	8. A
9. A	10. B	11. B	12. D
13. B	14. A	15. B	16. C
17. D	18. C	19. D	20. D
21. B	22. C	23. D	24. A
25. B	26. A	27. B	28. C
29. D	30. B	31. D	32. A
33. D			

ANSWER KEY - PRACTICE TEST 2 - SHORT ANSWER

1. genes; chromosomes
2. genome
3. linkage
4. evolutionary
5. evolution
6. mutate
7. natural selection
8. modules
9. language; mating
10. rules; elements
11. deep; surface
12. Chomsky; acquisition
13. similar stages
14. universal
15. sociobiologists
16. analogy; commonalities
17. stereotypes
18. heritability
19. individuals
20. adopted; identical (monozygotic) and fraternal (dizygotic)
21. .50; .60 to .80
22. group
23. prenatal care; malnutrition or exposure to toxins, or large family size, or stressful family circumstances
24. surface

ANSWER KEY - PRACTICE TEST 3 - ESSAY

1. A. The basic elements of DNA within the genes influence protein synthesis in the body by specifying the sequence of amino acids, which are the building blocks of the proteins. The sequence of amino acids are affected by the arrangement of the basic elements, which comprises a chemical code. Proteins then go on to affect virtually all structural and biochemical characteristics of the organism. Genes for alcoholism might influence the basic elements of DNA or their arrangement, which then go on to influence the amino acids, the proteins, and the structures or biochemistry of the body.

    B. This statement misinterprets heritability estimates. Heritability estimates do <u>NOT</u> apply to individuals, only to variations within a group. No one can determine the impact of heredity on any particular individual's trait. For one person, genes may make a tremendous difference; for another, the environment may be more important. This statement ignores the fact that even highly heritable traits can be modified by the environment. This statement ignores environmental influences.

    C. One might use a linkage study, which would examine large families in which alcoholism is common.

2. A. The feeling of disgust may have been useful in warding off contamination from disease and contagion.
    B. Intuition may have allowed people to anticipate others' behaviours based on their beliefs and desires and thereby prepare for problems.
    C. Self-concept may have been useful in knowing one's value to others.
    D. Feelings of kinship may have promoted protection and help to one's kin, thereby insuring their survival.
    E. Male promiscuity has the effect of increasing the offspring of any individual male, thereby continuing his genes.
    F. Female selectivity increases the chances of conceiving with the best genes.

3. Until the middle of this century, views about language acquisition suggested that language is learned (not inborn) bit by bit and that children learn to speak by imitating adults and paying attention when adults correct their mistakes. Chomsky stated that language was too complex to learn in this way. He said that children learn not only which sounds form words, but can apply the rules of syntax and discern underlying meaning. He said that the capacity for language is inborn and that the brain has a language acquisition device, or a "mental module" that allows children to develop language if they are exposed to an adequate sampling of speech. According to Chomsky, human beings are designed to use language. The following support his position:
    1. Children everywhere seem to go through similar stages of linguistic development.
    2. Children combine words in ways that adults never would, and so could not simply be imitating.
    3. Adults do not consistently correct their children's syntax.
    4. Even children who are profoundly retarded acquire language.

4. A. The study would use pairs of identical twins reared apart. IQ tests would be given to both members of the pairs and the following comparisons would be made:
    1. Scores of both members of the pairs of identical twins
    2. Scores of identical twins reared together
    3. Scores of siblings reared apart
    4. Scores of siblings reared together
    5. Scores of unrelated people

    The conclusions would depend on the results of these comparisons. Similarity of IQ scores based on genetic similarity, regardless of shared environment, would be supportive evidence for heritability estimates. Cautionary statements would include:
    1. Heritable does not mean the same thing as genetic.
    2. Heritability applies only to a particular group living in a particular environment, and estimates may differ for different groups.
    3. Heritability estimates do not apply to individuals, only to variations within a group.
    4. Even highly heritable traits can be modified by the environment.

    B. The following recommendations would be made:
    1. Develop a prenatal care program for mothers-to-be that involves education about drug use, nutrition, health, and environmental pollutants
    2. Nutrition program for young children
    3. Assistance related to exposure to toxins
    4. Information on the importance of mental stimulation
    5. Family therapy and support to reduce stressful family circumstances
    6. Training in parent–child interactions

ANSWER KEYS FOR CHAPTER FOUR

ANSWER KEY - PRACTICE TEST 1 - MULTIPLE CHOICE

1. D	2. B	3. A	4. D
5. A	6. C	7. C	8. D
9. A	10. B	11. A	12. A
13. B	14. C	15. B	16. D
17. B	18. B	19. C	20. A
21. B	22. D	23. D	24. B
25. A	26. A	27. B	28. C
29. D	30. B		

ANSWER KEY - PRACTICE TEST 2 - SHORT ANSWER

1. central; peripheral
2. somatic; autonomic
3. sympathetic; parasympathetic
4. cell body
5. dendrites; axon
6. myelin sheath
7. synapse
8. axon terminal; neurotransmitters
9. all or none
10. endorphins; neurotransmitters
11. endocrine
12. norepinephrine and serotonin; acetylcholine
13. androgens; estrogen; progesterone
14. electroencephalogram
15. magnetic resonance imaging
16. reticular activating
17. pons; medulla; cerebellum
18. thalamus
19. hypothalamus
20. limbic
21. pituitary gland; uterine contractions during childbirth
22. occipital; parietal; temporal; frontal
23. corpus callosum
24. Wernicke's; temporal; Broca's; frontal
25. behaviour
26. PET scans
27. neuroethics

ANSWER KEY - PRACTICE TEST 3 - ESSAY

1.   A.   The dendrites of neurons in the ear are stimulated and the message is sent to the cell body, which causes an inflow of sodium ions and an outflow of potassium ions that result in a wave of electrical voltage travelling down the axon. At the end of the axon, synaptic vesicles held in the synaptic end bulb release neurotransmitters, which cross the synaptic cleft and lock into receptor sites on the next neuron.

       B.   The sound causes neurons in the ear to fire, via sensory neurons to the thalamus, which directs the message to the auditory cortex in the temporal lobes, to the prefrontal lobes to figure out what to do and make a plan, to the motor cortex in the frontal lobe, out of the brain via motor neurons to the skeletal muscles to get up and move.

       C.   Information from the ears goes to the brain via the somatic nervous system of the peripheral nervous system. Once at the thalamus, it is in the central nervous system. As information exits the brain from the motor cortex, the somatic nervous system gets involved again as messages go to the muscles that allow you to cross the room. Your feeling nervous involves the autonomic nervous system, which carries messages from the central nervous system about your preparedness for the test to the glands and organs.

2.   A.   Hypothalamus
       B.   Thalamus
       C.   Prefrontal lobe
       D.   Broca's area
       E.   Hippocampus
       F.   Cerebellum

3.   It is difficult to say exactly, but the cerebrum, which is responsible for higher functioning, has been damaged. Parts of the brain stem, specifically the medulla, which is responsible for heart rate and respiration, are still in tact, but because Helen is not conscious, it is possible that the pons, which is responsible for sleeping and waking, may be damaged.

4.   A.   Frontal lobes; personality, planning, initiative
       B.   Parietal lobes; body senses and location
       C.   Occipital lobes; vision

5.   A.   Right
       B.   Left
       C.   Right
       D.   Left
       E.   There are problems with functions controlled by the left hemisphere, but not with the right hemisphere.

6.　　Neuroethics is an interdisciplinary field that has arisen to address the scientific, legal, and ethical implications of neuroscience research. Issues such as using brain scans in the future to determine what someone is thinking or feeling are addressed by this field.

ANSWER KEYS FOR CHAPTER FIVE

ANSWER KEY - PRACTICE TEST 1 - MULTIPLE CHOICE

1.	B	2.	C	7.	D	8.	D
9.	D	10.	D	11.	A	12.	C
13.	B	14.	C	15.	B	16.	C
17.	B	18.	C	19.	C	20.	D
21.	D	22.	B	23.	C	24.	D
25.	C	26.	D	27.	A	28.	C
29.	C	30.	D	31.	C	32.	A
33.	C	34.	B					

ANSWER KEY - PRACTICE TEST 2 - SHORT ANSWER

1. consciousness
2. circadian
3. suprachiasmatic nucleus
4. biological rhythm
5. desynchronization
6. hormones
7. REM sleep
8. spindles
9. inactive; active
10. lucid
11. manifest; latent
12. problem solving
13. interpreted brain activity
14. psychoactive
15. central nervous system
16. stimulants
17. tolerance
18. neurotransmitter
19. physical factors, experience with the drug, environmental setting, or mental set
20. "think-drink" effect
21. hidden observer
22. pseudomemories
23. dissociation
24. medical and psychological
25. sociocognitive
26. biological rhythm
27. narcolepsy

ANSWER KEY - PRACTICE TEST 3 - ESSAY

1.   .   A.   The definition of PMS is important because physical and emotional symptoms often appear on the same questionnaire. Because many women may experience physical symptoms, they are likely to have a higher score than if these two categories of symptoms were presented separately.

              B.   Negative moods are likely to be attributed to PMS when they occur just prior to the onset of menstruation, whereas negative moods that occur at different stages of the menstrual cycle are likely to be attributed to other factors. Another problem related to the self-reporting of PMS symptoms is the tendency to notice negative moods that occur before menstruation, and to ignore the absence of negative moods before menstruation.

              C.   Expectations can influence perceptions. The very title of a widely used questionnaire, the Menstrual Distress Questionnaire, can bias responders to look for and find certain symptoms, while ignoring other, more positive symptoms.

              D.   Research findings include

                    1.   Women and men do not differ in the emotional symptoms or number of mood swings they experience over the course of a month.

                    2.   For most women, the relationship between cycle stage and symptoms is weak or nonexistent.

                    3.   There is no reliable relationship between cycle stage and behaviours that matter in real life.

                    4.   Women do not consistently report negative psychological changes from one cycle to the next.

2.   A.   Sleep consists of REM and four distinct non-REM periods.

              B.   The extra alertness results from the fact that the body is synchronized to wake itself up as the morning approaches. Loss of sleep is not invigorating.

              C.   Although theorists do not agree on the exact functions of sleep, rest is one of its presumed functions. We can "catch up" on several nights of sleep deprivation in just one night.

              D.   Though people can function pretty well after losing a single night's sleep, mental flexibility, originality, and other aspects of creative thinking may suffer.

              E.   We display four to five REM periods each night, and laboratory research indicates that we dream every night.

3..   A.   Activation–synthesis theory or dreams as interpreted brain activity

              B.   Dreams as information processing

              C.   Dreams as unconscious wishes or psychoanalytic theory

              D.   Dreams as problem solving

4..   A1.   Depressant

              A2.   Disinhibition, anxiety reduction, slower reaction times, memory loss, poor coordination

              A3.   Death, psychosis, organic damage, blackouts

              B1.   Depressant

B2. Sedation, anxiety and guilt reduction, release of tension
B3. Tolerance and addiction, sensory and motor impairment, coma, death

C1. Opiate
C2. Pain reduction, euphoria
C3. Addiction, convulsions, nausea, death

D1. Stimulant
D2. Elevated metabolism and mood, increased wakefulness
D3. Nervousness, delusions, psychosis, death

E1. Stimulant
E2. Appetite suppression, excitability, euphoria
E3. Sleeplessness, sweating, paranoia, depression

F1. Psychedelic
F2. Hallucinations and visions, feelings of insight, exhilaration
F3. Psychosis, panic, paranoia

G1. Classification unclear, some say mild psychedelic
G2. Relaxation, increased appetite, culturally determined effects
G3. Controversial abusive effects

5. Hypnosis is associated with changes in sensations, perceptions, thoughts, feelings, and behaviour. Although people can perform uninhibited or even embarrassing acts while under hypnosis, they are turning over responsibility to the hypnotist. There is no evidence that individuals will actually violate their morals or put themselves into danger.

Hypnosis occasionally improves recall for forgotten experiences. However, it also tends to boost the number of errors someone makes. This is particularly problematic because hypnotized people are often convinced that their memories are completely true. There is little evidence that regression to childhood under hypnosis can help individuals re-experience long-ago events.

Hypnosis is used for many medical and psychological purposes. It can be useful for eliminating nail biting or smoking. It can boost the confidence of athletes and help reduce nausea for those undergoing chemotherapy. It has been used as an anesthetic for people undergoing dental procedures or even surgery. Hypnotic suggestions also have been used to reduce stress or extreme pain.

ANSWER KEY - PRACTICE TEST 1 - MULTIPLE CHOICE

1. C	2. C	3. A	4. C
5. B	6. A	7. A	8. C
9. D	10. A	11. B	12. A
13. B	14. C	15. D	16. D
17. C	18. B	19. D	20. D
21. A	22. B	23. C	24. A
25. B	26. A	27. B	28. C
29. C	30. A	31. B	32. D
33. C	34. A		

ANSWER KEY - PRACTICE TEST 2 - SHORT ANSWER.

1. perception
2. anatomical; functional
3. psychophysics
4. absolute
5. just noticeable difference (jnd)
6. sensory; decision
7. adaptation
8. brightness
9. retina
10. rods; cones
11. feature-detector
12. ground
13. closure
14. constancies
15. off
16. basilar membrane; cochlea
17. intensity or amplitude
18. salty, sour, bitter, and sweet; umami
19. culture
20. touch (or pressure), warmth, cold, pain
21. gate-control
22. kinesthesis; equilibrium
23. visual cliff
24. emotions, expectations
25. extrasensory perception
26. glial
27. inattentional blindness

ANSWER KEY - PRACTICE TEST 3 - ESSAY

1.   A.   When a person compares two stimuli (the scarf and the car), the size of the change necessary to produce a just noticeable difference is a constant proportion of the original stimulus. In this case, $2.00 is a much larger proportion of $10 than it is of $10,000. Therefore, $2.00 on the price of a car would not produce a just noticeable difference. Two dollars represents 1/5 of the price of the scarf. One-fifth of the price of the car would be $2,000 and would produce a jnd.

       B.   Signal -etection theory indicates that active decision-making is involved in determining an absolute threshold. The fatigue, as well as attention, of subjects may be interfering with decision making.

       C.   A reduction in sensitivity results from unchanging, repetitious stimulation or sensory adaptation. John may be having trouble feeling the glasses on his head because they have been there for a long time.

       D.   When people find themselves in a state of sensory overload, they often cope by blocking out unimportant sights and sounds and focusing only on those they find useful. Unimportant sounds are not fully processed by the brain. This capacity for selective attention protects us from being overwhelmed by all the sensory signals impinging on our receptors.

2.   Light, the stimulus for vision, travels in the form of waves. Waves have certain physical properties: length, which corresponds to hue or colour; amplitude, which corresponds to brightness; and complexity, which corresponds to saturation or colourfulness. The light enters the cornea and is bent by the lens to focus. The amount of light that enters the eye is controlled by muscles in the iris, which surrounds the pupil. The pupil widens or dilates to influence the amount of light let in. The light goes to the retina located in the back of the eye. The retina contains rods and cones, which are the visual receptors. The cones are responsible for colour vision; the rods for black-and-white vision and seeing things in dim light. The fovea, where vision is sharpest, is in the centre of the retina and contains only cones. Rods and cones are connected to bipolar neurons that communicate with ganglion cells. The axons of the ganglion cells converge to form the optic nerve, which carries information out through the back of the eye and on to the brain.

3.   A.   Three colours will be needed - blue, red, and green - corresponding to three types of cones. Combining such colours produces the human colour spectrum.

       B.   Four colours will be needed - blue, yellow, red, and green. They must be paired in a way that allows them to function as opposites.

4.   A.   Loudness is increasing as indicated by changes in the amplitude of the waves.

       B.   Pitch changes are related to changes in wave frequency.

       C.   The quality of sound, called timbre, is being altered by mixing various waves.

5. A. Proximity is the tendency to perceive objects that are close together as a group.
   B. Closure is the tendency to fill in gaps to perceive complete forms.
   C. Similarity is the tendency to see things that are alike as belonging together.
   D. Continuity is the tendency for lines and patterns to be perceived as continuous.

6. A. Your expectation could influence your interpretation of what you saw and what happened.
   B. Your belief about your neighbour's character could influence your perception that he was sneaking around.
   C. Your emotions could influence your perception that someone was at the door.

ANSWER KEYS FOR CHAPTER SEVEN

ANSWER KEY - PRACTICE TEST 1 - MULTIPLE CHOICE

1.	C	2.	B	3.	A	4.	D
5.	A	6.	C	7.	A	8.	A
9.	B	10.	C	11.	D	12.	B
13.	C	14.	D	15.	B	16.	C
17.	A	18.	C	19.	A	20.	B
21.	C	22.	D	23.	C	24.	A
25.	B	26.	C	27.	C	28.	C
29.	A	30.	A	31.	B	32.	B
33.	A						

ANSWER KEY - PRACTICE TEST 2 - SHORT ANSWER

1. learning
2. conditioned stimulus
3. extinction
4. higher-order
5. generalization
6. discrimination
7. predicts
8. counterconditioning
9. operant; consequences
10. reinforcement
11. reflexive; complex
12. primary; secondary
13. positive; negative
14. negative; punishment
15. reduces; increases
16. intermittent (or partial)
17. fixed-ratio
18. fixed-interval
19. shaping
20. extinction; reinforcement
21. extrinsic; intrinsic
22. biological
23. latent
24. observational
25. social-cognitive
26. restaurant phenomenon

ANSWER KEY - PRACTICE TEST 3 - ESSAY

1.   A.   CS = first and middle name; US = father's anger; UR = anxiety; CR = anxiety
       B.   CS = closet and leash; US = walk; UR = excitement; CR = excitement
       C.   CS = perfume; US = true love; UR = happy; CR = happy
       D.   CS = Park Place and Main Street; US = accident; UR = fear; CR = anxiety

2.   A.   Dogs are often disciplined by being swatted (US) with rolled-up newspapers (CS). Fear is a natural response (UR) to being hit and a learned response to such objects (CR). Furthermore, stimulus generalization is demonstrated in that the dog gives the CR to other types of rolled-up papers.
       B.   When attacked (US) by a Doberman (CS) in the past, Joan experienced fear (US). Since that time, she has been nervous about all Dobermans (stimulus generalization), though not around other dogs (stimulus discrimination). Her reduction of fear toward Dobermans represents extinction.
       C.   The sudden noise of screeching tires (CS) often causes people to tense up and flinch (CR). The lack of response during a car race is stimulus discrimination.
       D.   Getting sick (UR) from spoiled chicken (US) caused Bill to experience stimulus generalization to turkey (CS), which is similar to the chicken on which he originally became ill, and to experience a CR to the turkey.

3.   A.   The tendency to buckle-up is strengthened through negative reinforcement (the desire to eliminate the sound of the buzzer).
       B.   Punishment is weakening the tendency to smoke around the roommate. This becomes more complicated because of the addictive process, which negatively reinforces smoking by removing uncomfortable withdrawal symptoms.
       C.   Reinforcement is strengthening Warren's dishwashing behaviour.
       D.   Punishment is weakening Fred's tendency to go down the most difficult slopes.

4.   A.   Sara is on a partial reinforcement schedule. While this may be enough to maintain a behaviour once it is well established, when a response is weak it should be reinforced each time it occurs (continuous reinforcement).
       B.   By picking him up sometimes in response to his cries, Ari's parents have put him on a partial reinforcement schedule, which causes behaviours to be very persistent and difficult to extinguish. To change this pattern, they must consistently respond by not picking him up when he cries and eventually the behaviour will extinguish. It will take longer to do so now that he is on this intermittent schedule.
       C.   It appears that all the things the teacher is trying to use as punishment are reinforcing Sue's behaviour. They all involve extra attention, so by finding a consequence that is unpleasant and does not involve attention, this behaviour might be decreased by using punishment. She might also try teaching her and then reinforcing her for other types of attention.

5. The initial punishment occurs long after the marks are made and therefore may not be associated with the behaviour that is being punished. The parent is also scolding the child when he or she is feeling angry and therefore he or she may be harsher than usual. The child may also be aroused because of the punishment. Ideally, the behaviour should be directed to an appropriate medium, such as paper or colouring books, and then that behaviour should be reinforced.

6.   A.   Variable-interval
       B.   Fixed-ratio
       C.   Fixed-interval
       D.   Fixed-ratio

7.   Similarities
       1.   Agree about the importance of laws of operant and classical conditioning
       2.   Recognize the importance of reinforcers and the environment

       Differences
       1.   In addition to behaviours, study attitudes, beliefs, and expectations
       2.   Emphasize interaction between individuals and their environment

8.   Use positive reinforcement to get yourself to start assignments earlier. Choose a reward that is highly positive for you, and reward yourself for beginning an assignment early. Classical conditioning might be used to help condition you to have a study location. Choose a study location that you use only for studying. (When you start feeling tired or want to take a break, leave that location.) Over time, you should stay more focused at your study location as a result of classical conditioning. Studying on one's bed has the opposite problem: people are classically conditioned to feel sleepy when they are on their bed. Therefore, you shouldn't be surprised when you feel drowsy if you study on your bed!

ANSWER KEY - PRACTICE TEST 1 - MULTIPLE CHOICE

1.	A	2.	B	3.	B	4.	B
5.	B	6.	D	7.	D	8.	A
9.	A	10.	D	11.	C	12.	B
13.	A	14.	C	15.	D	16.	B
17.	A	18.	C	19.	C	20.	D
21.	D	22.	B	23.	C	24.	C
25.	A	26.	D	27.	D	28.	C
29.	A	30.	D	31.	B	32.	A
33.	D						
34.	A						
35.	C						

ANSWER KEY - PRACTICE TEST 2 - SHORT ANSWER

1. roles
2. two-thirds
3. roles
4. manners; entrapment
5. cognition
6. situational
7. dispositional; situational; fundamental
8. self-serving bias
9. just-world hypothesis
10. attitude
11. validity
12. coercive
13. obedience; conformity
14. openness to experience
15. diffusion of responsibility
16. uninteresting
17. deindividuation
18. altrusim
19. social
20. ethnocentrism
21. stereotype; prejudice
22. emphasize; underestimate
23. flipside
24. social
25. acculturation
26. groupthink

ANSWER KEY - PRACTICE TEST 3 - ESSAY

1.   The prison study   The students were either playing the roles of prison guards or prisoners. These roles were governed by norms of how prisoners and guards should behave. The students knew the roles and the norms that governed them and played the parts.

      The obedience study   The roles of the research subject and authority figure were known to the study participants, who then played the role of subject. Knowing the norms for both sets of roles made it difficult for subjects to violate their roles and defy the authority figure.

2.   A.   Dispositional attribution
        B.   Just-world hypothesis
        C.   Situational attribution - self-serving bias
        D.   Situational attribution

3.   You might want to use some techniques of friendly persuasion. You could use the validity effect by repeating that you have worked very hard in this class. Repeatedly referring to your effort may make it seem more believable to the faculty member. You also might want to refer to a class you have taken by a well-respected colleague in which you did very well. This is attempting to influence your teacher's attitude by using the respected colleague's opinion. Finally, you might try to link your message with a good feeling by telling your professor how much you enjoyed the class.

4.   To reduce social loafing, Dr. Wong should make sure each student is responsible for a different part of the project that is essential to the whole project. She might make part of the grade an individual grade and part of the grade a group grade. To reduce groupthink, she might want to make grades dependent on the presentation of multiple points of view and different positions and approaches. She will want to structure the project so that success depends on the co-operation and interdependence of all students. Finally, to promote altruism and independent action, she might want students to volunteer at a homeless shelter to get to know some homeless people personally.

5.   A.   Underestimating differences within other groups
        B.   Accentuating differences between groups
        C.   Producing selective perceptions
        D.   Illusory correlations

6.   Factors that contribute to the persistence of prejudice include
        1.   Socialization - children learn prejudices from their parents.
        2.   Social benefits - prejudices bring support from others who share them and the threat of losing support when one abandons the prejudice.
        3.   Economic benefits and justification of discrimination - when economic or social times are difficult, prejudice increases.

        Reducing prejudice: efforts that have not been particularly successful include - the contact hypothesis, efforts aimed at individuals, such as education, and the legal approach.
        A program to reduce prejudice must include - multiple efforts, the co-operation of both sides, equal status and economic standing of both sides, comprehensive support from authorities and the opportunity to work and socialize together, formally and informally.

7.   The following are mentioned in your text as characteristics of brainwashing often used by groups to recruit new members. The person is put under physical or emotional stress. The person's problems are reduced to one simple explanation. The leader offers unconditional love, acceptance, and attention. A new identity based on the group is created. The person is subjected to entrapment—gradually but steadily increasing commitment. The person's access to information is controlled.

ANSWER KEY - PRACTICE TEST 1 - MULTIPLE CHOICE

1. C	2. A	3. C	4. C
5. D	6. C	7. A	8. D
9. A	10. D	11. B	12. B
13. C	14. B	15. B	16. B
17. A	18. B	19. C	20. C
21. C	22. B	23. D	24. C
25. D	26. B	27. C	28. D
29. A			

ANSWER KEY - PRACTICE TEST 2 - SHORT ANSWER

1.   mental
2.   concept
3.   basic
4.   proposition; cognitive schema
5.   subconscious
6.   nonconscious
7.   must; is probably
8.   formal; algorithm
9.   dialectical reasoning
10. reflective
11. quasi-reflective
12. mental sets
13. availability heuristic
14. dissonance
15. metacognition
16. psychometric approach; cognitive approach
17. biased; culture
18. general; multiple
19. triarchic; contextual
20. componential, experiential, contextual
21. motivation; cultural attitudes
22. lower
23. displacement; productivity
24. anthropomorphism
25. Benjamin Whorf

ANSWER KEY - PRACTICE TEST 3 - ESSAY

1. A. Coat   B. Horse
    C. Dog   D. Uncle

2. A. The ship's position must be deduced. The position of the North Star and the formula are two premises that, once known, will allow the conclusion to be determined with certainty.

    B. Scientists of all types rely on inductive reasoning. Enough cases must be collected before a conclusion can be drawn.

    C. The overall process is dialectical reasoning, which is likely to incorporate inductive and deductive reasoning. It will be necessary to assess potential outcomes, risks, losses, and appropriate considerations.

    D. Again, the overall process is dialectical reasoning, which will probably incorporate inductive and deductive reasoning.

3. A. Availability heuristic   B. Cognitive dissonance
    C. Confirmation bias

4. A. Componential intelligence   B. Contextual intelligence
    C. Experiential intelligence

5. A. Evidence supporting cognitive abilities in nonhumans:
    1. Evidence on herons, sea otters, and assassin bugs related to their food-gathering habits reflects behaviours that appear intelligent.
    2. Some chimpanzees use objects as rudimentary tools, and there is evidence for some summing abilities and the use of numerals to label quantities.
    3. Some primates demonstrate the ability to use some aspects of language like - learning signs from sign language, understanding words and some sentences, using signs to converse with each other, ability to manipulate keyboard symbols to request food without formal training, use of some simple grammatical rules.
    4. Other evidence about dolphins and parrots exists.

    B. Evidence against cognitive abilities in nonhumans:
    1. The meaning of these abilities is questioned; human meaning may be attributed to these actions.
    2. Early studies were overinterpreted and biased.
    3. It's unclear whether the use of signs and symbols were strung together without any particular order or syntax.
    4. While an animal may be "conscious," in the sense of being aware of its environment, it does not know that it knows and is unable to think about its own thoughts in the way that human beings do.

6.   Gardner advocated adding items such as musical intelligence, kinesthetic intelligence, insight about oneself, insight about others, and insight about the natural world. Some have criticized this approach, saying that musical and kinesthetic "intelligence" are better thought of as talents, and insight into oneself and others (collectively known as emotional intelligence) might instead be a collection of personality traits. Perhaps the proliferation of intelligences leads the term to lose all meaning.

ANSWER KEY - PRACTICE TEST 1 - MULTIPLE CHOICE

1. A	2. D	3. D	4. D
5. B	6. C	7. D	8. D
9. C	10. A	11. B	12. C
13. A	14. C	15. D	16. D
17. D	18. A	19. C	20. A
21. C	22. B	23. A	24. D
25. A	26. B	27. C	28. D
29. D	30. C		

ANSWER KEY - PRACTICE TEST 2 - SHORT ANSWER

1. reconstructive
2. source
3. stable
4. suggestive
5. recall; recognition
6. explicit
7. implicit; priming
8. information processing
9. encode; store; retrieve
10. sensory; short-term (memory)
11. parallel distributed processing
12. chunks
13. semantic
14. network
15. semantic; episodic; declarative
16. serial position
17. maintenance; elaborative
18. epinephrine
19. decay
20. retroactive; proactive
21. retrieval; cue-dependent
22. state-dependent
23. amnesia

ANSWER KEY - PRACTICE TEST 3 - ESSAY

1.   To be remembered, material first must be encoded into the form in which it is to be retained. Storage takes place in various areas of the brain, which appears to correspond to structural changes in the brain. Retrieval is the process by which stored material is located for current use.

2.   Information entering through the senses is briefly held in sensory memory, where preliminary sorting and encoding take place. It is then transferred to short-term storage, where it is rehearsed. Finally, as a result of deep processing or elaborative rehearsal, it is forwarded to long-term storage, where it is indexed and organized to become part of the network of more permanent material.

3.   A.   Procedural memory
     B.   Episodic memory
     C.   Semantic memory

4.   Memory processes are subject to distortion in recall. Selection pressures bias information within sensory memory. Short-term memory simplifies, condenses, and even adds meaning as information is being processed. In long-term storage, information is organized and indexed within the preexisting framework, allowing memories to become intermixed. As information is retrieved, distortion can result from interferences and reasoning involved in reconstructing the event.

5.   A.   According to decay theory, virtually all the details should be forgotten because of the long-time interval involved. The only memories remaining should be those used from time to time as the person grew older.
     B.   The absence of retrieval cues is often a source of forgetting. The example suggests that the mental image created by the description of the homeroom was a cue that released a set of associated memories.
     C.   Some emotionally unpleasant situations may be forgotten more rapidly and may be harder to recall than other situations. For the sake of emotional comfort, Henry may be motivated to forget situations associated with personal distress.

6.   Interference arises as memory incorporates similar material in succession. Assuming there is greatest similarity between Italian and Spanish, these should be kept as separate as possible, as well as overlearned and frequently reviewed. Breaks would also help as you go from one topic of study to another. A sequence like Italian, math, English, history, and Spanish would be better than Spanish, Italian, English, math, and history.

ANSWER KEYS FOR CHAPTER ELEVEN

ANSWER KEY - PRACTICE TEST 1 - MULTIPLE CHOICE

1. D	2. C	3. A	4. B
5. D	6. C	7. C	8. B
9. D	10. C	11. B	12. B
13. A	14. A	15. D	16. D
17. B	18. D	19. B	20. C
21. B	22. C	23. B	24. C
25. C	26. D	27. A	28. D
29. C	30. D	31. A	

ANSWER KEY - PRACTICE TEST 2 - SHORT ANSWER

1.   face
2.   basic
3.   facial feedback
4.   amygdala; cerebral cortex
5.   sympathetic (or autonomic); epinephrine, norepinephrine
6.   patterns
7.   physiological; cognitive
8.   attributions
9.   appraisals
10.   cognitions; emotions
11.   primary; secondary
12.   prototypes
13.   display rules
14.   work
15.   nonverbal
16.   cultures
17.   provocation; sensitive
18.   perceptions
19.   power
20.   express
21.   sadness, happiness, contempt, disgust, surprise, anger, fear
22.   left prefrontal cortex
23.   amygdala

ANSWER KEY - PRACTICE TEST 3 - ESSAY

1. A. The facial-feedback hypothesis assumes that emotion and facial expression are intimately interconnected. Distinct facial expressions not only identify emotions but contribute to them as well. By posing the face, performers may actually engender emotions in themselves.
    B. They indicate that outward expressions can be masked or even faked. More importantly, they indicate that learning is important in the expression of emotion.
    C. Emotion work might be defined as the ability to intentionally alter facial expression and body language to simulate a chosen emotion.
    D. For Darwin, facial expression was biologically wired because of its adaptive communication value. Because the face rather than the body is the focal point of social interaction, body expressions need not be similarly wired.

2. A. An increase in epinephrine and norepinephrine is brought about by the adrenal glands and under the control of the autonomic nervous system. Involvement of the amygdala, limbic system, and cortex contribute to this arousal response.
    B. The patient is functioning according to the display rules for men, which dictate that men should not feel fear or anxiety. The nurse is doing the emotion work associated with the role of a nurse. Nurses are supposed to be comforting and pleasant to patients.

3. These results are consistent with the idea that it is our interpretation of events that is instrumental in the experiencing of emotion rather than the event. The students' reactions are based on their explanations and interpretations of why they got those grades. Larry studied hard and expected a better grade. His depressive reaction may have to do with the fact that since he studied and did not do better, he may see himself as stupid, which is an internal and stable interpretation. Curly studied a little bit for the test so he felt relieved that he got a C. The grade has no bearing on his view of himself. He did not expect to fail, but did not really expect a better grade. Moe did not study at all, so he interpreted the grade as very lucky. The grade did not influence his view of himself, but rather he interpreted it as due to external luck.

4. A. Display rules govern the recipients of gifts.
    B. Emotion work involves acting out emotions not truly felt.
    C. The facial expression of anger is universally recognizable. Moreover, the husband's familiarity with Mary should make any idiosyncratic expressive features easily identifiable.
    D. The emotion work is implied by gender roles.
    E. She has a combination of lower status, high familiarity, sexual similarity, and gender.
    F. All of the reactions do.

ANSWER KEYS FOR CHAPTER TWELVE

ANSWER KEY - PRACTICE TEST 1 - MULTIPLE CHOICE

1. C	2. B	3. C	4. A
5. A	6. D	7. C	8. C
9. D	10. D	11. A	12. C
13. B	14. B	15. C	16. D
17. C	18. B	19. D	20. D
21. D	22. D	23. A	24. A
25. A	26. A	27. B	28. A
29. A	30. C	31. B	32. C

ANSWER KEY - PRACTICE TEST 2 - SHORT ANSWER

1. toward; away
2. drives
3. set point
4. diet; exercise
5. performance
6. passion; commitment
7. trust
8. attachment
9. express
10. economic
11. testosterone
12. similar
13. partner approval; peer approval
14. misperceptions
15. dominance
16. sexual
17. cultural norms
18. industrial/organizational
19. achievement
20. opportunity
21. temperament
22. proximity and similarity
23. secure, anxious-ambivalent, and avoidant
24. passionate love

ANSWER KEY - PRACTICE TEST 3 - ESSAY

1. Lessons from motivational research which could apply include:
   a. Seek activities that are intrinsically pleasurable, even if they don't pay off.
   b. Focus on learning goals, not only performance goals.
   c. Assess working conditions.
   d. Take steps to resolve motivational conflicts.

2. <u>Information that supports homosexuality as a choice and refutes the biological argument</u>
   a. The fluidity of women's experiences
   b. There are flaws in the biological evidence
      *Methodological problems in the findings on brain differences
      *The majority of homosexuals do not have a close gay relative
   c. Psychological theories have not been well-supported

   <u>Information that supports the biological information and refutes the choice position</u>
   a. Research findings that women with a history of prenatal exposure to estrogen are more likely to become bisexual or lesbian
   b. Research findings on differences in brain structures of homosexual and heterosexual men
   c. Studies that show a moderate heritability

   <u>Political implications include</u> If homosexuality is biological, then it is a fact of nature and not a choice, and therefore, people should not be prejudiced. Those who are prejudiced against homosexuals suggest that the biological evidence says that it is a "defect" and should be eradicated or "cured." Those who say it is a choice, say it can be "unchosen."

3. A. Avoidance–avoidance conflict
   B. Approach–approach conflict
   C. Approach–avoidance conflict

4. People sometimes try to meet needs simultaneously. In other words, they might try to satisfy needs lower on the pyramid and needs higher on the pyramid at the same time. Some people do not focus on the higher needs, such as self-actualization, even when their lower needs have been met. Others will sacrifice needs at the lower levels in order to reach higher needs (such as enduring pain in sacrifice for a cause they believe in).

ANSWER KEYS FOR CHAPTER THIRTEEN

ANSWER KEY - PRACTICE TEST 1 - MULTIPLE CHOICE

1. C	2. A	3. C	4. C
5. C	6. D	7. C	8. C
9. D	10. D	11. C	12. A
13. A	14. C	15. A	16. C
17. C	18. D	19. A	20. B
21. D	22. D	23. C	24. D
25. B	26. C	27. C	28. A
29. A	30. A	31. D	32. A

ANSWER KEY - PRACTICE TEST 2 - SHORT ANSWER

1. behaviour; thoughts
2. objective; inventories
3. Allport; central; secondary
4. agreeableness; conscientiousness
5. reactive
6. heritability
7. nonshared
8. reciprocal determinism
9. expectations; reciprocal determinism
10. collectivist
11. collectivist
12. psychodynamic
13. id; realities; superego
14. defence mechanisms
15. sublimation
16. Horney
17. collective; archetypes
18. representation
19. falsifiability
20. self-actualized; functioning; unconditional positive
21. anima, animus
22. shadow

ANSWER KEY - PRACTICE TEST 3 - ESSAY

1. A. Cognitive social-learning approach
   B. Trait approach
   C. Psychodynamic approach
   D. Humanistic approach

2.   A.   According to the reality principle, the ego would seek to prepare for the test.
      B.   The id seeks pleasure and immediate gratification, according to the pleasure principle.
      C.   The id seeks pleasure and is not concerned with the consequences of reality.
      D.   The ego is appraising reality.
      E.   The internalized parental values of the superego are discouraging him from cheating.
      F.   The ego is defending against threats from the superego.
      G.   Violations of the superego produce guilt.

3.   A.   Reaction formation   D.   Denial
      B.   Projection   E.   Regression
      C.   Repression   F.   Displacement

4.   A.   Phallic stage   C.   Phallic stage
      B.   Oral stage   D.   Anal stage

5.   A.   Adler
      B.   Jung
      C.   Horney
      D.   Object-relations school

6.   Abraham Maslow
      Self-actualization was a basic need for Maslow. However, its achievement depended on gratifying even more fundamental needs, such as physiological drives and social needs.

      Rollo May
      May believes that alienation, loneliness, and helplessness are basic components of human existence. The person strives to overcome these through effective choices.

      Carl Rogers
      According to Rogers, self-actualization and full functioning are related to the presence of unconditional positive regard. However, most children and adults live in situations in which they receive conditional positive regard.

7.   A.   Low levels of neuroticism, high levels of extroversion, and agreeableness
      B.   High levels of conscientiousness, and probably agreeableness, and a low level of openness to experience
      C.   High levels of neuroticism and openness to experience, but a low level of extroversion

ANSWER KEY - PRACTICE TEST 1 - MULTIPLE CHOICE

1. C	2. D	3. B	4. D
5. B	6. A	7. A	8. C
9. B	10. B	11. D	12. D
13. A	14. C	15. A	16. D
17. C	18. D	19. B	20. C
21. B	22. A	23. C	24. C
25. A	26. B	27. B	28. D
29. B	30. A		

ANSWER KEY - PRACTICE TEST 2 - SHORT ANSWER

1. socialization
2. germinal; embryonic; embryo
3. placenta; X-rays; drugs
4. teratogens
5. terry-cloth; contact comfort
6. Ainsworth; strange situation
7. avoidant
8. mothers; temperament
9. eleven; symbolic
10. Piaget
11. schema; assimilation
12. object permanence
13. egocentrism; preoperational
14. concrete operations
15. ten
16. socialization
17. menarche; menopause
18. individuate
19. transgendered
20. eight; crisis
21. fluid; declines; crystallized; stable
22. induction

ANSWER KEY - PRACTICE TEST 3 - ESSAY

1. A. Fetal abnormalities and deformities
    B. There is an increased likelihood of miscarriage, premature birth, abnormal fetal heartbeat, and underweight babies; after the child's birth, there are increased rates of sickness and Sudden Infant Death Syndrome; in later childhood, hyperactivity and difficulties in school.
    C. Fetal alcohol syndrome
    D. Effects vary with specific drugs; extreme caution must be exercised, even with prescribed and over-the-counter drugs.

2. A. Newborns should have the following reflexes: rooting, sucking and swallowing. They should follow a moving light with their eyes and turn toward a familiar sound. They should be able to distinguish contrasts, shadows, and edges, and be able to discriminate their primary caregiver.
    B. Newborns are sociable from birth and show a preference for the human face. They can distinguish their primary caregiver by smell, sight, or sound almost immediately.

3. A. The child is in the preoperational stage and is demonstrating egocentric thinking.
    B. The child is incorrectly trying to use assimilation; she should use accommodation.
    C. The younger child is in the preoperational stage and lacks the ability to conserve; the older child is in the concrete operations stage.
    D. Johnny is in the sensorimotor stage and has developed object permanence.

4. At 4 months old - Jennie would cry and coo and respond to high-pitched and more varied verbalizations in which the intonation is exaggerated. She can recognize her own name.
    At 10 months old - she would be increasingly familiar with the sound structure of her native language. She might be making babbling sounds such as "ba-ba" or "goo-goo."
    At 14 months old - she could begin using gestures.
    At 23 months old - she would use telegraphic speech because she is not yet able to use articles and auxiliary words. She would probably say, "Apple table."

5. Most children who have experienced early trauma are resilient. They eventually recover from adversity. Resilience appears to be rather ordinary and associated with personality traits (easy going temperament, self efficacy), a history of secure attachment, and strong family and/or community relationships. We are constantly interpreting our own experiences.

ANSWER KEYS FOR CHAPTER FIFTEEN

ANSWER KEY - PRACTICE TEST 1 - MULTIPLE CHOICE

1.	A	2.	C	3.	A	4.	D
5.	D	6.	B	7.	A	8.	D
9.	A	10.	C	11.	A	12.	A
13.	D	14.	C	15.	B	16.	C
17.	B	18.	A	19.	B	20.	C
21.	C	22.	D	23.	C	24.	A
25.	B	26.	C	27.	D	28.	D
29.	D	30.	A	31.	D	32.	A
33.	B						

ANSWER KEY - PRACTICE TEST 2 - SHORT ANSWER

1. health
2. Selye; alarm; resistance; exhaustion
3. widowed men
4. worse; higher
5. antigen; immune
6. psychoneuroimmunology
7. immune
8. hostility
9. emotional inhibition
10. optimistic; illusions
11. control
12. primary; secondary
13. coping
14. emotion-focused; problem-focused
15. Reappraising
16. compare
17. reduce; cause
18. psychological
19. "pop-health"
20. either-or
21. forgiveness

ANSWER KEY - PRACTICE TEST 3 - ESSAY

1.   A.   Air traffic controllers are likely to face a higher degree of daily irritation and uncontrollable events than fishermen.

   B.   Type A people, particularly if they have antagonistic hostility and experience greater stress.

   C.   Those with an external locus of control are less likely to feel that they can predict and control their environments, and prediction and control reduce stress.

   D.   Generally, those with social networks experience buffers to stress.

   E.   Pessimistic explanatory styles result in the perception that the stressor is unchangeable, therefore these people will feel less control over the stress.

2.   A.   The alarm phase will be the most prominent as the person is being captured. Bodily resources will be mobilized as the person attempts to fight or flee.

   B.   Resistance will coincide with early captivity. Its duration is related to the victim's capacity to manage potentially overwhelming events. Signs of arousal will be prominent and bodily preparedness is the rule. Biologically, use of energy resources will be above normal. Psychologically, the victim is actively fighting the situation.

   C.   The timing of exhaustion depends on individual characteristics, such as coping styles. Biologically, it is signalled by bodily fatigue and susceptibility to illness. Psychologically, the person shows signs of giving up and wearing down.

3.   A.   Prolonged stress is capable of suppressing the disease and infection-fighting cells of the immune system. As this happens, bodily defences are impaired and susceptibility to symptoms increases.

   B.   Though the evidence is mixed, it is possible that the depression is contributing to his illness by affecting the immune system. It is also possible, however, that his continuous illness is contributing to the depression. It may be that poor health habits are causing both or that an entirely different thing is causing both. Finally, the depression and the illnesses could be mutually influencing each other.

   C.   David must examine his personality for antagonistic hostility; his personal style of evaluating and managing changes, daily hassles, and problems; the quality and quantity of his social relationships and interest; and everyday habits relating to rest, exercise, and diet.

4.   A.   Margaret is rethinking the problem and using some denial.
   B.   The situation is being directly attacked with a problem-focused strategy.
   C.   Frank is reappraising the problem using social comparisons.
   D.   Tony is using an emotion-focused strategy.
   E.   Joan is trying to live with the problem.

ANSWER KEYS FOR CHAPTER SIXTEEN

ANSWER KEY - PRACTICE TEST 1 - MULTIPLE CHOICE

1. C	2. A	3. B	4. A
5. C	6. B	7. C	8. B
9. D	10. C	11. B	12. C
13. D	14. A	15. D	16. C
17. C	18. B	19. D	20. B
21. C	22. D	23. A	24. D
25. A	26. A	27. A	28. D
29. A	30. D	31. C	32. D
33. B	34. A	35. D	36. B
37. C			

ANSWER KEY - PRACTICE TEST 2 - SHORT ANSWER

1. cultural
2. *Diagnostic and Statistical Manual of Mental Disorders* (DSM-IV)
3. over-diagnosis
4. generalized
5. posttraumatic stress disorder
6. interpret
7. social phobia
8. agoraphobia
9. obsessions; compulsions; anxiety
10. behavioural, cognitive
11. depression
12. attachment
13. personality
14. inhibition
15. vulnerability–stress; stresses
16. rumination
17. common; clinicians
18. sociocognitive
19. biochemistry
20. learning
21. psychosis
22. delusions; hallucinations
23. genetic; prenatal
24. virus
25. projective; reliability; validity
26. hopelessness
27. prefrontal cortex

ANSWER KEY - PRACTICE TEST 3 - ESSAY

1.   A.   This definition considers the violation of norms and standards to be abnormal. Jason violates norms governing social interaction, appearance and good taste.

        B.   Maladaptive behaviour is behaviour that results in disharmony and distress to oneself or others.. Jason is behaving disruptively toward others.

        C.   This definition emphasizes signs of subjective distress. Jason is apparently seeking forgiveness based on some internal experience of guilt or anxiety..

2.   A.   Included
        B.   Excluded
        C.   Excluded
        D.   Included
        E.   Included

Explanation - The DSM-IV classifies disorders on five axes: primary diagnosis, ingrained aspects of personality, relevant medical conditions, current stressors and overall level of functioning. The included items reflect those axes and the others do not.

3.   A.   Abnormal: panic attack
        B.   Abnormal: obsessive–compulsive disorder
        C.   Normal
        D.   Abnormal: phobia
        E.   Abnormal: posttraumatic stress disorder

4.   A.   Mood disorders involve emotional, behavioural, cognitive, and physical symptoms.

        B.   In bipolar disorder, mania alternates with depression.

        C.   Antidepressant drugs raise the levels of serotonin and norepinephrine.

        D.   There is no change.

        E.   Negative thinking seems to be both a result and a cause of depression.

        F.   Repeated failure can be a source of learned helplessness, a characteristic related to depression.

5.   A.   Josephine has delusions. The fact that she believes that airplanes dirty the streets and sidewalks by dripping oil, that pilots have a power called "telectic penetration," and that she is being used as a radar are all examples of delusions.

        B.   Josephine is experiencing hallucinations. She hears the pilots talking to her about her location.

        C.   Josephine is demonstrating incoherent associations, including "telectic penetration," her latitude and longitude, and airplanes.

        D.   Josephine's behaviour is inappropriate in that she withdraws and is unable to speak.

        E.   From the description, it is unclear if Josephine is exhibiting emotional flatness.

6.   Danger signs for suicide include talking about it, past suicide attempts, a history of depression, revealing specific plans for carrying it out, giving away prized possessions, listlessness and withdrawal, and access to a lethal method, such as a gun. It's important to

emphasize that if someone talks about suicide, they really are at risk. Suicide threats should be taken seriously. You should ask your friend questions. Your friend might be relieved to talk about the issue with someone. Don't try to deny the person's experience through unrealistic cheerfulness, or try to talk your friend out of it by saying that suicide is wrong. Don't leave your friend alone. Try to get your friend professional help through counselling, a suicide hotline, hospitalization, etc. The worst thing to do is to do nothing.

ANSWER KEYS FOR CHAPTER SEVENTEEN

ANSWER KEY - PRACTICE TEST 1 - MULTIPLE CHOICE

1. A	2. A	3. D	4. D
5. A	6. D	7. D	8. A
9. A	10. B	11. B	12. C
13. D	14. C	15. A	16. C
17. A	18. B	19. C	20. C
21. A	22. D	23. C	24. B
25. A	26. A	27. D	28. B
29. D	30. C		

ANSWER KEY - PRACTICE TEST 2 - SHORT ANSWER

1. schizophrenia; psychoses
2. tardive dyskinesia
3. antidepressant
4. Lithium carbonate
5. relapse
6. prefrontal lobotomy
7. electroconvulsive therapy
8. psychodynamic; free association
9. transference
10. systematic desensitization
11. exposure (or flooding)
12. evidence; interpretations
13. emotive behaviour
14. client-centred; unconditional
15. family
16. research
17. coercive
18. empathy; genuineness
19. cognitive; anxiety
20. behavioural
21. coercion
22. multiple personality disorder
23. community; rehabilitation
24. deep brain stimulation
25. scientist-practioner gap

ANSWER KEY - PRACTICE TEST 3 - ESSAY

1. Medical treatments feature drugs and other forms of organic intervention. Drugs are very useful for psychotic disorders, and, in combination with psychotherapy, are effective against other disorders, including major depression, bipolar disorder, and some anxiety disorders.

    Psychotherapies attempt to change thinking, emotional, and behavioural processes. They are designed to help clients think about their lives in new ways in order to find solutions to the problems that plague them. They have been shown to be very useful with mood disorders, anxiety disorders, and eating disorders.

    Community services tend to be problem-oriented and offer counselling, support groups, and skills training. They can be useful for those with mental or physical disabilities, including schizophrenia.

2. A.   Anxiety disorders: minor tranquilizers
    B.   Mood disorders: antidepressants
    C.   Psychotic disorders: antipsychotics

    Drug treatments are limited by the complications of side effects and finding the right dosage. They may not be effective for everyone or may work effectively only in the short-term. Often there is little research on the effects of long-term usage. Moreover, drugs relieve symptoms and do nothing to help people learn new coping skills.

3. Psychodynamic therapies strive for insight into the unconscious processes that produce a problem. With insight and emotional release, symptoms should disappear. The goal of treatment is not to solve an individual's immediate problem, since it is only the tip of the iceberg. Techniques include free association and transference. Psychoanalysis was the original model proposed by Freud in which a patient was seen multiple times in a week for many years.

    Cognitive therapy aims to correct distorted, unrealistic thoughts, beliefs, and expectations. Techniques vary but revolve around examining negative thoughts, formulating reasonable responses, and using realistic perspectives.

    Behaviour therapy attempts to eliminate maladaptive responses and behaviour patterns. Techniques are based on learning principles and include systematic desensitization, aversive conditioning, flooding, and operant strategies.

    Humanistic therapy is designed to increase self-esteem, positive feelings and self-actualization. Approaches include client-centred therapy and existential therapy. Client-centred therapy utilizes unconditional positive regard, empathy, and genuineness.

Family therapy aims to correct the forces in the family that are contributing to the expression of a problem. The family may be analyzed from a multigenerational standpoint, using a genogram, or as a social system.

The shared features include - support factors, which allow the client to feel secure and safe; learning factors, which allow the client to see and experience his or her problems in a new light and think about how to solve them; and action factors, which allow the client to reduce fears, take risks, and make necessary changes.

4.   Client features - commitment to therapy, willingness to work on their problems, and expectations of success; co-operativeness with suggested interventions and positive feelings during the therapy session.

Therapist features - empathy, warmth, genuineness, and imagination; make clients feel respected, accepted, and understood; expressive and actively invested in the interaction with the client.

Therapeutic alliance: a relationship in which both parties respect and understand one another, feel reaffirmed, and work toward a common goal.

5.   Coercion by the therapist to accept the therapist's advice, sexual intimacies, or other unethical behaviour. Bias on the part of a therapist who doesn't understand the client because of the client's gender, race, religion, sexual orientation, or ethnic group. Therapist-induced disorders can be harmful, such as when therapists so zealously believes in the prevalence of certain problems that they induce the client to produce the symptoms they are looking for.

ANSWER KEYS FOR APPENDIX

ANSWER KEY - PRACTICE TEST 1 - MULTIPLE CHOICE

1. C	2. B	3. A	4. C
5. D	6. A	7. B	8. D
9. A	10. D	11. B	12. B
13. C	14. A	15. C	16. C
17. B	18. D		

ANSWER KEY - PRACTICE TEST 2 - SHORT ANSWER

1. frequency
2. polygon
3. mean; mode
4. central
5. range; deviation; mean
6. percentages; z-scores
7. normal
8. negatively
9. null
10. statistically

ANSWER KEY - PRACTICE TEST 3 - ESSAY

1. A. These descriptive statistics are measures of central tendency and describe data by a single, representative number.
    B. These descriptive statistics measure variability and reflect the spread of obtained scores.
    C. These statistical pictures are used to organize data in terms of an overall visual summary.
    D. These transformations are used when scores are put in a standardized format for easier comparisons.

2. A. This statement is justified because the mean and mode are equal in a normal distribution.
    B. This statement is unjustified because the normal distribution is symmetrical, with either side of the mean mirror-imaging the other.
    C. This statement is justified because less than 16 percent of the population receives a score about one standard deviation from the mean.
    D. This statement is unjustified because this curve is likely to be skewed to the right given that basketball players are chosen for their height.

3.	A.	The null hypothesis is rejected whenever results are statistically significant.
	B.	Statistical significance occurs when differences between the experimental and control groups are very unlikely to be caused by chance or random errors.

NOTES

NOTES

NOTES